25 BEST
Off-the-Beaten-Path
MONTANA FLY-FISHING STREAMS

MOLLY J. SEMENIK

STONEFLY PRESS

Copyright © 2015 by Stonefly Press

All rights reserved, including the right of reproduction
of this book in whole or in part in any form.

640 Clematis St. #588
West Palm Beach, FL 33402
FAX: 877-609-3814

For information about discounts on bulk purchases, or
to book the author for an engagement or demonstration,
please contact Stonefly Press at inquiries@stoneflypress.com,
or visit us at Stoneflypress.com.

stoneflypress.com

Printed in the United States

19 18 17 16 15   1 2 3 4 5

Library of Congress Control Number: 2015952634

Stonefly Press

Publisher: Robert D. Clouse

Acquiring Editor: Robert D. Clouse

Front Cover Photo: Molly Semenik fishing the Stillwater River near Columbus, Montana.

Back Cover Photo: Rainbow photo by Molly Semenik.

*To my parents, Jo and Charlie Moore,
who filled my life with adventure, pride,
and a "just do it" attitude*

Montana native Westslope cutthroat trout. Peter Lami

Contents

Acknowledgments vi
About the Author vii
Introduction ix
Montana Rivers and Streams xi
Packing Your Fly Box xiii
Montana Facts xvi
Montana Fishing Facts xvii
Wildlife Safety xviii
Stream Accessibility and Wading Challenge xxi
Weather xxii
Trout Fishing in Montana xxiii
Fly Fishing Strategies for Small Streams xxv

BILLINGS REGION

1. Rock Creek (Red Lodge) 3
2. West Rosebud Creek 9
3. East Rosebud Creek 13
4. Stillwater River 17
5. West Fork of the Boulder River 23

BOZEMAN REGION

6. Gallatin River 29
7. East Gallatin River 33
8. Hyalite Creek 37
9. Ruby River 41
10. Lower Madison—Bear Trap Canyon 45

WHITEFISH REGION

11. North Fork of the Flathead River 51
12. Middle Fork of the Flathead River 55
13. Swift Creek 59
14. Lake Creek 63
15. Thompson River 67

HELENA REGION

16. Boulder River 73
17. Little Prickly Pear Creek 77
18. North Fork of the Blackfoot River 81
19. Monture Creek 85
20. Little Blackfoot River 89

MISSOULA REGION

21. Rock Creek 95
22. East Fork of the Bitterroot River 99
23. West Fork of the Bitterroot River 103
24. Seymour Creek 107
25. Wise River 111

References 115
Index 119

Acknowledgments

I WAS VISITING with Terry Gunn in the Lees Ferry Anglers booth at the International Sportsmen's Exposition in Phoenix in 2012 when Terry asked me, "Have you ever thought of writing a book?" So, that was the beginning of this journey.

As I look back over the ten months that went into the writing of this book, I think mostly about the support of my friends and family through every step in the process; I also met many wonderful new people who helped significantly.

During the early stages, my friends Jean and Alan Kahn helped me with the initial concept of the book. Author and friend Tom Rosenbauer shared important how-to pointers with me that proved invaluable. (In a less direct way, Tom's *Orvis Fly-Fishing Guide* has been helping me as far back as 1988.) When I agreed to take my own photographs for this project, I was not well versed in the many technical aspects that would be involved, and cannot thank Peter Lami enough for his patience with my modest photography skills and his tutelage in the medium.

During research and development, several friends join me in taking notes, checking out cafés, visiting a few bars, and fishing the streams. The research and development process was in itself an adventure, not unlike the ones I hope readers will experience for themselves when out on the water, following the recommendations in this book. The camaraderie on the road was absolutely my favorite part of this project. On my first and second visit to the Rosebuds, I was accompanied by my loving and supportive husband, Rich Semenik, who helped dig a swatch through the snow for the Suburban after 38 inches fell in Absarokee, Montana, in early October. Jean Kahn joined me for the Missoula chapter (and she thought she was just going fishing). Peter Lami joined me in Whitefish. Bill Toone came along for both Bozeman and Helena. And Mark Ozog helped me wrap up in the Helena region.

Having been a guide myself, I understand the scheduling constraints my peers have during the fishing season. I am very appreciative of the time they made available to me. Thanks to Andy Szofram of Fly Fishing Only Adventures, Chris Fleck from Stillwater Anglers, Jim Mitchell of Montana Hunting and Fishing Adventures, Rob Weiker of Lakestream Outfitters, Robert Winstrom of KRO (Kootenai River Outfitters) and KRO Fly Shop, and Austin Trayser of Trayser Media Group. This book greatly benefited from their in-depth knowledge of their home waters.

During the final stages of this project, my friends Bill Toone and Rick Williams were of immense help in editing a draft to submit to my publisher.

Of course, a project like this would never have succeeded without the support of Robb Clouse, publisher and co-founder of Stonefly Press, and his team of researchers and editors.

Finally, I wish to thank my husband, Rich, and my daughter, Andrea, for all their support and positive energy.

About the Author

MOLLY SEMENIK was a guide in Livingston Montana from 2001-2014. Molly currently resides in Birch Bay Washington where she continues to own and operate Tie The Knot Fly Fishing and continues to return to Montana with her women's fly fishing destination trips. Molly and her team primarily worked on the Yellowstone and Madison Rivers, nearby spring creeks, and local lakes. A nationally recognized fly fishing instructor, Molly teaches fly fishing for warmwater, coldwater, and saltwater species, as well as Spey casting with a two-handed rod for steelhead and salmon. In 2001, she began offering select women's fly fishing destination trips in and around Montana.

Molly is devoted to several fishing- and conservation-related nonprofit organizations. She is very active as a Certified Master Casting Instructor and serves on the Casting Board of Governors for the International Federation of Fly Fishers (IFFF). She's been involved with Trout Unlimited ever since first fishing Michigan's Au Sable River in her early teens.

Molly's father, the late Charlie Moore, noted her keen interest in fly fishing and nurtured her development as an angler. The Orvis bamboo rod he gave his teenage daughter was on display at the American Museum of Fly Fishing in Manchester, Vermont, during an exhibition titled A Graceful Rise: Women in Fly Fishing, Yesterday, Today, and Tomorrow.

The Au Sable River was Charlie and Molly's favorite spot, and they often fished together along the banks of property once owned by George Mason, who in September 1959, together with a group of fellow trout fishermen, founded

Photo by Peter Lami.

Trout Unlimited. Being tutored in the organization's local history at such an early age planted the seed for Molly's lifetime dedication to trout-water conservation.

In an 18-foot RV filled with fishing gear, photography equipment, and various Apple devices, Molly embarked on the ultimate Montana road trip, visiting and fishing each stream you'll find in this book. Every cast sent her thoughts back to those early times with her father so many years ago. Charlie would have loved to be part of this project—as it turns out, he very much is.

North Fork of the Blackfoot. Molly Semenik

Introduction

WHO DOESN'T WANT more adventures in life? Fly fishing is a great way to fulfill that desire. That's what I love about this sport—the adventure and the discovery. When I approach a river for the first time, I often feel like I am the very first person ever to fish there. What could be more exciting and adventurous than that? The adventure lies in exploring the river, finding places to stay and eat, and meeting new people. The discovery in fishing is figuring out where to fish, what to use, how to present the fly, and what you might catch. There may be a few bumps along the way, both literally and figuratively, as well as some pleasant surprises and lifelong memories.

When asked to choose 25 of the best small streams in Montana, I was undecided at first about how to approach the topic. After discussing this challenge with a few friends and colleagues, I decided to focus on waterways within driving distance of five Montana airports. That's how Regions 1 to 5 came about. Depending on the number of available fishing days, an angler can visit just one stream in a region or connect to all five. Readers on an extended fishing trip can hit two regions and visit ten streams. In my experience, the best scenario is to work west from Billings and visit all five regions over a five-week period—now, that's the trip of a lifetime! Not all creeks will fit everyone's style and interests, of course. Within every region, there are also larger rivers that may be fished with outfitters and guides, if desired.

Narrowing down all the praiseworthy streams took time. When I studied the 2013 and 2014 *Montana Fishing Regulations* (a publication of Montana Fish, Wildlife & Parks), the Western and Central Districts alone listed over 103 creeks! I wish I'd had the time and resources to visit every one of them, as well as others that weren't specified by the parks department. I chose the 25 small streams in this book based primarily on my personal knowledge of Montana's water systems, with a few suggestions by friends and colleagues. In between guide days and teaching classes, I did get to visit or revisit all 25 streams, and I had a fantastic time! I was fortunate enough always to have a friend tag along with me—in many ways, the best part of this adventure. I'd already fished most of the creeks numerous times before; in the course of writing this book, I discovered a few more. Because I wanted to suggest eating establishments, bars, lodging, and other amenities in the area profiles, I did need to familiarize myself with the communities nearest the streams, as well. At times, I felt more like a field researcher than a fishing guide and author. Not surprisingly, I enjoyed this project very much.

So, what makes a small stream good to fish? I recommend the following features:

Good access
Mostly walk-and-wade only
Small enough for an angler to move easily from one
    fishing hole to the next
Beautiful, lesser known, and hopefully solitary waters
    (depending on time of year and day of the week)
Interesting and attractive local geography—it should
    be fun to get there
An area where the more adventurous angler can
    further explore the profiled waters or find other
    fishable streams nearby
Healthy fluvial habitat with wild trout
Watercourses free of environmental stress and
    excessive angling pressure.

I've included different types of small streams in these pages: some are easy outings as far as approach and technique, while others pose more of a challenge when it comes to access and expertise. Some of the creeks are recommended especially for the young family and for novices. Fish size depends on the type of stream and the amount of food available to the trout. The high-mountain streams, such as Rock Creek near Red Lodge or the Rosebuds, are steeply graded with fast pocketwater. Their fish are smaller as a result of the harsh environment and short growing season. Glacier waters near Whitefish, for example, have very few nutrients, as you will see from the size of the fish. Don't equate fish size with toughness, however—the 14-inchers can really fight!

Rivers such as the Little Blackfoot and Stillwater start out as mountain headstreams with steep descents, but once they flow down into valleys, they exhibit the typical long riffle runs, deep pools, and undercut grassy banks common to valley hydrography. The fish in lower valley streams enjoy more temperate conditions, a long growing season, and abundant food—and the easy living shows in their physiques. Some of those low stretches are close to the main rivers that they feed and, in spring and fall, may hold large spawning fish. Higher-elevation streams support grayling and brook and cutthroat trout, which can tolerate cold water temperatures. The larger trout in lower elevations include rainbow, brown, and bull trout.

I've provided general information about Montana's wildlife, weather, and the Stream Access Law for your review. You will also find strategies for fishing small streams, casting tips included. (As a Certified Master Casting Instructor, I could not neglect casting technique!)

My hope is that this book will inspire you to plan a trip to Montana. Add a few maps of your own and a venturesome spirit, and you will be well on your way. Do keep in mind that *25 Best Off-the-Beaten-Path Montana Fly Fishing Streams* is merely a glimpse of what you can discover in Big Sky Country. Do your own digging. Blaze your own trails. Enjoy!

As a last note—please confirm all lodging and eating venues before your arrival. While the places I've suggested are currently in operation as of this writing, things have a way of changing quickly in the rural West. I do apologize to those businesses I did not have the privilege of learning about and visiting.

—Molly J. Semenik

North Fork of the Flathead. Peter Lami

Montana Rivers and Streams

MONTANA'S RIVERS are mostly wild and undammed. The Yellowstone River, for example, is the longest undammed river in the contiguous United States. The river flows from Wyoming for approximately 692 miles before it meets up with the Missouri River.

Spring Runoff

Larger rivers with dams are not so affected by snowmelt as the smaller rivers and streams you will be fishing. With no dam to temper the flows, springtime brings with it a deluge of muddy, frothy, dangerous water. We call it spring runoff. Water levels are measured in feet of depth and cubic feet per second (CFS). Cubic feet per second is the amount of water that passes a given point per second. From January to April, flows maintain their winter level. Spring changes that dramatically. Estimating when the spring runoff will occur is a challenge anglers in the area face annually, taking into account snowpack and daytime and nighttime temperatures. If we have warm days early in April, runoff will start sooner than in years when April is cold. Every year is different, and the timing is tricky to predict.

There are seasonal variations depending on the location of the stream. Generally speaking, I would say that pre-runoff fishing is best from mid-March to mid- and late April. With the season's unpredictable weather, planning a spring trip can be uncertain. By early April, water temperatures begin to warm up to the 40s, which gets the bugs moving. March and April hatches include Blue-winged Olives, midges, March Browns, caddis, and *Skwala* stoneflies. Water temperatures can reach 50 to 54 degrees Fahrenheit by late April. Spring is my favorite time of the year to fish, personally—but include risky weather conditions especially for those traveling great distances. As July approaches, water levels begin to drop and visibility improves. As a general fishing rule, it is best to have about 18 inches of visibility and water levels that are either stable or dropping—not rising. The higher the stream elevation, the colder the water temperatures will be. The higher-elevation creeks generally clear before the lower sections, however. Most of the streams in this book are branches of larger rivers, feeders that will clear up before the main stem does. The water flow, volume, and temperature will be major factors in determining when to visit as well as the fishing regulations. Check with a fly shop in the area for the most up-to-date local report.

Photo by Molly Semenik

Packing Your Fly Box

SMALL-STREAM fly selection is not complicated. The higher-elevation creeks have trout that survive primarily on terrestrials and feed eagerly to take advantage of the short growing season. Dry flies are a pleasure to fish, and most anglers prefer them to nymphs or streamers. When choosing a dry fly, pick one that's not too difficult to see. In fast pocketwater, good visibility is the key to detecting a strike and keeping the float drag free. Fly imitations can fit in a single box. I myself carry way too many flies, probably because I've gotten used to relying on the large bag of flies I keep in my drift boat.

A basic **dry fly** collection might include the following patterns in sizes 10 to 18:

Parachute Adams
Royal Wulff
Humpy
Elk-hair Caddis
Stimulator
terrestrials (beetles, moths, ants, hoppers)
a few exact imitations (Pale Morning Dun,
  Golden Stone)

When selecting **nymphs,** include some with weight, some with a standard beadhead, and one or two with a tungsten bead. You'll mostly be fishing sizes 8 to 18:

Prince Nymph
Gold-ribbed Hare's Ear
Pheasant Tail
Lightning Bug (up to #12)
soft-hackle wet fly (such as the Partridge and Orange,
  #12–16)

Streamers might be useful in lower elevations and, during spring and fall, near the confluence of tributaries and larger rivers:

Woolly Bugger (black or olive, #2–10)
Sculpin (black, olive, or tan; #2–10)
rubber-leg pattern (#4–12)
Yuk Bug
leech (black, brown, and olive; #6–12)

MONTANA HATCH CHART

The emergence dates I indicated include all five regions of the book, therefore they are somewhat general. Patterns are the most common from my personal experience. Every fly shop will have their favorites, along with a few locally tied flies. Please support the local fly shops.

INSECT	EMERGENCE	PATTERN: DRY	PATTERN: WET
Mayfly			
Blue-winged Olive, 14–22	Mar–Apr, Sept–Nov	Blue-winged Olive Parachute Rusty Spinner, Comparadun Cripple pattern	Sawyer, Pheasant Tail Gold-ribbed Hare's Ear
Western March Brown, 12–14	Mar–May	March Brown Dun March Brown Comparadun Cripple pattern	Golden-ribbed Hare's Ear March Brown Soft Hackle
Pale Morning Dun, 14–18	June–August	PMD Sparkle Dun PMD Emerger	PMD Soft Hackle PMD Split Case Gold-ribbed Hare's Ear
Green Drake, 8–12	June–July	Green Drake Quigley Cripple Green Drake CDC Winged Emerger Green Drake Dun	Olive Hare's Ear
Grey Drake, 10–12	July–Oct	Parachute Grey Drake	Pheasant Tail
Trico, 18–22	July–Sept	CDC RS2-Black Parachute Trico CDC Spinner, Trico Cripple	Trico Emerger
Mahogany Dun, 12–16	Aug–Oct	Thorax Mahogany Sparkle Dun Mahogany	Pheasant Tail
Caddis			
Grannom, 14–16 (Mother's Day Caddis)	Apr–June	Elk-hair caddis, brown to olive X-caddis, Olive Lime Trude (when all else fails)	Pupa: wired lime, Sparkle Caddis Pupa, lime Larva: BH Serendipity, lime, red, tan
Spotted Sedge, 10–14	May–Oct	Elk hair Caddis, brown to tan X-Caddis, tan to olive	Pupa: Sparkle caddis, tan to olive
Little Black Caddis, 18–22 (Microcaddis)	July–Aug	Elk-hair caddis, brown to black	Soft hackle, brown to orange Copper Brassie
Brown Sedge, 14–16 (Evening)	Aug–Oct	Elk-hair caddis, brown	Pupa: Sparkle caddis, tan
October Caddis, 6–8	Aug–Oct	Stimulator-orange Elk-hair caddis, orange	Larva: Cased caddis, brown Pupa: Sparkle caddis, orange to brown
Stonefly			
Skwala, 6–10	Mar–May	Stimulator, Sofa Pillo, brown to Olive	Kaufman's Stonefly, dark brown Rubber Legs, dark brown
Salmonfly, 4–8 (dark brown to orange)	May–June	Improved Sofa Pillow Stimulator Godzilla	Girdle Bug Yuk Bug Prince Nymph
Golden Stone, 6–8	May–September	Stimulator, yellow Chubby Chernobyl, Gold	Bead Head Golden Stone Nymph Girdle Bug, black to brown BH Gold Ribbed Hare's Ear
Little Yellow Sally, 14–16	June–August	Lawson's Yellow Sally Stimulator, yellow	Yellow Sally nymph Hare's Ear

MONTANA HATCH CHART continued

INSECT	EMERGENCE	PATTERN: DRY	PATTERN: WET
	JAN FEB MAR APR MAY JUN JUL AUG SEP OCT NOV DEC		
Midge Midge, 16–22 (black and tan)	All year, prominent spring and fall.	CDC Midge CDC Midge Emerger Griffith's Gnat Renegade	Brassi, red and green BH Black Zebra Midge Disco Midge Candy Cane Midge
Attractors	Summer	Royal Wulff, 10-16 Stimulator, 8–16 Royal Trude, 12–14 Humpies (red, yellow), 12–16 Purple Haze, 12–18 Parachute Adams, 12–18 Chubby Chernobyl's, 10–14	Prince Nymph, 8–16 Copper Johns (red or green), 12–16
Streamers 2–10	All year, prominent in the spring and fall		Black and Olive Woolly Buggers Black, Olive and Tan Sculpins Yuk Bug Black and Gray Zonkers
Leeches 6–12	All Year		Black, Olive, Brown
Aquatic Worms 10–16	All Year		San Juan Worm (red, tan or brown)
Terrestrials Grasshoppers, 6–14	July–September	Chernobyl Hoppers Dave's Hopper Morish Hopper (tan, yellow, pink)	
Crickets	June–Aug		
Beetles, 12–16	June–Aug		
Ants, 16–20	July–Oct	Black Flying Ant Cinnamon Ant	
Spruce Moth, 12–14 (9–2:00 and 6:00 p.m.)	August	Elk-hair caddis (trim the belly hackle off and splay the wings) Spruce Moth Patterns	

Montana Facts

PEOPLE OFTEN FIND that Montana has an interesting and unusual history and character. Here are some interesting facts about the state.

- Paleo-Indians are believed to have used stone tools in Montana around 11,000 B.C.E.
- Modern tribal nations derive from earlier nomadic indigenous cultures that have existed in the state for several thousand years.
- French explorers, traders, and trappers arrived in Montana in the early 1740s, hoping to discover the fabled Northwest Passage.
- In 1803, the United States acquired much of the region from France as part of the Louisiana Purchase.
- Great Britain ceded Western Montana to the United States as part of the Oregon Treaty of 1846.
- Montana became the 41st state on November 8, 1889.
- In 2010, the population was 989,415.
- The state capital is Helena.
- The economy is based on agriculture (wheat, barley, rye, oats, flaxseed, sugar beets, and potatoes). Sheep and cattle make a significant contribution, as do the lumber, outdoor recreation, and tourism industries.
- Montana's mining history began with the gold rush of 1864. Copper, lead, zinc, manganese, and coal extraction followed. During World War I, Butte was the richest town in the country. Today, 3,800 people in Montana are employed in 254 mines.
- There are eight tribal nations and 12 tribes in Montana.
- There are 56 counties in Montana—only half of those have a traffic light!

My favorite fact about Montana will become obvious to you as you drive across the state and fish the streams detailed in this book: the total area is 147,138 square miles. Fourth-biggest state in the USA. Forty-fourth most populous state in the nation. That's the reason we have so much open road, undeveloped land, and miles of endless sky!

Montana Fishing Facts

WHEN PEOPLE think of Montana, they imagine ranches, wildlife, open spaces and big skies, hunting, and fishing. Here are some fun fishing facts.

- Robert Redford's screen adaptation of Norman Maclean's novella *A River Runs Through It* was filmed in Montana in 1992.
- In Montana, *creeks* is pronounced *cricks*.
- Montana's oldest fish species is the pallid sturgeon—76 million years old.
- Montana has thousands of named rivers and streams; 450 of those river miles are designated Blue Ribbon trout fisheries.
- Montana manages most of its rivers for wild trout.
- Wild trout populations are self-sustaining and not supplemented with hatchery-raised fish.
- The Yellowstone River is the longest undammed river in the Lower 48: approximately 692 miles.
- Native game species include westslope cutthroat trout, Yellowstone cutthroat trout, bull trout, redband trout, Arctic grayling, lake trout, and mountain whitefish.
- The rainbow trout, brown trout, brook trout, and cutbows (a rainbow–cutthroat hybrid) found in Montana's waterways are nonindigenous species.

Miles of endless sky. Peter Lami

Wildlife Safety

As you travel throughout Montana, encounters with wildlife can pose a danger, and the risks involved vary depending on your location. Each stream profile notes whether wildlife is present in that area, but be alert to your surroundings at all times.

Bears

Montana Fish, Wildlife & Parks (FWP) provides the following advice about how to respond to a bear encounter (http://fwp.mt.gov/recreation/safety/wildlife/bears/bearEncounter.html):

> With a little knowledge you can keep a bear encounter from becoming a conflict. The following is a list of recommended responses to minimize the likelihood of attack or chances of human injury:
>
> Make certain you have *bear pepper spray* at the ready and know how to use it.
> Always maintain a *safe distance* from bears.
> *Stay calm.*
> Immediately *pick up small children* and stay in a group.
> Behave in a *nonthreatening manner.*
> *Speak softly.*
> Do *NOT* make eye contact.
> *Throw a backpack* or other object (like a hat or gloves) on the ground as you move away to distract the animal's attention.
> *Slowly back away,* if possible. Keep a distance of at least 100 yards.
> *Do not run from a bear.* Running may trigger a natural predator–prey attack response and a grizzly can easily outrun the world's fastest human.
> *Don't climb a tree* unless you are sure you can get at least ten feet from the ground before the bear reaches you. Many experts recommend against climbing trees in most situations.
> *Do not attempt to frighten away or haze a grizzly bear* that is near or feeding on a carcass.
> *If a grizzly bear* charges, your first option is to remain standing and direct your pepper spray at the charging bear. The bear may "bluff charge" or run past you. As a last resort, either curl up in a ball or lie facedown (flat). Leave your pack on to provide protection, cover your neck and head with your arms and hands. Do not attempt to look at the bear until you are sure it's gone.
> *If a black or grizzly bear attacks,* and if you have a firearm and know how to use it safely and effectively, Montana law allows you to kill a bear to defend yourself, another person, or a domestic dog. If you do kill a bear in self-defense, you must report it to FWP within 72 hours.
> If you are armed, *using a weapon on a grizzly bear does not guarantee your safety.* Wounding a grizzly bear will put you and others in danger.

Moose

I love to see moose—from a distance! Moose have an excellent sense of smell. Their ears move independently of each other; therefore, they can both hear well and track the direction of a sound. Their eyes move independently as well—all the better to see you with.

I am every bit as concerned about moose as I am about bears. Moose need food and cover. They browse on leaves and twigs, and their favorite food source, the willow, is often found along streambeds. Aquatic plants in lakes and ponds are another favorite. Moose overheat easily. In the summer months, you may see them trying to stay cool by standing in water.

A cow with its young is most likely to be aggressive, but every moose is dangerous. If you get too close, their ears will lie flat and the hair on the back of their necks will stand up. Moose may start with a false charge and then stop advancing. When really threatened, they may follow through on the attack. They strike with their hooves and are known to cause serious injury. Be particularly careful whenever you walk through thick willows. It may be best to walk around willow stands entirely. Before hitting the stream, ask locals if moose frequent the area you wish to fish.

Mountain Lion

According to the parks department (http://fwp.mt.gov/recreation/safety/wildlife/lion/lionEncounter.html):

> Knowing what to do if you do encounter a mountain lion can reduce the potential for a conflict.
>
> *Do not approach a lion*—Most mountain lions will try to avoid a confrontation. Give them a way to escape.
> *Do not run from a lion*—Running may stimulate a mountain lion's instinct to chase. Instead, stand and face the animal. Do not turn your back. Make eye contact. If there are small children nearby, pick them up if possible, so they don't panic and run. Although it may be awkward, pick them up without bending over or turning away from the mountain lion.
> *Do not crouch down or bend over*—A person squatting or bending over looks a lot like a four-legged prey animal. When in mountain lion country, avoid squatting, crouching, or bending over, even when picking up children.
> *Appear larger*—Raise your arms. Open your jacket if you are wearing one. Again, pick up small children. Throw stones, branches, or whatever you can reach without crouching or turning your back. Wave your arms slowly and speak firmly in a loud voice. The idea is to convince the mountain lion that you are not prey and that you may be a danger to it.
> *Be vocal*—Talk calmly and regularly.
> *Teach others how to behave*—One who starts running could initiate an attack.
> If a lion attacks:
> *If you are unarmed,* you can use bear pepper spray to deter the lion. Many potential victims have also fought back successfully with rocks, sticks, caps, jackets, garden tools, and their bare hands. Since a mountain lion usually tries to bite the head or neck, try to remain standing and face the attacking animal.
> *If you have a firearm,* and know how to use it safely and effectively, Montana law allows you to kill a mountain lion to defend yourself, another person, or a domestic dog. If you do kill a lion in self-defense, you must report it to FWP within 72 hours.

Snakes

Ten snake species live in Montana; only the prairie rattlesnake (Western rattlesnake) is venomous. It can be found in open, arid country and often dens on the south-facing slopes of areas with rock outcrops. Rattlesnakes rarely bite humans. Of the hundreds of thousands of hunters, hikers, and backpackers traversing Montana, only five or six report being bitten annually, according to the Rocky Mountain Poison and Drug Center in Denver. The center also notes that there was not a single death among the 45 reported prairie rattlesnake bites in Montana during the last eight years.

Here are a few safety notes that I have gathered over the years:

- Snakes don't like vibrations, so stomp your feet. Throw rocks or use a wading staff to tap on any rocks that you may need to scurry over.
- If you are about to be bitten and you are able to defend yourself, kick the bottom of your shoe out to the snake and let it strike the tread or sole.
- Striking distance is between a third to half the snake's length.
- Wear leather boots that cover past the ankle at least.
- Keep your eyes on the ground.
- Don't stick your hands into snaky areas, rocks, logs (firewood), or brush. Use a stick or object if you need to reach into places snakes find attractive.
- Rattlesnakes are cold-blooded and prefer to be active in 65 to 85 degrees Fahrenheit. They hibernate when cold temperatures arrive.
- If you see a snake, try to relax and detour around it.
- Do not touch a dead snake; it can still bite for some time after it has died.

First Aid for Snakebites

If you or a companion is bitten, heed this advice from snakebite experts:

1. Note the time of the bite.
2. The victim should be kept calm, and exertion should be avoided. Physical activity increases absorption of the venom.
3. Immediately remove rings, bracelets, and other constricting jewelry or clothing.
4. Immobilize the bitten limb with a splint or sling (applied loosely so circulation is not cut off), and keep it lower than heart level.
5. Walk the victim at a steady but relatively slow pace back to a vehicle, and provide transport to the nearest medical facility. Or go to the nearest house and ask for assistance.

Ticks

In Montana, tick season lasts from the onset of warmer weather in the spring until about mid-July, when heat and low relative humidity cause the ticks to become inactive. Rocky Mountain wood ticks are the primary disease vectors in Montana. A soft-bodied tick that transmits relapsing fever has recently been found in Montana as well. The black-legged ticks that can carry Lyme disease are not known to occur in Montana. The foregoing information comes from http://fwp.mt.gov/recreation/safety/wildlife/ticks/. The parks department site also gives directions on how to remove ticks that have latched on to you: http://fwp.mt.gov/recreation/safety/wildlife/ticks/removal.html.

I suggest long-sleeved shirts and pants for walking through bushes, and a tick check at the end of the day.

Moose. Molly Semenik

Stream Accessibility and Wading Challenge

THE SCALE I USE throughout the book is based on a rating from 1 to 5, with 5 being the most challenging.

I rated stream accessibility by comparing several factors, including how plentiful access is and what physical demands are required of an angler getting to the stream (for instance, crossing uneven ground, scaling gradients, or bushwhacking through a forest). The scale refers to the areas near the obvious access points identified in the chapter. If an angler is willing and able to venture away from obvious access points, then the scale is not so relevant.

Wading challenge is a bit tricky to classify because of how variable a stream's character can be. I tried to look at the stream as a whole and consider it from many different vantage points.

One could certainly choose to stay near an area that is less challenging than another just 50 yards away. When deciding on a rating, I reviewed the riverbed character along with the streambank character.

Another important quality is the slickness of the rocks. Lastly, water speed is critical when gauguing wading safety. Spring runoff can turn a mountain stream into an extremely difficult and dangerous environment. During the summer months, the water speed in a narrow river channel might be very different from that of a wider, more meandering watercourse. My scale for ease of wading is based on midsummer months in areas close to the obvious access points.

Weather

MONTANA holds the world record for the greatest temperature shift in 24 hours. On January 14 and 15, 1972, in Loma, the mercury climbed from 54 degrees below zero to 49 degrees Fahrenheit—a change of 103 degrees! I have seen great temperature swings for myself, and can testify that layers are key to streamside comfort and safety. Pack a warm hat, gloves, and raingear—even in high summer. Conditions in Montana fluctuate so constantly that when remarking upon the weather, locals usually quip, "Just wait ten minutes."

Spring really has two phases. Early spring, which includes March and April, is a fine time to fish when the weather cooperates; however, snow and wind still occur with regularity during those "pre-runoff" months. Late spring—that is, May and June—is the season for high muddy water. Checking in with a local fly shop for water conditions is recommended.

Summer in Montana runs from July through September, and is generally sunny and dry. Heat waves begin around the Fourth of July. Two or three hot spells occur every summer and reach into the upper 90s. Each one lasts a few days to a week, with the longer heat waves becoming more common now than in years past. It can snow in Montana even during July and August, a phenomenon I've witnessed twice in 13 years. Summer snow tends to occur in the higher elevations, always short-lived. Afternoon thunderstorms are more typical this time of year, and they can be serious. At the first onset of thunder or lighting, stop fishing immediately and seek shelter. Summer begins to wind down around early September. The higher elevations receive the first dusting of snow, as a rule. Occasionally, snow reaches the valley floor, but does not last long.

Autumn weather in Montana begins in late September and goes through November. It's a very unpredictable time of year, with really cold and snowy conditions setting in by the middle of November. Periods of cold temperatures and snowy conditions occur anytime during the fall months, so be prepared. Late September through October is the season for fall color. Snowcapped mountains, trees turning to gold, and crisp air mark the approach of winter. I love to take full advantage of the photographic smorgasbord as well as the good fishing this time of year.

In winter, it is very common for the areas east of the Continental Divide to be in a deep freeze of subzero temperatures while over in Missoula and Kalispell, the temperature registers 50 degrees warmer. Many rivers are open year-round and can be counted on for good fishing when the weather permits.

Threatening Sky. Peter Lami

Trout Fishing in Montana

IN 2013, over 322,000 fishing licenses were sold to residents and nonresidents. Iconic Montana scenes often include bears, horses, eagles, and most certainly trout.

Trout and Fishing Regulations

A conservation license and Montana fishing license are required for anglers over the age of 15. Special regulations exist for anglers younger than 15 years old. The annual *Montana Fishing Regulations* booklet may be picked up at any of the state's fly shops or in a Montana FWP office, as well as via the Montana FWP website: http://fwp.mt.gov/. Always refer to the current year's regulations for up-to-date information, help with fish identification, and river maps. Familiarize yourself with this little book; regulations are specific for each river and stream. A note on the term "possession," which you will see used in the regulations: "Possession limit" means the number of fish you may possess at any time in any form, including fresh, stored in a freezer, smoked, or otherwise preserved (*2013 Montana Fishing Regulations,* page 49).

Native fish found in Montana streams include Arctic grayling, mountain whitefish, and the Westslope cutthroat, Yellowstone cutthroat, bull, and Columbia River redband trout. Exotics were introduced into Montana's river ecosystems beginning in the 1890s. Nonnative rainbows and browns took to local waters particularly well, and their populations are healthy and abundant. Unfortunately, the same can't be said of some Montana natives. Cutthroat trout, redband trout, and Arctic grayling are listed by FWS as species of concern, bull trout are threatened, and Montana's ancient sturgeon are endangered.

The Yellowstone cutthroat trout is the jewel of the Yellowstone River and drainages. Sadly, its numbers are dropping and species survival has been jeopardized after the introduction of lake trout in Yellowstone Lake. Gillnetting in Yellowstone Lake and restocking programs are countermeasures meant to effect a recovery.

The westslope cutthroat trout is the Montana state fish. Westslope cutthroat are holding steady west of the Continental Divide, while populations in the upper Missouri basin (east of the divide) have dwindled to less than 5 percent of their original range. Restoration projects have been launched in the hopes of reversing that decline. Like Yellowstone cutthroat, westslope cutthroat are distinguished by slash marks on their lower jaws and small irregular black spots mostly on the back and toward the tail. Average size is 6 to 12 inches.

Fishing for bull trout in Montana is allowed *only* on the South Fork of the Flathead River, as bull trout are protected under the Endangered Species Act. A valid Bull Trout Catch Card (available for free at the FWP Region 1 Headquarters in Kalispell) is required when targeting bull trout. Any bull trout caught by accident must be released immediately. Bull trout are most easily identified by the white leading edges on their fins and by an absence of black coloration on their dorsal fin: "No black, put it back."

Please familiarize yourself with your quarry by studying the "Fish Identification Key" on the first pages of *Montana Fishing Regulations*.

Aquatic Invasive Species

An aquatic invasive species is a nonnative waterborne organism that threatens the diversity or abundance of native flora and fauna in our streams and lakes. As anglers change fishing locations, they risk transporting invasive species, particularly when switching drainages. Aquatic nuisance species may include single-celled didymo algae, Eurasian water milfoil, whirling disease, and New Zealand mudsnails.

While conducting research on this topic, graduate student Kiza Gates discovered that the average angler who does not clean their wading boots is transporting 16.78 grams (.59 oz.) of sediment from one access site to the next. Gates determined that in 2005, angler boots moved more than 6,300 pounds of sediment between access sites in southwestern Montana. Of course, transferred mud can contain unwelcome invaders, so we must make sure our boots are clean when moving between waters.

Responsible anglers follow these simple steps to remove aquatic hitchhikers:

1. **Inspect.** Carefully examine all your equipment at the end of a trip to see if there is any sign of unwanted material attached. That includes any plants life as well as mud traces. If you see anything questionable, clean your gear.
2. **Clean.** First remove the visible material by hand; then use water to wash your equipment clean. It's okay to clean with water from the site where you fished because you will be leaving behind any problems you may have picked up there. Never clean your equipment at your put-in spot, however, since you may end up dispersing hitchhikers that have been with you since your last fishing trip. If you cannot clean before you leave a river, make sure to do so at home, where there is no chance an invader can reach the fishery.
3. **Dry.** A thorough drying of your equipment will kill any live invaders you may have picked up. If you are counting primarily on the drying process to eliminate hitchhikers, you must make sure every bit of hidden moisture is gone for it to be truly effective.

For further information, please look up the Invasive Species Action Network's website: www.stopans.org.

Montana Stream Access Law

The Montana Stream Access Law states that rivers and streams capable of recreational use may be so used by the public, regardless of streambed ownership. The law permits fishing within the ordinary high-water mark. The ordinary high-water mark means the line that water impresses upon land by covering it for a time sufficient to cause different characteristics below the line. The beginning of permanent vegetation is usually a good landmark. Floodplains next to streams are considered to be above the high-water mark. It is illegal to reach a stream by trespassing. However, anglers may gain legal access to rivers and creeks by means of a county road right-of-way at bridge crossings, state fishing access sites, or with permission from the immediate landowner. Suspension of recreational access may be imposed by a county commission for public safety reasons, and not all bridge crossings offer rights-of-way. Exceptions to the Stream Access Law should be posted.

Historically, Montana landowners and recreationalists have cooperated with mutual respect. The citizens of Montana are grateful for the Stream Access Law and work hard to protect it. If you must portage around obstructions, do so in the least intrusive manner possible. If you are unclear about whether you may be trespassing on private land, please ask or seek permission from a landowner.

Fly Fishing Strategies for Small Streams

I HAVE BEEN LEARNING to fly fish for 45 years. I will continue to explore and analyze throughout my remaining years. In this section, I wish to share with you my approach to fishing small streams. I will start at my car and end by releasing a trout. While I've benefited greatly from books, videos, and the wisdom of friends and fellow professionals, most of my schooling has taken place on the water—all types of water, from large rivers to high-mountain headstreams, to lakes and ocean flats.

For me, fishing small streams is the most solitary and peaceful of all angling experiences. Creeks make great classrooms. They give you the time and the privacy to observe and reflect on all the pieces that come together in the sport of fly fishing: rigging tackle, observing hatches and fish behavior, reading the water, approaching the water, and casting. Small waterways provide an intimate atmosphere in which to develop as an angler.

Tackle

It is important to have an idea of suitable tackle before making a purchase, especially if you are from an area far away from Western streams.

Fly Rods

If you can bring only one fly rod to Montana, I suggest an 8½- or 9-foot, 5-weight rod with medium action. Consider the size of the stream and the vegetation found along the water when selecting rod length. Longer rods allow for easier line management—from keeping the line off the water to manipulating it during mending—but longer rods can be a nuisance in small streams bordered by thick brush. If carrying two rods, I personally like a 7½-foot 3-weight rod for mountain brooks and an 8½- or 9-foot 5-weight for larger streams. Manufacturers may offer rod lengths an inch or so longer or shorter than my recommendations, which do just as well for fishing small streams.

Another alternative that some anglers might find both fun and unusual is to bring along a Tenkara rod. Tenkara is a traditional Japanese method of fly fishing that uses only rod, line, and fly. The concept is simplicity itself, which for many Tenkara devotees is the whole point. I've heard this style of fishing described as simple, fun, and intimate. (I have yet to try it.) The telescoping graphite Tenkara rods are generally 11 to 13 feet in length and utilize 5X tippet, so they are best for small and medium-sized fish. In smaller streams, the extra length on Tenkara rods can be a drawback; however, they work quite well on larger creeks and small rivers. At the time of this writing, two companies—Tenkara USA and Temple Fork Outfitters—offer new telescoping rods better suited for small-stream fishing, in lengths of 8½ to 11 feet. Many of the creeks in this book have enough clearance for fishing with Tenkara rods.

Fly Lines

The basic rule for fly lines is to match the weight of line to the weight of the rod. That rule can sometimes be broken. Most fly rods are designed to function (flex) with 30 feet of fly line extended beyond the rod tip. A few small-stream rods are designed to bend with 20 feet of fly line beyond the rod tip. That difference is important when fishing smaller waters. Casting distance in a small stream is short—frequently 10 to 15 feet or less. It may be to your advantage to over-line your smaller rods by one line weight to allow the rod to bend at shorter distances. The heavier line will also be an advantage when casting larger flies. Standard weight-forward floating lines are sufficient; I am partial to double-taper lines on all my rods smaller than a 4-weight. Weight-forward lines assist with longer casts; but small-stream fishing casts are short. Therefore, I prefer a double-taper fly line, where both ends of the line are identical. When one end wears out, I just switch the line by moving the reel end of the line to the front—two lines for the price of one! There are a couple of creeks described in this book that have very deep pools, namely the Middle Fork of the Flathead and the North Fork of the Blackfoot, where a sinking-tip line might be used.

Reels

In small-stream fishing, reels just hold the line. If you choose average- or better-than-average-quality reels, they will last many years. I consider the aesthetics and weight of the reel, and large-arbor versus regular-arbor options. I like lightweight reels on my smaller rods, which usually means a regular arbor. Large-arbor reels have the benefit of a faster line retrieve.

Leaders

Most manufacturers of trout leaders offer lengths in 7½ and 9 feet. A few outfits sell leaders that are 6 feet in length. I always carry at least two 7½- and 9-foot leaders. When fishing smaller flies, I use 4X or 5X tippet, but for larger streamers or nymphs, I might go with a tippet as big as 3X. If I know the fish could be sizable, like browns in the fall on the Ruby River, I may use a 2X leader to keep from breaking off. In the smallest mountain streams, a 7½-foot 5X leader is a good choice. If you decide to tie your own leaders, 6½ feet is ideal. As the waters (and fish) grow in size, I switch to a 9-foot 4X leader. Leader length is all about being stealthy. The slower and clearer the water, the more time the trout has to scrutinize your fly. Smaller tippet sizes (4X and 5X) work best, while faster, turbulent water means quick grabs requiring the use of heavier tippets (2X and 3X). Over the years, I have tried many leaders. Often I tie my own, which is enjoyable during the cold winter months. When buying leaders, you can't do better than a standard nylon knotless leader with a stiff butt section.

Observation, Approach, and Position

Learning how to approach and read a stream can have a great impact on your success.

Regardless of my familiarity with a stream, every outing begins with careful observation, from the moment I take my first step. Observations include wind direction, clouds or sun, sun angle, insects, birds, and any other indicator that may set the stage for me. Once I am 10 to 12 feet from the water's edge, I watch for aquatic insects in the air, on bushes, or on the water's surface. I look to see if any birds are feeding. I look to see if fish are eating below the surface or on top. I listen for the sounds of fish feeding. It takes time to meld with my surroundings. So as not to spook the fish, I cautiously examine the banks of the river from a distance: Are there trout on or near the bank? On many occasions I have spooked a trout as I approached the stream, ruining a good opportunity. I cannot emphasize enough the importance of observation. Analyzing your environment is an acquired skill that gets easier the more you do it.

Once I am well oriented to my surroundings, I begin to focus more on the creek itself. Where are the fish holding? Trout need food, oxygen, and protection (from current, birds, and predators). They avoid places where there is no food, where the water is stagnant, or where there is no place to hide. Make note of those places and avoid them. Remember also that trout need to consume more calories than they expend. Typical holding water will start to stand out to you clearly the more you fish.

Basic trout-stream features consist of pools, runs, and riffles, which alternate along the length of the stream or river.

- **Pools** have four parts: head, belly (deepest part), edges, and tailout. Pools generally have fine sediment bottoms; whereas riffles occur over coarse bottoms. All sections of a pool can hold fish, especially the head and the tailout.
- **Runs** are similar in structure to pools, but typically have a faster center current and a coarser rubble or gravel bottom than pools do. Fish hold in the same spots in runs as they do in pools.
- **Riffles** are shallower than pools, and their choppy water provides protection from prey. Riffles can hold a great deal of trout food, particularly caddis and stoneflies. Start fishing riffle sections at the edge and work toward the middle.

Here are some other water features relevant to where fish will hold:

- **Drop-offs,** like pools and riffles, hold many fish. An example of a drop-off would be water that is flowing over a rocky shelf and into a pool. The trout will be facing the edge of the shelf where food is concentrating and being pushed into the drop-off. The pool provides cover.
- **Seams** are fishy, too. They form wherever two different current speeds meet. For example, an inside bend in a stream will have a slower current than the water near the outside of the bend. The point where the two differing current speeds meet is the seam. Fish will hold in the slower water near the edge of the faster water. The faster current acts like a conveyor belt of food. Fish are protected from the current in the slower water. Trout dart out into the faster water to grab food as it passes by.
- **Foam lines,** those foam bubbles traveling downstream in an obvious line, have many benefits for a trout. The foam lines provide cover, and the bubbles trap food; this feature marks a feeding lane or a place where food has concentrated. If no foam line is present to show you the current holding the most food, throw a small piece of wood or leaf onto the water, and watch its progress downstream. The trajectory can tip you off to the places food is being funneled.
- **Color changes** in the depth of water indicate where a trout may be. Again, trout survive by eating more than they burn off. They favor depressions that shield them

from the current. In addition to color changes, look for changes in surface texture.

- **Rocks** provide good habitat for trout, as everyone knows. My favorite situation is a long string of larger rocks creating overlapping holding water. Fish will hold in front of rocks before the water splits to either side. Once the water splits, it jets around the sides of the rock and then starts to move back to the center behind the rock, forming a teardrop shape or triangle. Fish station themselves in the water along the seams separating the faster water on the outside and the slower water on the inside of the triangle. Fish also hold where two currents merge at the bottom point of the triangle below the rock. Stay clear of the frothy wavy water just behind the rock; the turbulence will pull your fly under. Instead, target the softer water just behind the turbulent water—not an easy task. Rocks also create another holding area in the small 6-inch shadows along their edge. Try to place a fly along the shadow line. Trout hide just under the curve of the rock and will see a fly running along its edge; however, this maneuver works only if the current is not too fast.
- **Woody structure** creates another likely fish-holding location, so long as the current delivers food. A structure that runs parallel with the bank is better than a structure that sticks out into the current. The closer you can fish to them, the better. Any flies that catch on the woody structure can be retrieved after you've fished the hole; my dad used to say to me, "If you are not losing flies, you are not close enough."
- **Undercuts banks,** especially along grassy streamsides, can be the best location of all and frequently hold the largest fish. Terrestrials (ants, grasshoppers, and the like) fall off the grass into the water to become sizable meals. The wind is your friend when fishing these brinks in the heat of the summer.

After careful observation, think of how you will approach the water and where you will stand. Decide if you are going to fish upstream, across stream, or downstream. Obstructions, the stream's size, and the location of good holding water will often determine your approach to the stream. For heavily obstructed banks, I like to wade upstream, especially when fishing a dry fly. Because fish face upstream, my approach from below is less likely to be noticed. Additionally, the stirred-up river bottom left in my tracks will be moving downstream, away from the fish. When fishing upstream, it is easier to avoid snagging streamside vegetation, particularly on your backcast.

Molly fishing Swift Creek. Peter Lami

Fishing across stream is a good method as well, but does require more room for the backcast. When fishing across stream, you'll want to be slower and more precise. Mending the line is easier when fishing across stream. Downstream presentation works as well, as I will describe in detail in the "Casting Techniques" section of this chapter. If you need to hike upstream before fishing back downstream, stay clear of the streambank, as fish are easily spooked.

My proximity to the stream and how close I am able to get to the fish depend on several factors. Fast, turbulent pocketwater allows you to get closer to the fish than you would in slower, calmer water. Fast water disguises the disturbance created by wading, whereas slower water holds surface waves for a longer time. When fish are feeding, you can carefully wade close, as they are focused on the food. After fishing to feeding fish for a few minutes, you may notice them start to feel your presence and move farther away or stop feeding entirely. When that happens, have a seat and wait ten minutes or so to let the hole rest. Once they resume feeding, you can fish again, though you'll want to move even more slowly and carefully than before. I have spent close to an hour fishing to rising fish by taking breaks and letting the hole rest. Nevertheless, the most productive fishing will take place with the first several casts. After that, the fish will become increasingly finicky until you decide it's time to move on. Another method at close quarters is to use brush, trees, and boulders to hide your profile. Every stream will have its own threshold for how close you can get. Start slow, move slow, and then be as still as a heron.

Just prior to casting, be aware of your actual position. Look around for obstructions—even when the fish are rising and your body is trembling with excitement! When first fishing a hole, try to fish from the bank before you enter the water. Our footsteps in the shallows make noise, create vibrations, and send ripples along the surface of the water. Move your feet slowly, try not to lift them completely out of the water as you take a step. I learned this method of walking in water from bonefish guides: step gently and move as little water as possible. Keep a low profile if you can; trout see tall objects more easily than profiles low to the ground. If you need to false cast in order to measure your casting distance, do so in an area away from the trout. I often do a practice cast when I have the space. I will cast parallel with the bank, adjust my length, then turn and present the fly to the trout. Watch for shadows cast by your rod action and body profile.

When you are prospecting the selected area, I advise gridding out the water. Emmett Heath, a well-known guide on the Green River in Utah, taught me how to look at the water and imagine lines that make a grid. Fish every section of the grid systematically, starting close and working your way out. This method will not be so necessary on smaller streams, but it can be helpful on your larger waters. Move on after you have covered the water.

Casting Techniques

Finally, it is time to cast. I always find it worthwhile to go back to the basics and think about how a fly rod works. In the basic overhead cast, two forces are acting together: body motion (mostly arm movement) and the weight of the fly line. The casting stroke, coupled with the weight of the fly line, bends the rod. When the casting stroke is stopped, the rod unloads its stored energy into the fly line, sending the line off the rod tip in the direction of the casting stroke. Meanwhile, the fly just goes along for the ride. In overhead casting, two strokes are used—one for the forward cast and another for the backcast—both equally important and mirror images of each other.

In a small stream where there's not much room, every casting stroke counts. Again, it is the weight of the fly line that bends the rod. On small streams, very little fly line will travel beyond the rod tip, which can make it difficult to load (bend) the rod. To help bend the rod, prior to picking up the line off the water, remove all slack and keep the rod tip close to the surface before initiating your backcast. Casting on larger streams may call for more than one backcast before presenting the fly, but most smaller streams will need only a single backcast. Smaller rods sizes (2- and 3-weight.) can bend with less line beyond the rod tip. With all casts, minimize the amount of line used and cast as few times as possible.

The casts described below may be studied online (YouTube clips are especially helpful), on DVD and video, and in how-to books and articles. For a hands-on tutorial, consider contacting one of the Certified Casting Instructors listed on the International Federation of Fly Fishers website: www.fedflyfishers.org.

I've taught fly casting for over 30 years. While it is beyond the scope of this book to offer detailed fly-casting instruction, I shall define each cast relevant to small-stream fishing and share some important tips. The pointers derive from my experiences as a casting instructor and from more than 13 guiding seasons. If you are new to fly fishing, I highly recommend a few months' worth of lessons to get yourself ready for your Montana adventure. The big fishing trip will be more enjoyable without the distraction of learning how to cast onsite. Besides, whether you're just learning to cast or brushing up on your technique, preseason training is fun!

Basic Overhead Cast

In a basic overhead cast, the line is picked up off the water with a backcast. Start with a slow, lifting move and a firm wrist; then when the fly line–leader connection begins to leave the water, speed up to a crisp stop. The stop is followed by a pause long enough for the line to straighten. A forward cast is then executed, which lays the line back down on the water. Begin with the rod tip close to the water; strip in any slack line on the water so when the rod tip starts to move, there is direct contact with the fly line, which loads or bends the rod.

For most backcasts, the stop position is the point at which the casting hand reaches the caster's ear (that is, answering a phone; thumb vertical). The rod tip should travel in a straight line. The straight-line rod path creates tight loops that cut through wind, travel farther, and are more accurate than a larger, wider loop. Wide loops are caused by the rod tip traveling in a dome shape. If the caster's rod tip travels too far back (often past the straight-up noon position; thumb at two o'clock), the loop shape will widen.

Start the forward cast once the loop starts to unfold (the pause) and the leader is about to straighten. The line should not have started to drop behind or lose energy. Begin the forward and end with a crisp stop just like the backcast. After the forward stop, allow the rod tip to follow the line down to the water. Upon lowering the rod tip, the caster is ready to fish or is positioned for the next backcast.

Here are some pointers for small streams:

- After my fly is tied on to my leader and I'm ready to make my first cast, I hook the fly on a guide, then pull the line off the reel. Once I have the desired amount of line off the reel, I hold the fly by the bend of the hook, hook point facing away from me, and shake out all the fly line beyond the rod tip. Make the backcast and release the fly. This motion should keep your fly from catching on the ground. A roll cast can also be used during the first initial cast.

- Learn to cast over both shoulders (dominant and nondominant sides); the cast is the same for each side. You can cast throughout with your dominant hand, but change the line placement from your dominant shoulder to your off-shoulder simply by changing the angle of the rod. Just tilt the butt section (the rod just above the cork) a few inches toward your nondominant side to cast off your nondominant shoulder or back a few inches to cast off your dominant side.
- Learn to cast at different angles, from vertical to horizontal. Fish that are tucked under streamside bushes are easier to reach when you tilt your body and use a sidearm horizontal cast for presentation.
- Learn to change your trajectory up or down as needed. Trajectory is the path of the rod tip, and thus of the fly line. A horizontal trajectory is parallel to the water. An upward trajectory raises the forward cast and lowers the backcast, while a downward trajectory lowers the forward cast and raises the backcast. A downward trajectory cast is extremely useful in fishing small streams. For short casts, the backcast should be aimed nearly straight up to the sky, and the forward cast down to the water. If a longer cast is required, the trajectory will need to tilt more toward the horizontal so the line does not crash on the water. A high backcast will also reduce the number of fly-and-tree encounters.
- Rod arc is the angle change of the rod's butt section between the backcast and the forward cast. The arc is shaped like a piece of pizza. Most casters cast with too wide an arc for the amount of bend in the rod, which creates a dome-shaped rod tip path and results in a wide loop. On small streams with short casts, the rod barely bends. Consequently, a small arc with the fly line trajectory down in the front and high in the back will result in tight loops and accurate presentations. My clients are often amazed at how little rod movement is actually required for short casting distances.

Roll Cast

The roll cast is an extremely versatile and often underutilized cast. The roll cast uses only a small loop of line positioned behind the caster's rod, with the remainder of the line anchored on the water in front of the caster. (There is no backcast.) When the forward cast is made (basic cast), tension from the water helps load the rod. After the forward stop, a loop travels off the rod tip toward the target, lifting the line off the water and finally straightening out to the target.

The roll cast has many uses: removing slack from the line at the start of fishing, lifting heavily weighted fly line from the water, casting when obstacles are present behind the caster, casting when wind is blowing from the caster's back, and removing flies that are stuck on an obstacle (a classic scenario in a small stream).

A roll cast is half a cast. In small streams, begin with a few feet of line on the water. Slowly raise the rod tip to the one o'clock position, ending with your rod hand at head height; then stop. Look to see if some fly line is behind the rod tip, forming a rounded loop behind the rod (the D-loop). Tilt the rod away slightly from the shoulder, so the fly line is not behind your back. Keep the elbow in toward your body, hand positioned outside the elbow. Start the forward cast slowly and drive the elbow downward. (This loads the rod.) The elbow leads the cast; the hand follows the elbow but finishes toward the intended target. Finish with a crisp stop at the conclusion of the forward stroke, making sure not to drop the rod tip below horizontal.

As in all good forward casts, the rod tip must travel in a straight line. Power occurs at the end of the forward stroke. The roll cast requires more power than a standard forward cast. To avoid having the fly line crash into itself, if the target is left of center, the fly line (D-loop) must be placed behind the right shoulder, while targets to the right require fly line placement behind the left shoulder. Roll casting on small streams is easy and will probably constitute 50 percent of your fishing time.

Mastering the roll cast will add versatility to your casting and fishing experiences. Two common casting problems occur in the early stages of learning the roll cast:

1. **The casting loop is too big.** The caster may have started the cast with the rod tip too far back, below the straight-line path of the rod tip. In this case, the loop will be directed upward initially, rather than forward toward the target. Alternatively, the caster may have started the cast with too much power. The power occurs at the end of the stroke.

2. **The line crashes onto the water.** Crash landings happen when the forward cast stop is aimed too low. The caster raises the forward cast trajectory and directs the loop forward, rather than downward.

When roll casting in small streams:
- Practice roll casting off both sides of the body.
- Practice a sidearm roll cast off both sides of the body.

Dapping and Jigging

Dapping can be used in very tight conditions where a backcast is not an option. Dapping is done with the rod tip. The rod tip is lifted and placed either directly over the target or a foot or so upstream and then lowered so the fly just touches the water's surface. Only the fly touches the water. Jigging would be when using an imitation that sinks. I have lowered nymphs down between the limbs of a log and caught brook trout that were otherwise unreachable.

- When dapping:
- Keep the leader short, maybe six feet or less.
- Be careful during the hook-set; otherwise, your backcast may go off into the bushes behind you.
- If it is a windy day, a small split shot can be placed six inches or so above either a dry fly or wet fly.

Bow-and-Arrow Cast

The bow-and-arrow cast is fun! Use it when a short cast is needed and you have little room for a backcast. Take hold of the fly (at the bend of the hook) with your free hand and trap the line with the forefinger of your rod hand. Only the leader may pass beyond the rod tip. Pull the fly back (keeping the point away from you) until the rod is bent like a bow. Direct the rod tip toward the target and release the fly. You may wish to practice this maneuver before you use it on the stream. For a longer cast, you can fold the fly line in the hand that is holding the fly. When I am using a large dry fly, I often take hold of the fly material rather than the bend of the hook.

Beyond the Basic Casts

For in-depth descriptions of more technical casts—such as the reach, curve, pile, tuck, puddle, and parachute casts—you will want to consult the Internet or books and videos for instruction. Supplemental casts are fun to learn and very useful tools for small-stream fishing.

Fishing Upstream

When fishing upstream, cast at a slight angle either left or right rather than directly upstream of your body, to keep from placing the line over the fish. Our goal is a fly-first presentation! A curve cast would be a good tactic as well. As the fly floats back toward you, strip fly line in to match the speed of the current. While stripping, begin to lift your rod as the fly nears; this movement will allow you to lift the fly line off the water as the fly approaches the side of your body. At that point, recast. The trout will be wary of your body. If you wish, mentally grid out the water; then start fishing with a 45-degree angle cast to the left of your center. Now work sequentially across, casting directly upstream, and progressing out to 45 degrees to the opposite side of the river.

Fishing Across the Stream

Casting across the stream and then allowing your fly to drift downstream is a great and popular angling technique, and a method that requires you to be slow and precise. In the across-stream presentation, you drift the fly down to the fish. Cast across stream or slightly upriver. Depending on the current, you may need to mend the fly line, usually upstream, in order to have a drag-free float. *Mending* is the manipulation of the fly line before it lands on the water (the aerial mend) or after it lands on the water (a water mend). If the speed of the water is the same from your feet to the fly, mending line may not be necessary; however, if the water is faster near your feet than at the fly, then an upstream mend is in order. If the water is slower near your feet than near the fly, a downstream mend applies. Mending is key to a drag-free float. Sometimes, you need only one initial mend; other times, multiple quarter mends are needed to set up and follow through on a good drift.

Perform a water mend immediately once the line touches the water after the cast. The longer you wait, the more challenging it will be to mend your line. Remember to lift the line, direct the line (creating the mend), and lower the rod tip. Lift the line upward to break its tension with the water; then direct the line with your rod tip (use the spring of the bend in the rod) to fling your line in the direction you want it to go—like a half cast. Finally, lower the rod and prepare to set the hook. The size of the mend is dictated by the water speed, with faster currents requiring larger mends. The most common mistake I see anglers make is not breaking the line-water connection first when attempting a water mend. If you don't lift the line off the water, your fly will get dragged across it by the fly line.

An aerial mend is basically a reach mend. After the forward stop, reach in the direction of the intended mend with your hand and rod while slipping line through the fingers of your rod hand. In a proper aerial mend, your arm and rod are about parallel with the streambank. Slipping the line will prevent your fly from being pulled back toward you during the reach. Alternatively, you may want to intentionally pull the fly back in your direction (setting up a drag-free drift in a specific feeding lane), restrain the line with your forefinger, and pull the fly back by raising the rod tip to the desired position. You then lower the rod tip to begin your drift as a drag-free presentation. Be ready to set that hook when a fish takes your fly! All aerial mending actions take place before the line lands on the water. This method requires practice.

Getting the reach mend in before the line lands on the water is a timing issue. Be patient—the precision will come. Once perfected, the reach cast (go ahead and think of it as a mend) will have a permanent place in your fly fishing.

Fishing Downstream

When you're fishing in slower water, a downstream presentation is effective. I often use a downstream presentation for rising fish. The downstream presentation is the trickiest approach because the fish are facing upstream, which creates a timing issue with regard to setting the hook. If the set is too fast, you will pull the hook out of the trout's mouth before the fish gets a hold of it.

Another useful downstream presentation is to cast with slack in the line, so that there's no drag as it travels downstream. A downstream slack-line presentation can be made using a pile cast. In a pile cast, the rod tip and fly line need to have an upward trajectory during the forward cast, while the backcast will have a downward trajectory. Once the rod stops on the forward cast, slowly lower the rod tip down toward the water, creating slack. The cast works best with slow line speed; too much acceleration will pull the slack out of the line before it lands on the water. There are often times when I find myself presented with a dry fly hatch downstream of me, and have no other way to reach the rising trout. While the pile cast can be difficult to master, learning it is worth your while. The cast is not good for distance or in the wind, however.

Add the puddle cast to your follow-up research for a bonus downstream technique.

Dry Fly

Fishing with a dry fly is the ideal fly fishing experience. Dry fly fishing is visual! Dry fly fishing is exciting! When it's dry fly fishing you're after, then small streams are where you want to be. Most of the time, matching the hatch is unnecessary. Popular attractor patterns will generally suffice; however, at lower stream elevations, where the water can be slower and possibly larger, a more precise match may be required. Trout do not need to be rising in order for anglers to fish dry flies. That's true not only on small streams, but larger rivers as well.

If you find yourself in a situation with rising fish, then you already know where the trout are—they gave away their location. Take time to watch the rise and to examine the food the fish are eating. I carry an inexpensive white aquarium net so I can scoop up the bugs or catch them in the air. Look to see if the trout are eating just below the surface (an emerger pattern) or if their heads are leaving the water's surface to take a dry fly. When matching a hatch, duplicate the length of the abdomen, the bug's shape (thick or thin), and lastly its color. Hatches are generally the heaviest in the evenings, but mornings are good, too. They can occur in pools, including at the tailouts, or in back eddies.

When you're fishing to rising trout, a drag-free drift is paramount; however, there are situations in which drag can give you an advantage. Twitching dry flies can attract a trout's attention. As your fly is drifting naturally, occasionally make the fly twitch by squeezing and releasing the cork rod handle. Maybe add a slight twitch of the rod tip, moving the fly only an inch or two at most. This method works great with a Salmonfly, stonefly, caddis, or with terrestrial imitations.

Skating is another way to tantalize the trout. Skating flies need to float well to stay on the surface. The idea is to imitate a fly getting blown by the wind or one trying to break free of the water's surface. Cast across stream and let the fly begin to drift downstream. Mend the line upstream, locking the line to the cork, and drag the fly across the stream. Lastly, if I'm fishing in fast pocketwater, I will skate the fly with the high-stick method typically used for nymphing.

Nymphing

In small streams, nymphing is most commonly used when the water is cold, high, or off-color. Nymph fishing can be done upstream, across stream, or downstream. Mending line to achieve a drag-free float is just as important when nymphing as it is when using dry flies. Because you can't see the fly, an optional indicator may come in handy for detecting trout strikes.

When fishing short leaders in fast water, I forgo indicators. With short leaders, I like to keep most of my fly line off the water by holding my rod tip high. I learned this high sticking technique from guide friends in California who are now at Confluence Outfitters.

High-sticking works best with a short cast, short leader, and a single weighted nymph. When nymphing in larger, deeper water, use longer leaders with added weight, strike indicators, and two flies. From the downstream position, just lob or fling the rig upstream; the water's tension on the line will bend the rod, assisting you. Before I lob, I like to turn my wrist so the reel and butt of the rod are facing my intended target. Cast upstream enough to give the nymph time to sink to the proper water depth. Next, lift the rod horizontally so the fly line is off the water. It is important to have a nearly tight leader and fly line from the nymph to the rod tip. Move the rod at the same speed as the nymph or slightly ahead of the nymph as you move downstream. Watch for any unnatural movement in the fly line, leader, or strike indicator (if in use). If you sense a bite, lift the rod a few inches with intent, but leave the rig in the water rather than pulling it all out like a backcast. A backward motion leads only to a ruined drift and most likely a web of leader in a tree. If no trout, lower the rod tip and continue your drift. During the drift, line management (pulling in line or letting it out) will be necessary to keep the proper tension in the line.

Another great nymphing method that will instantly increase fishing effectiveness is the Leisenring Lift. If you have ever accidentally caught a fish at the conclusion of your drift while initiating a backcast, you used the Leisenring Lift, popularized by avid fly fisherman Jim Leisenring prior to World War II.

An across-stream presentation is best for this technique. Cast across stream, mend, and allow the fly to get down to the proper depth. Continue with your typical drag-free drift. As the end of the drift approaches, lock or anchor your fly line to the cork with your forefinger and let the fly swing through the current with tension and drag on the line. As it swings, the sunken fly will ascend or lift in the water column to imitate a natural insect emerging to the surface. Try to place the cast so that the swing occurs in prime trout territory. For more enticement, add a twitch as the fly ascends. With that tight line, there will be no doubt when the trout eats the fly!

The Leisenring Lift can also be used with streamers and dry flies. When dry fly fishing, your swing will initiate a skating maneuver across the surface.

Streamer Fishing

I love streamer fishing. I first learned how to streamer fish from my friend Emmett Heath on the Green River in Utah. I like to use streamers in the spring or fall or when the stream holds mainly brown trout. Streamer fishing still takes a backseat to dry fly fishing, in my opinion, so I'll cast streamers only when dry flies are not effective. Streamer fishing may not fit the bill if your goal is quantity, but the trout you do land on a streamer should be sizable. When fishing streamers, I cover a significant amount of water, not only because I cast them farther than I do nymphs or drys, but also because I move through the stream quickly, covering prime water much faster than when nymphing or dry fly fishing. If the trout are in the mood for a streamer, they will travel out of their way to get it. And when they take, you know it.

If I see small forage fish in the water, I use a Woolly Bugger. If I see sculpin darting around the rocks, I use a sculpin pattern. When in doubt, use a Woolly Bugger. Streamers are best suited to larger streams found in the valleys, especially in spring and fall.

Smaller streamers patterns can be fished with a dead drift like a nymph. I will often dead-drift small streamers with a nymph tied onto the bend of the hook with 18 inches of tippet. I dead-drift the streamer, and then at the end of the drift, use the Leisenring Lift along with a few strips. The other more classic method of fishing with a streamer is to cast across stream, mend so the fly can sink down to the preferred depth, and then begin to strip. The speed and length of the strip are dependent on the water temperature, the bait you are imitating, and the mood of the trout. When stripping in colder water, slow down the strip; the smaller the bait, the shorter the strips. Cast under fallen wood or as close to the bank as possible. Brown trout love undercut banks. Over the years, I've learned that if after an hour or so I have not picked up a fish on a streamer, I can probably assume the trout just aren't in the mood for streamers. That may not be the most scientific approach, but fishing with streamers is kind of a gut-feeling thing; the angler has to believe the streamer will work, and the trout have to want it.

Releasing a Fish

Fish mortality depends largely on how an angler handles the fish. Below, I list precautions that will help to improve the survival rate for landed trout.

- If the fish is out of the water, hold your breath to remind yourself that during this time (for example, over 20 seconds), the mortality rate increases substantially the longer your fish is out of its element.
- Try to avoid catching fish less than 6 inches in size; little fish are delicate and very hard to release.
- The warmer the water, the higher the mortality rate. Try to bring in the fish as quickly as possible, and avoid handling it.
- If you're not going to photograph the fish, try to release the fish in the water without ever touching it, by taking hold of the bend of the hook with fingers or hemostats and working the hook out in the direction that it went in.
- If you are taking a photograph, leave the fish in a net and in the water while setting up the snapshot. Photographs can be taken while the fish is in the water (best case) or by quickly lifting the fish for the shot, and quickly returning it to the net.
- Wet your hands before handling a fish.
- When holding a fish, grasp it firmly around the base of the tail and support its weight with your other hand.
- Use a rubber net to protect the slime layer on the fish; avoid cotton or hard nylon nets.
- When releasing the fish into the water, face it upstream. Don't let go until the fish has recovered. Hold the fish at the base of the tail until it is strong enough to swim away. If it appears slow to recover, gently move

the fish forward and back in the stream to let water move through its gills but only in slow moving water.
- If the fish has swallowed a hook so deeply that you can't reach it, cut the tippet and leave the hook. Your hook will eventually come out, and leaving it be is better than damaging the fish by retrieving a fly with hemostats.

Summary

Time on the water is the best teacher. If you are a beginner, the learning curve may seem a bit steep at first. Be patient with yourself and remember: fly fishing is supposed to be fun! It does not take long to become a proficient angler in small streams. For those of you who are a little further along, hopefully the foregoing casting and fishing strategies offer something new to try. Keep in mind:

- One can never take too many casting lessons or practice too much.
- While fishing, keep casting to a minimum.
- Keep casts as short as possible.
- Be strategic.
- Be patient.
- Learn to manipulate your fly line.
- Keep line on the reel when it's not in use.
- Look around for obstacles.
- If you snag your fly on structure in a prime location, consider breaking off the fly and continuing to fish. Once the spot has been fished, retrieve the fly.
- Wade slowly and quietly.
- Be a predator.
- Smile when you catch a tree, it will not be the last!
- Keep a journal.

Bill Toone releasing a fish. Molly Semenik

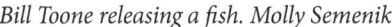

BILLINGS

ROCK CREEK

WEST ROSEBUD CREEK

WEST BOULDER RIVER

EAST ROSEBUD CREEK

STILLWATER RIVER

Billings is located in south central Montana,
140 miles east of Bozeman on the I-90 interstate.
(All Billings streams are in the FWP Central District, **Region 5.**)

▶ **Location:** Billings is the largest city in Montana. In 2010, its population was reported at 104,170, which makes it the only city in Montana with more than 100,000 residents. Of all the cities in our state, Billings is experiencing the largest growth. The Bakken oil field region, which includes Eastern Montana and North Dakota, has created phenomenal growth in the wake of the largest oil discovery in U.S. history. Billings was established as a railroad town back in 1882, and is named for Frederick H. Billings, a former president of the Northern Pacific Railroad. To this day, Billings is the major trade center for Montana and surrounding states.

Montana Avenue, in downtown Billings, which runs between 22nd and 26th Streets, has great dining and fun shopping, including a few unique antique shops specializing in Western history.

A day trip to the Little Bighorn Battlefield National Monument (about an hour's drive from Billings) is worth a visit. The history of General Custer and the Native Americans of this region is well documented throughout the museum with both indoor and outdoor displays.

Another recommended day trip is a guided fishing day on the Bighorn River. The Bighorn begins in Wyoming and flows north through Montana into the Yellowtail Reservoir. The Yellowtail Afterbay Dam, built in 1967, controls the flow of the Bighorn River. Rainbows and browns stocked back in the 1960s now reproduce there naturally. With an abundance of food and steady water flows, the river supports an astonishing 7,500 fish per mile! To avoid crowds, fish early or late (or both); a drift boat is your best option for a day of fishing, since walking and wading can be difficult due to limited river access.

There's also the option of hiring a guide with a motor craft and fishing Bighorn Lake for carp and smallmouth bass. I spent the day with Ryan Kitts (guide) and Matt Clawson (outfitter, 406-670-6866) from the Bighorn River Lodge (www.bighornriverlodge.com). The landscape was spectacular, and the smallmouth bass and carp fishing were excellent.

▶ **Travel Routes:** Here are two route options for the Billings region. Route A includes the famous and beautiful Beartooth Highway (a National Scenic Byway reaching 10,947 feet) and Yellowstone National Park. The Beartooth Highway opens at the end of May or in early June, depending on snowmelt. (Charles Kuralt, "On the Road" television correspondent, called this highway "the most beautiful drive in America.") Route B keeps you closer to the Billings area and does not cut through Yellowstone National Park.

REGION

Route A

Billings to Red Lodge—1 hour (62 miles)
Fish Rock Creek
Red Lodge to Cooke City—2 hours (68 miles)
Scenic drive over the Beartooth Highway
Cooke City (through Yellowstone Park) to
    Gardner—1 hour 20 minutes (52 miles)
Drive or fish your way to Gardner (or do both)
Gardner to Big Timber—1 hour 30 minutes (89 miles)
Stop to tour the town of Livingston
Fish West Boulder River
Big Timber to Columbus—45 minutes (40 miles)
Fish Stillwater River
Columbus to Absarokee or Fishtail—20 minutes
    (15 miles)
Fish West Rosebud Creek
Fish East Rosebud Creek

Route B

Billings to Red Lodge—1 hour (62 miles)
Fish Rock Creek
Red Lodge to Absarokee—45 minutes (33 miles)
Fish West Rosebud Creek
Fish East Rosebud Creek
Absarokee to Columbus—20 minutes (15 miles)
Fish Stillwater River
Columbus to Big Timber—45 minutes (40 miles)
Fish West Boulder River

FLY SHOPS

Bighorn Fly & Tackle Shop
485 S. 24th St. W
Billings, MT 59102
406-656-8257
www.bighornfly.com

East Rosebud Fly & Tackle
805 24th Street W
Billings, MT 59102
406-839-9397
www.eastrosebudflyandtackle.com

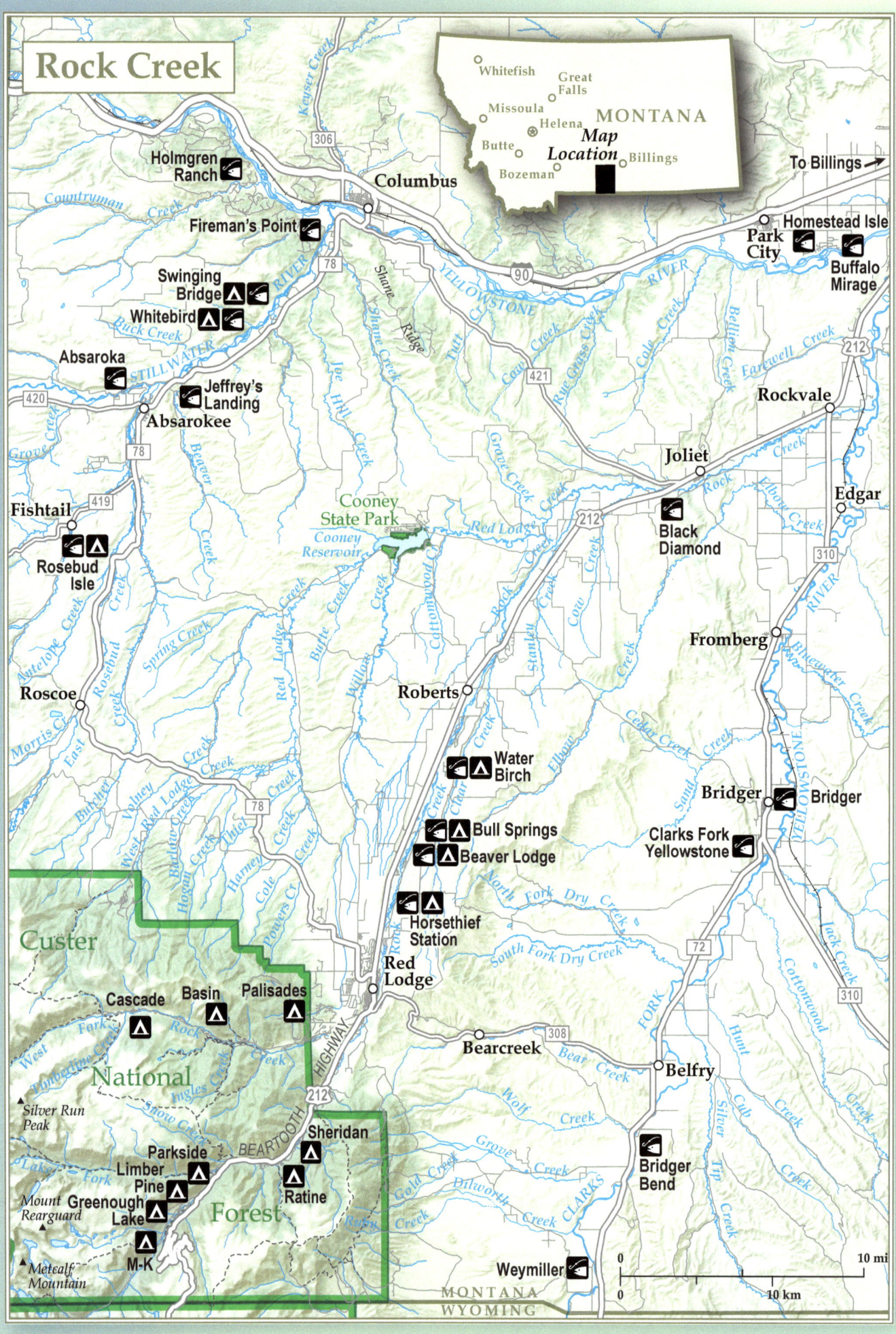

1 · Rock Creek *(Red Lodge)*

Guide Interview

Sitting at a charming table outside the popular Café Regis with Andy Szofram, I knew within minutes that I was in for a great day with a seasoned and knowledgeable guide. This man lives fly fishing! Before our food arrived, Andy said, "If I'm not fishing, I'm tying flies. If I'm not tying, I'm talking fishing."

Andy showed me the upper section of Rock Creek. He said, "I love fishing small creeks, even if the fish are small. Most of my guiding is done on the bigger waters, so this is a treat." Andy made a point of mentioning that anglers need to be careful of hazards such as woody deadfalls and holes in the ground near the creek. Andy guides for steelhead in the winter, and during the summer he's on the Yellowstone and Stillwater Rivers, as well. He has been guiding in the Red Lodge area since 1990. I appreciated the time Andy spent with me exploring Rock Creek and its tributaries. (Fly Fishing Only Adventures, Red Lodge—Andy Szofram, www.flyfishredlodge.com, 406-425-1761.)

▶ **Location:** Red Lodge is 60 miles southwest of Billings along Highway 212. To get to Red Lodge from Billings, take I-90 W/US 212 W toward Butte (15.7 miles). Take exit 434 and merge onto US 212/US 310 toward Laurel/Red Lodge. Turn left onto US 310 S/US 212 S. Stay on US 212 S for about 44 miles.

Red Lodge is tucked in a valley that was carved out by glacial movement and the swift waters of Rock Creek. According to census takers in 1887, the town then consisted of "19 tent houses and 5 saloons." Two years later, the East Side coal mine was in operation and the railroad arrived. This is truly a charming town. It perches at an elevation of 5,555 feet in the foothills of the magnificent Beartooth Mountains, surrounded by Custer National Forest. Downtown shopping on Broadway Avenue offers a variety of stores to visit and enjoy: Montana Candy Emporium, the Beartooth Gallery Fine Art, and Sylvan Peak Mountain Shop (sporting goods and bear spray), among many others.

Many spots south of Red Lodge to pull off along highway. Molly Semenik

Montana has two rivers named Rock Creek; one in southwest Montana near Missoula (see chapter **TK**); and the Rock Creek in southeast Montana near Red Lodge, profiled here. Rock Creek near Red Lodge is the lesser known of the two. Rock Creek originates in the mountains of the Absaroka-Beartooth Wilderness. The river flows for 55 miles from the

Above. Andy Szofram fishing a small pocket.   *Facing top. Many spots south of Red Lodge to pull off along the highway. Molly Semenik*

Absaroka-Beartooth Wilderness to the Clarks Fork of the Yellowstone River. The lower section of Rock Creek does get dewatered from irrigation in the mid- to late-summer months; therefore, the fishing quality suffers significantly. However, fishing improves the closer you get to Red Lodge itself.

The following four access sites are north (downriver) of Red Lodge. In this section, the water character has less of an elevation drop and is more meadowlike, with easy approaches from the fishing access points. Fish the pools and riffle areas. Water Birch is the first fishing access site worth mentioning. It is located 30 miles from the mouth of Rock Creek and 8.1 miles north of Red Lodge, on US 212. Undesignated camping is available at this site. Bull Springs is 32 miles from the mouth of Rock Creek. At 5.3 miles north of Red Lodge, turn east onto Fox/E. Bench Road, travel 0.4 mile; then turn north onto Two Mile Bridge Road. Primitive camping is available. Beaver Lodge is 34 miles from the mouth of Rock Creek. At 5.3 miles north of Red Lodge on US 212, turn east on Fox/E. Bench Road; travel 0.4 mile, turn south on Two Miles Bridge Road, and continue for 1 mile. Horsethief Sportsman Access is 36 miles from the mouth of Rock Creek. At 5.3 miles north of Red Lodge on US 212, turn east on Fox/E. Bench Road, travel 0.4 mile, then turn south on Two Mile Bridge Road and continue for 3 miles.

Upriver (south) of Red Lodge, Rock Creek becomes a high-elevation creek with fast flows, boulders, and pocketwater. Once you're in the Forest Service area, river access is easy—look for popular turnouts: mile markers 58 and 61 are two good ones. Eleven miles south of Red Lodge on US 212, you can turn right on Rock Creek Road (Forest Service Road 2421). Continuing along, you will cross over Rock Creek and pass Limber Pine Campground. The road is dirt and rough. Although the first few miles can be driven without all-wheel drive, you will need it as you travel farther. The road ends at the 8-mile mark, rewarding you with an outstanding view of the Beartooth Mountains. You can fish anywhere along the road except for its last 2 miles, which cross into the state of Wyoming. Look for low-gradient meadow areas. While fishing, watch for uneven ground. Carry bear spray and make

Rock Creek midway up Rock Creek Road. Molly Semenik

noise when walking through thick brush. Several nice campgrounds are located on or near Rock Creek: Limber Pine Campground and Greenough Lake Campground are two.

Two fun and easy-to-access small tributary creeks to Rock Creek itself are the West Fork and Lake Fork. Each creek has a hiking trail running alongside it. Lake Fork Trail meanders through a forest for 10 miles, and West Fork Trail is 4 miles long, ending at Quinnebaugh Meadows. More detailed descriptions can be found on a Custer National Forest map.

The section south of Red Lodge (upstream) holds small cutthroat, rainbow, and brook trout measuring 6 to 13 inches. These higher-elevation fish live in cold water with a short feeding season. The higher up you get, the smaller the trout. North of Red Lodge (downstream), you will find rainbow and brown trout, and your best brown trout fishing will be in the lower prairie sections of Rock Creek, as is true in the Stillwater River and the Rosebuds. Streamers fished around deadfalls and near or under the banks are a good bet for drawing out the larger browns, especially as fall approaches.

Be sure to mark your calendar to join (or steer clear of) motorcycle enthusiasts as they gather in Red Lodge for the enormous Beartooth Rally, generally held the third week of July (www.beartoothrally.com).

➤ **Hatches:** Rock Creek will take some time to warm up and become fishable in its higher elevations. (The Stillwater River, mentioned later in this chapter, holds the region's first reliably fishable waters.)

Pre-runoff in April can be good downstream of Red Lodge, using typical spring imitations such as Blue-winged Olives, March Browns, and caddis. You'll want to wet a line during warmest parts of the day: 10 A.M. to 3 P.M. June is generally mudded out as a result of spring runoff.

Middle to late July, the water begins to clear and levels drop, kicking off prime fishing season. August is the best month to fish, except for during afternoon thunderstorms. September continues to host great fishing; grasshoppers (use imitations when you see or hear them) will keep enticing trout through most of this month. During October, the rainbows and browns start to color up and get aggressive, switching their focus to streamers as dry fly activity tapers off.

When you consult the Montana Hatch Chart (page xiv), note that the following flies are especially suited to Rock Creek:

Elk-hair Caddis, #14–16
Royal Wulff, #14–16
Stimulator, #14–16
Parachute Adams, #14–16
small terrestrials
Beadhead Hare's-ear Nymph, #12–16
Beadhead Pheasant Tail Nymph, #12–16

➤ **Fishing regulations:** Rock Creek and its tributaries are open the entire year. Fishing regulations are general. The combined daily limit for trout is five fish, only one over 18 inches in possession. All grayling and cutthroat must be released immediately.

➤ **Tackle and strategy:** South of Red Lodge, the stream is small, a great place for a 7½-foot 3-weight with a 7½-foot 4X leader. North of Red Lodge, where the water is slower and larger, the 4X leader may be lengthened to 9 feet.

South of Red Lodge, roll casts and high-stick nymphing will serve you best. Fishing upstream is the easiest method on these waters. Move often—a few casts per hole, and then on to the next spot. Do be careful of uneven ground. Downstream of Red Lodge, all fishing tactics will work. Mornings when the water is still cold and the early season are optimal for nymphing. Fish any riffles, small pools, or foam lines.

Be careful around Rock Creek's round, slick rocks and fast current. As the summer months arrive and the water drops, wading will get easier. A wading staff and felt or cleated boots are a must, along with slow and tentative steps. The water temperature is very cold due to the high elevation of the stream's headwaters. In the heat of the summer, the cold water feels good.

Left. Andy Sxofram fishing below the Beartooth Mountains. Molly Semenik

Below. Typical high mountain trout. Molly Semenik

FLY SHOP
There are no fly shops in this area; however, fishing licenses may be obtained at
Red Lodge True Value Hardware
1 N. Oakes Ave.
Red Lodge, MT 59068
406-446-1847

OUTFITTERS
Fly Fishing Only Adventures (Red Lodge)
Andy Szofram
406-425-1761
www.flyfishredlodge.com

Montana Trout Scout (Red Lodge)
Craig Beam
406-855-3058
www.montanatroutscout.com

LODGING
Yodeler Motel
601 S. Broadway Ave.
Red Lodge, MT 59068
866-446-1435
www.yodelermotel.com

Pollard Hotel
2 N. Broadway Ave.
Red Lodge, MT 59068
406-446-0001; toll-free 800-765-5273
www.thepollard.com
(historic upscale hotel)

Comfort Inn
612 N. Broadway Ave.
Red Lodge, MT 59068
406-446-4469
www.comfortinn.com

Lupine Inn
702 S. Hauser Ave.
Red Lodge, MT 59068
888-567-1321
www.lupineinn.com

Beartooth Hideaway Inn
1223 S. Broadway Ave.
Red Lodge, MT 59068
406-446-2288
www.beartoothhideaway.com

CAMPGROUNDS
Perry's RV Park and Campground
Rock Creek mile marker 67, US-212
406-446-2722
contact@perrysrv.us

Red Lodge KOA
7464 Hwy. 212
Red Lodge, MT 59068
800-562-7540
www.koa.com/campgrounds/redlodge

Custer National Forest campgrounds
877-444-6777
www.forestcamping.com/dow/northern/custinfo.htm

LIBATIONS
Red Lodge Ales Brewing Company
1445 N. Broadway Ave.
Red Lodge, MT 59068
406-446-4607
www.redlodgeales.com
(brewery and taproom)

Foster & Logan's Pub & Grill
17 S. Broadway Ave.
Red Lodge, MT 59068
406-446-9080
(20 beers on tap, full bar)

DINING
Bear Creek Saloon & Steakhouse
101 W. Main St.
Bearcreek, MT 59007
406-446-3481
www.redlodge.com/bearcreek
(home of Bear Creek Downs pig races, held Thursday–Sunday from Memorial Day to Labor Day; 7 miles east of Red Lodge)

Bridge Creek Backcountry Kitchen & Wine Bar
Red Lodge, MT 59068
406-446-9900
www.eatfooddrinkwine.com
(lunch, afternoon bar menu, dinner)

Bogart's
11 S. Broadway Ave.
Red Lodge, MT 59068
406-446-1784
www.redlodgerestaurants.com/bogarts
(big burgers, Mexican fare)

Mas Taco
304 N. Broadway Ave.
Red Lodge, MT 59068
406-446-3636
www.facebook.com/mastaco
(limited dine-in seating; takeout)

Carbon County Steakhouse
121 S. Broadway Ave.
Red Lodge, MT 59068
406-446-4025
www.carboncountysteakhouse.com
(casual fine dining; reservations recommended)

The Pub at The Pollard
2 N. Broadway Ave.
Red Lodge, MT 59068
406-446-0001
www.thepollard.com
(casual fare, billiards, live music)

Vintage One Bistro
2 N. Broadway Ave.
Red Lodge, MT 59068
406-446-0001
www.thepollard.com
(the Dining Room at The Pollard; breakfast and dinner)

Cafe Regis
501 S. Word Ave. (at 16th St.)
Red Lodge, MT 59068
(breakfast, coffee; a favorite with locals)

Prindy's
407 S. Broadway Ave.
Red Lodge, MT 59068
406-446-0225
(breakfast)

COFFEE SHOP
Coffee Factory Roasters
22 S. Broadway Ave.
Red Lodge, MT 59068
406-446-3200
www.coffeefactoryroasters.com
(free Wi-Fi)

EMERGENCY MEDICAL HELP
Beartooth Billings Clinic
2525 N. Broadway Ave.
Red Lodge, MT 59068
406-446-2345, toll-free 877-404-9442
www.beartoothbillingsclinic.org

Mountain View Clinic
10 Robinson Ln.
Red Lodge, MT 59068
406-446-3800

CELL PHONE SERVICE
Cell service is available in the town of Red Lodge. Reception drops off the farther out of town you travel.

STREAM ACCESSIBILITY
3 above Red Lodge; **1** below

WADING CHALLENGE
2 above Red Lodge; **4** below

WILDLIFE ALERTS
Bear, moose

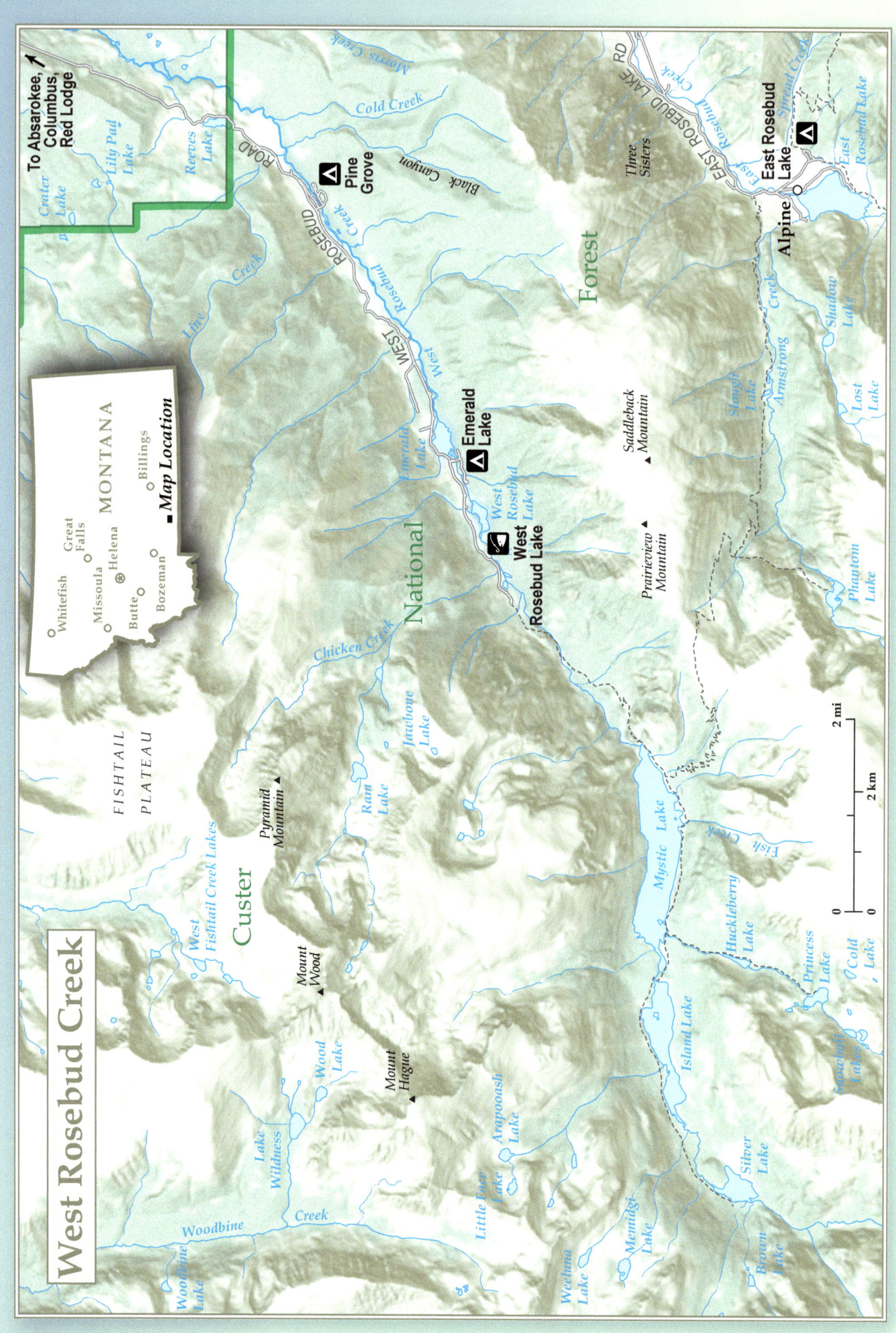

2 · West Rosebud Creek

➤ **Location:** Both the West and East Rosebuds can be reached from the towns of Red Lodge, Columbus, and Absarokee. The area near Red Lodge is described in the Rock Creek chapter. Columbus is profiled in the Stillwater chapter.

From Red Lodge on Montana Highway 78, the town of Absarokee (*ab-sor-kee*) is 33 miles to the northwest. From Columbus to Absarokee on MT 78, it is 13 miles.

From Absarokee to Fishtail is 7 miles: Head south on MT 78 for 2.8 miles. Turn right onto Nye Road/County Road 419; drive 3.4 miles. (Nye Road is 0.3 mile past Nitche Road)

> While you're in Fishtail, a must-visit is **Fishtail General Store** (406-328-4260). Crossing its threshold is like stepping back in time. The shop has a great deli counter with good food to go. Prices range from a PBJ at $2.75 to a sandwich special for $8.

As you leave Fishtail, drive 1.5 miles and turn left on West Rosebud Road. In approximately 6.5 miles, you will see a sign on the left for Emerald Lake Campground (W. Rosebud Road, No. 72 sign); turn left. The road turns to dirt for the next 13 miles. In 9 miles, you will come to Pine Grove Campground; in another 4 miles, you will reach Emerald Lake Campground.

If I had time enough to fish only one of the Rosebuds, I would choose the West Rosebud. Locals say it has greater fish numbers than its sister stream. The Rosebud Creeks are nestled in high prairie just to the north of the Absaroka-Beartooth Wilderness area. The scenery at both Rosebuds is outstanding. These creeks merge and join the Stillwater River just above the town of Absarokee. The waters are crystal clear and surrounded by trees, brush, or open meadows. Both streams offer fast pocketwater in their upper sections and more meadowlike water in the lower sections.

Mystic Lake can be a fun side jaunt on your Rosebuds excursion. It is certainly worth driving up to the lake to admire its beauty and see whether any fish are rising. The western lakeshore, where the outhouse is located, would be the best spot to fish.

Back on the stream, there are good access and fishing below Emerald Lake and between the two campgrounds.

Yellowstone cutthroat trout, brook trout, rainbow trout, and brown trout swim in both Rosebuds. You might also catch golden trout and mountain whitefish. In the upper section, closer to Emerald Lake, fish range from 6 to 13 inches. As you descend into more meadowlike areas, the fish will get larger—13 to 16 inches, with an occasional 18-inch trout.

Fishtail General Store. Molly Semenik

➤ **Fishing regulations:** The season runs from the third Saturday in May through November. The combined daily limit for trout is five; in possession, only one over 18 inches. All grayling and cutthroat must be released immediately.

From early spring until the end of July, Both Rosebuds are too swollen from snowmelt for worthwhile and safe angling. These high mountain streams improve as the waters recede, with excellent fishing through the end of October. Snowpack and spring temperatures will dictate when the rivers become fishable from year to year.

➤ **Hatches:** The trout in these high-altitude streams are eager and willing feeders. Your selection of flies is the same here as in Rock Creek.

Top. Lower West Rosebud. Molly Semenik

Inset left. The drive from Red Lodge to Roscoe. Molly Semenik

Inset right. Mystic Lake. Molly Semenik

Facing page. Andy Szofram holding a rainbow. Molly Semenik

Locals favor the following patterns:

Elk-Hair Caddis, #14–16
Royal Wulff, #14–16
Stimulator, #14–16
Parachute Adams, #14–16
small terrestrials
Beadhead Hare's-ear Nymph, #12–16
Beadhead Pheasant Tail Nymph, #12–16

➤ **Tackle and strategy:** Both Rosebuds are small fly rod creeks, calling for a 7½-foot 3-weight with a 6- or 7½-foot 4X leader. The creeks are not very wide.

Work the deeper pools and logjams. Drift large drys throughout the riffles and above and below the boulders. If you fish the clear, still waters of Mystic Lake, lengthen your leader accordingly; a 9-foot 5X leader may be needed.

Small but cute. Molly Semenik

Fly Shop and Outfitter
Stillwater Anglers Fly Shop & Outfitters
637 N. Ninth St., #130
Columbus, MT 59019
406-322-4977, toll-free 1-855-STILLWTR
www.stillwateranglersmt.com

Campgrounds
Rosebud Isle fishing access site
In Fishtail, just before the bridge crossing West Rosebud Creek
(a few campsites)

Emerald Lake Campground
Turn onto West Rosebud Rd., #72 and travel 12.6 miles.

Pine Grove Campground
Turn onto West Rosebud Rd., #72 and travel 8.7 miles.
http://www.forestcamping.com/dow/northern/cust.htm

Lodging
Stillwater Lodge
28 S. Woodward Ave.
Absarokee, MT 59001
406-328-4899
www.stillwaterlodge.net
(six rooms only; call ahead)

Dining
Rosebud Cafe
18 S. Woodward Ave.
Absarokee, MT 59001
406-328-6969

Itti Bitti Bistro
30 S. Woodward Ave.
Absarokee, MT 59001
(breakfast and lunch)

Cowboy Bar & Supper Club
1 Main St.
Fishtail, MT 59028
406-328-4288
www.cowboybar.co
(breakfast, lunch, dinner)

Montana Jack's
1383 Nye Rd.
Dean, MT 59028
406-328-4110
www.mtjacks.com
(brunch and dinner; locally sourced ingredients)

Grizzly Bar and Grill
1 Main St.
16 E. Rosebud Rd.
Roscoe, MT 59071
406-328-6789
www.wherethehellisroscoe.com
(lunch, dinner, full bar)

Libations
Cowboy Bar & Supper Club
(see left)

Montana Jack's
(see left)

Grizzly Bar and Grill
(see left)

Emergency Medical Help
Stillwater Billings Clinic
710 N. 11th St.
Columbus, MT 59019
406-322-1000
www.stillwaterbillingsclinic.com

Cell Phone Service
In the town of Absarokee. As you leave town, service is limited.

Stream Accessibility
2

Wading Challenge
3

Wildlife Alerts
Bears and moose

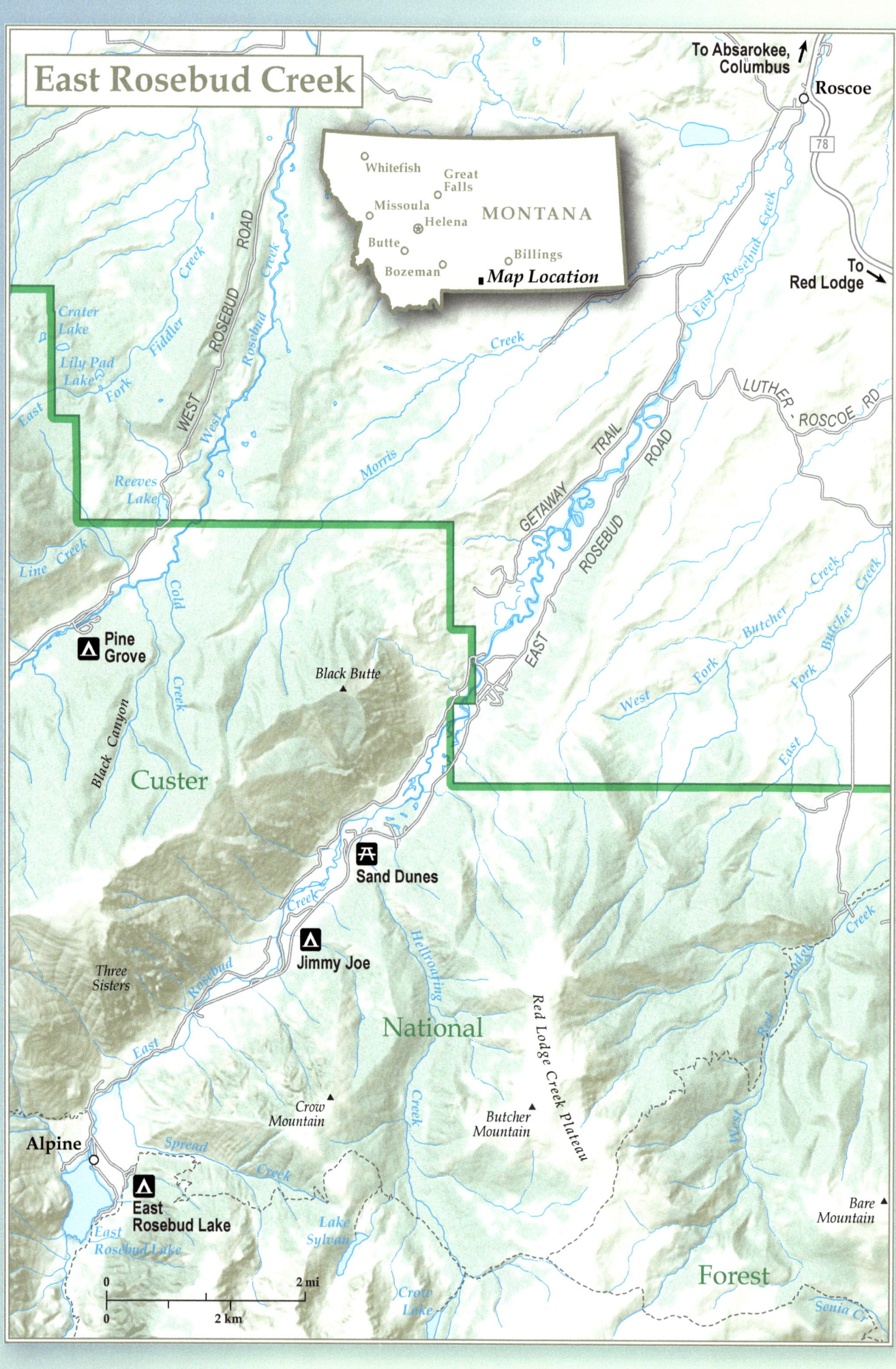

3 · East Rosebud Creek

▶ **Location:** Once in the town of Roscoe, turn onto East Rosebud Road. Roscoe is on Highway 78 south of Columbus or north of Red Lodge. Travel a few miles, and you will come to a bridge crossing the river. Stay right, and drive along the dirt road through a meadow area (you will pass vacation and summer homes), until you reach the Custer National Forest. Jimmy Joe Campground is another two miles down the paved road. From the Jimmy Joe Campground, continue another mile. (The road turns back to dirt.) Look for places where the creek is close to the road, and park. From the dirt road, there are three miles of fishing until you come to the East Rosebud Lake.

From East Rosebud Lake, the East Rosebud flows for 50 miles until it merges with the West Rosebud just above the town of Absarokee. The mountain section of East Rosebud Creek flows through Forest Service land and has a road paralleling the creek until East Rosebud Lake. These upper three miles of river offer the best fishing access. Park along the road, and fish wherever it looks good. The lower section of East Rosebud Creek flows through mostly private land with a few bridge crossings. In 1996, the Shepard Mountain Fire burned in this area, leaving its mark to this day.

See the West Rosebud Creek chapter for information on the fish, fishing season, access, flies, and tackle, which will likewise pertain to this sister stream.

East Rosebud Lake. Molly Semenik

Above. Spring run-off just below East Rosebud Lake. Molly Semenik

Below. Lower East Rosebud. Molly Semenik

Above. Spring run-off just below East Rosebud Lake. Molly Semenik

Grizzly Bar in Roscoe. Molly Semenik

CAMPGROUND
East Rosebud Lake Campground
After you turn onto E. Rosebud Rd., it is 14.5 miles to the campground.
http://www.forestcamping.com/dow/northern/cust.htm

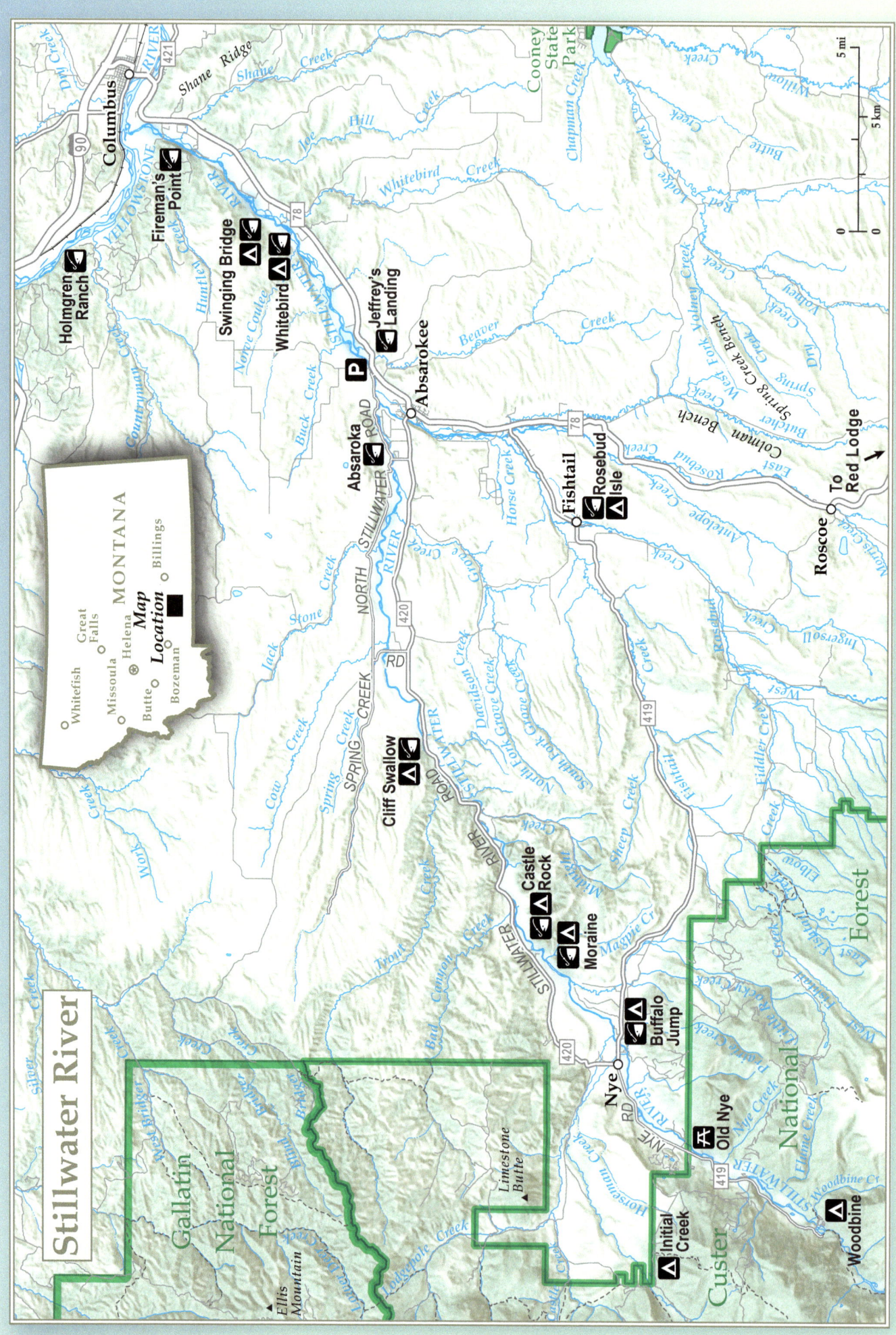

4 · Stillwater River

> **Guide Interview**
>
> Chris Fleck became a guide in 2003, two years after retiring from the marines. When asked, "How do you describe the Stillwater?" he replied, "The Stillwater has a great character and personality. In one day, you can experience all types of water—from riffles to runs to pocketwater." Chris guides both the Yellowstone and the Stillwater. He loves guiding because, as he puts it, "Every day is a different day, no two days are the same, and guiding is a constant learning process."

▶ **Location:** Like the Rosebud Creeks, the Stillwater River originates in the Beartooth range just north of Yellowstone National Park. Lake Abundance marks the headwaters of the Stillwater, which then flows for 70 miles to meet the Yellowstone River in Columbus. The Stillwater valley is a classic rural setting: deer, turkeys, sandhill cranes, and geese are a permanent fixture in farmers' fields.

Columbus can serve as your hub for both the Stillwater River and the two Rosebuds. The town has a great fly shop, modest hotels, and casual eating establishments. Other Columbus attractions include the Montana Silversmiths headquarters, the New Atlas Bar (one of Montana's oldest licensed bars, with 50 unusual animal head mounts), and a nine-hole golf course running along the Yellowstone River.

Flies and up-to-date local fishing information can be obtained from Stillwater Anglers, owned by Chris Fleck. For additional information and photographs of the Stillwater River, visit *Montana Fly Fishing Magazine* (www.mtflyfishmag.com). Chris writes in the June 2012 issue, "The Stillwater is one of those fisheries that can offer anglers of all skill levels a variety of angling experiences."

Yellowstone cutthroat, rainbow, cutbow, brown, brook trout, and whitefish can all be caught in the Stillwater River. The average size of the rainbows and browns is 12 to 14 inches. A fish of the day would be 15 to 16 inches. These wild trout really give you a good fight in fast water.

Columbus to Absarokee

This section of the Stillwater River is the easiest to wade, and the fish tend to be a bit larger here than in the upper river. You'll have a good chance of spotting big browns, too.

Access points are listed below and start from the town of Columbus on Highway 78:

Fireman's Point (2 miles, camping available)
Swinging Bridge (5 miles, camping available)
White Bird (6 miles, camping available)
Jeffrey's Landing (12 miles)

Just past Jeffrey's Landing is North Stillwater Road. Turn north onto this road and cross the bridge. Turn left onto a dirt road after crossing the bridge, and follow the riverside drive toward Absarokee. You will pass two bed-and-breakfasts on the way: River Haven Bed & Breakfast (owned by Betty Olsen), and the Magpie Nest (owned by Pat and Jack Ross). Just past the Magpie Nest is the Absaroka Fishing Access site; this is a good place to fish. Another quarter mile beyond Absaroka, a bridge crosses the river to get you back on the main road, Stillwater River Road.

Abarokee to Nye

Turn right on Spring Creek Road, go to the community center, and park. Fish the bridge access either up or down.

Cliff Swallow (23 miles, camping available)

From Cliff Swallow downstream, the river will begin to braid up and the water will slow some. Brook, brown, and rainbow trout dwell in this section. The fish will start to get larger, averaging 12 to 14 inches.

Castle Rock (31 miles, camping available)
Moraine (32 miles)

In a few miles, turn left on Stillwater Mine Road and go over the bridge toward Nye. "At the Custer's Camp sign", turn right, and continue on Nye Road.

Nye to Woodbine

This length of the river travels through mostly private meadows just before it enters the Custer National Forest. Once you reach the end of the road, you will have access again at the Woodbine Campground. From there, only foot travel will take you farther up the Stillwater. Cutthroat and brook trout are found in these upper reaches. Many of the lakes in this area hold golden trout.

▶ **Hatches:** The Stillwater has a prolific caddis hatch that occurs just prior to runoff (March and April). If runoff is early, the caddis hatch may not be fishable due to the high and muddy water. The caddis hatch is always a wait-and-see game that runs on a day-to-day basis from the end of April to early May. After runoff—late June and early July—the entire river fishes well.

Pre-runoff (March, April, early May) patterns for the lower Stillwater are listed in *Table 1 on page 19*.

In post-runoff (beginning late June, early July), switch to the following in *Table 2 on page 19*.

▶ **Fishing regulations:** Open all year. The combined limit for trout is two fish daily; only one over 13 inches in possession (includes cutthroat trout).

▶ **Tackle and strategy:** A 5-weight fly rod will be best. Use a 9-foot leader with 2X tippet when casting large nymphs or streamers, and 3X tippet for average-size imitations. If the water is slow and clear, consider a 4X tippet.

With its fast current and deep pools, the Stillwater is made for nymphing. Another classic setup is to use a dry–dropper rig. By this I mean the dry fly (a mayfly or attractor—like a Stimulator) is the top fly, and tied to a 3X tippet generally. The second fly is attached to the bend of the hook and called the dropper. The attached piece is tied on to the bend of the hook and is approximately 18 inches in length; the tippet may be 3X or 4X, depending on the size of the fly being attached. A good dropper could be a beadhead nymph, such as a Flashback Pheasant Tail or Prince Nymph. Tippet size on this river is not critical: the water is so fast and the season so short, the fish do not want to miss out on the chance of a meal.

During the heat of summer, I look for trout in the frothy water upstream of boulders. When you're in fast pocketwater—start your rig well above your target and let it drift into the foamy mix—and up will come a trout to eat your large dry fly, very exciting! I have been known to use a size 8 Royal Wulff when fishing the heavy waters upstream and downstream of rocks.

Sign to Spring Creek Community Center. Peter Lami

TABLE 1: Pre-runoff

Drys
Blue-winged Olive, #16–18
Beadhead Midge, #16–22
March Brown, #12–14
Caddis (late April), #12–16

Nymphs
Flashback Pheasant Tail, #14
Zebra Midge, #16–22
Beadhead Hare's-ear, #14
March Brown Spider Soft Hackle, #14
Black Stonefly, #10–12
Caddis Larva or Pupa, #12–16
Prince Nymph, #14

TABLE 2: Post-runoff

Drys	Nymphs	Time of Year
Caddis, #12–16	Olive Caddis Pupa, #12–16	All summer
Golden Stone, #6–8	Golden Rubber Leg, #6–10	July–Aug.
Yellow Sally, #14–18		July–Aug.
Pale Morning Dun, #14–18	PMD emerger or Soft Hackle, #14–18	July–Aug.
Attractor, #10–16		
Royal Wulff		
Red & Yellow Humpy		
Parachute Adams		
Stimulator		
Terrestrials, include an assortment of grasshoppers		

Author casting. Peter Lami

Above. From Woodbine Bridge. Peter Lami
Inset. Nice Rainbow photo by Molly Semenik.

Near Castle Rock. Peter Lami

West Fork of the Stillwater River

The West Fork can be accessed roadside from Nye for just a few miles, after which a trail follows the creek another 20 miles. Although the lower section is tough to access, larger browns and rainbows can be found there. The upper portions holds cutthroats and rainbows.

New Atlas Bar located in Columbus. Peter Lami

FLY SHOP AND OUTFITTER
Stillwater Anglers Fly Shop & Outfitters
637 N. 9th St., #130
Columbus, MT 59019
406-322-4977, toll-free 855-STLLWTR
www.stillwateranglersmt.com

LODGE
Yellowstone River Lodge, Cabins and B&B
1936. Highway 10
Columbus, MT 59019
406-322-8474, cell 406-670-4552
www.yellowstoneriverlodgemt.com

CAMPGROUND
Itch-Kep-Pe Park
On the Yellowstone River.
Free campsites. Thirty or more campsites, some with pull-throughs. No hook-ups. Flush and pit toilets. Water. Drive all the way to the back of the park for the best riverside sites.
http://freecampsites.net/#!1460&query=sitedetails

LODGING
Super 8
(next to the Town Pump)
From I-90, Exit 408
Columbus, MT 59019
406-322-4902
www.Super8.com
(free Wi-Fi)

DINING
307 Bar & Grill
842 E. Pike Ave.
Columbus, MT 59019
406-322-4511
www.307grill.com
(casino, free Wi-Fi)

Apple Village Restaurant
565 N. Ninth St.
Columbus, MT 59019
406-322-5057

Uncle Sam's Eatery
619 Clough Ave. S
Columbus, MT 59019
406-322-6227
(lunches to go)

LIBATIONS
New Atlas Bar
528 E. Pike Ave.
Columbus, MT 59019
406-322-9818

307 Bar & Grill
(see above; casino, free Wi-Fi)

EMERGENCY MEDICAL HELP
Stillwater Billings Clinic
710 N. 11th St.
Columbus, MT 59019
406-322-1000
www.stillwaterbillingsclinic.com

CELL PHONE SERVICE
Good service in the towns of Columbus and Absarokee

STREAM ACCESSIBILITY
2

WADING CHALLENGE
4, due to the swiftness of the river

WILDLIFE ALERT
Bears

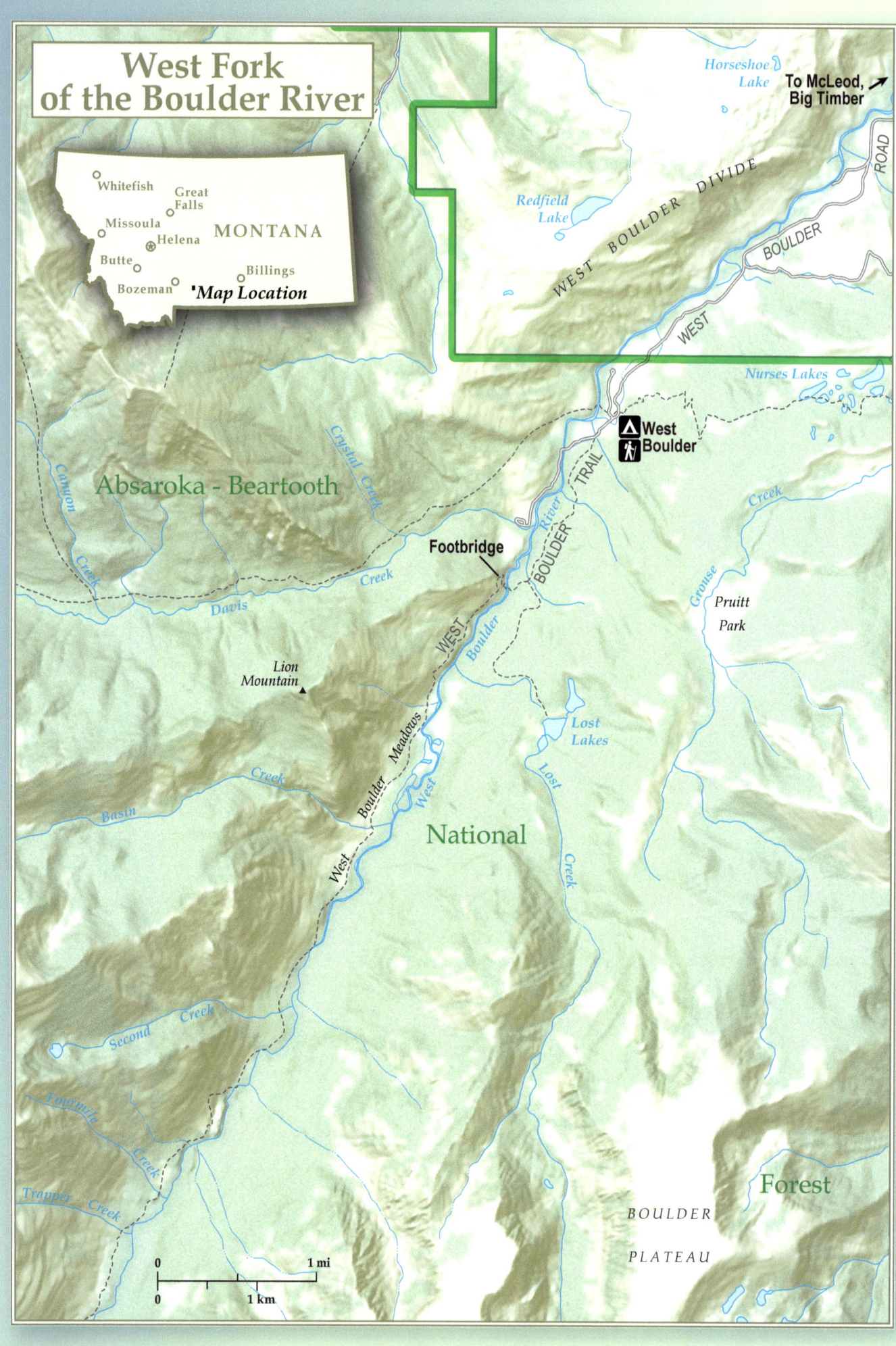

5 · West Fork of the Boulder River

➤ **Location:** The West Boulder is a remote and magnificent river. Its headwaters are in the Gallatin National Forest in the Absaroka-Beartooth Wilderness. The river flows for 29.3 miles until it reaches the Boulder River near the town of McLeod.

From the river's mouth up to about 25 miles, brown trout are common, and they average 12 to 14 inches long, while rainbows are not so common. Mountain whitefish are found in the first 25 miles, as well. From mid-river to 25 miles or so up from the mouth, cutthroat trout are present, averaging 14 inches—with a few reaching 18 inches.

From Big Timber, take MT 298 south for 16 miles until you reach McLeod. Just past McLeod is MT 295, a gravel road. Turn right onto MT 295 and travel approximately 5 miles until you reach the sign for West Boulder Road, where you'll turn left. (This intersection is also marked with a National Forest sign.) Continue another 7 miles to the end of the road, and find a spot in the parking area.

If you are traveling from Livingston, drive east out of town, cross over the Yellowstone River, and in 1 mile, turn right onto Swingley Road. In 15 miles, just after crossing the West Fork of the Boulder River (West Boulder River), turn right onto West Boulder Road. Follow West Boulder Road to the end, about 7 miles, and park your car in the designated area.

Walk through the gate and over the cattle crossing, where it says DO NOT ENTER. (The warning refers to autos only.) In 200 yards, you will see a trailhead sign: TRAIL NO. 41—WEST BOULDER.

The West Boulder Meadows trail is well maintained. The first mile passes through thick berry bushes before opening up with great views; after that, there's a steady uphill climb for the next three miles into the Absaroka-Beartooth Wilderness. The hike takes approximately 1½ hours. (Carry bear spray and make noise during the first mile of thick brush.) When you reach a footbridge over the river, you're at the halfway point.

➤ **Hatches:** Along with those patterns mentioned in the Montana Hatch Chart on page xiv, the Black Flying Ant (#16–18) and Beadhead Hare's-ear Nymph (#16) are particularly effective on these waters.

➤ **Fishing regulations:** West Boulder is open the entire year; however, I would not fish there until mid to late July because the river needs time to warm up.

The combined daily limit for trout (including cutthroat) is two fish, and only one in possession over 13 inches

➤ **Tackle and strategy:** You'll want 4- or 5-weight four-piece or pack rods 8 to 8½ feet long, with floating line. If the skies are overcast and there's wind, a 4X tippet and a 9-foot leader should do you. With sun overhead and no wind, you may need 5X tippet.

Author crossing bridge. Peter Lami

West Boulder's waters stay cold all summer, but waders are optional. While I did carry my hip waders, I did not really need them.

Approach the eastern edge of the river's meadow section first. Trout are stacked up just above where the river narrows for its descent into the canyon. Fishing here is good; a slightly weighted Hare's-ear Nymph or small Leech will do the trick. Moving west along the shore, you come into superb sight fishing for cutthroat. I have found a Black Flying Ant (#16) to be a hot pattern for these fish during early to mid-August.

Continue along from the meadow section and fish the braided area beyond it, or return to the trail and hike onward to the river section above the meadows. How far up you should go depends on the amount of daylight remaining. (Hiking back down in the dark is not recommended.) Consult Google Earth to get an idea of what the river looks like above the meadow section.

Meadow section. Peter Lami

Author on trail approaching meadows section. Peter Lami

Author dressing an ant pattern. Peter Lami

Author with cutthroat. Peter Lami

Skip the area just below the meadow, as it's hard to access, and I didn't find the fishing very productive. There's some nice access near the campground parking area that's fun to fish, but downriver from the campground, access is difficult. It's possible to wade from the bridge, but the rocks there are very slippery and the fishable section is limited.

You'll find good fishing in the West Boulder until the weather gets too cold for comfort. Fall is a beautiful time to wet a line on this stream.

> **Livingston** is one of my favorite towns in Montana. Northern Pacific Railway Company founded Livingston in 1882, and for over 100 years, Livingston was the gateway town for Yellowstone National Park. From historic Main Street, shops, museums, art galleries, and amazing restaurants are all within walking distance. The town rocks during the Fourth of July weekend with celebrations and a world-class rodeo. For more information, visit: www.livingston-chamber.com.

FLY SHOP AND OUTFITTER
Sweet Cast Angler
119 First Ave. W
Big Timber, MT 59011
406-932-4469

George Anderson's Yellowstone Angler
5256 US 89 S
Livingston, MT 59047
406-222-7130
www.yellowstoneangler.com

Dan Bailey's Fly Shop
209 W. Park St.
Livingston, MT 59047
406-222-1673
www.dan-bailey.com

Hatch Finders Fly Shop
5237 US 89 S, Suite 12
Livingston, MT 59047
406-222-0989
www.hatchfinders.com

Sweetwater Fly Shop
5082 US 89 S
Livingston, MT 59047
406-222-9393
www.sweetwaterflyshop.com

OUTFITTERS
Brant Oswald Fly Fishing Services
117 S. 9th St.
Livingston, MT 59047
406-222-8312
www.brantoswaldflyfishing.com

Kinsey Outfitting
326 S. 13th St.
Livingston, MT 59047
406-222-4494
www.secludedwater.com

Long Outfitting
P.O. Box 1224
Livingston, MT 59047
406-222-6775
www.longoutfitting.com

CAMPGROUND
A small campground and Forest Service cabin are located at the end of West Boulder Road. The cabin may be reserved via www.recreation.gov. (Make your reservation at least six months in advance.) Type "West Boulder cabin, MT" into the page's search field and check availability, or call 1-877-444-6777. Two campsites are located on the West Boulder in the meadow area. They are operated on a first-come, first-served basis.

LODGING
The Grand Hotel Bed & Breakfast
139 McLeod St.
Big Timber, MT 59011
406-932-4459
www.thegrand-hotel.com

Super 8 Big Timber
5400 Southgate Dr.
I-90 and US 10 W
Big Timber, MT 59011
800-536-1211
www.super8.com

The Murray Hotel
201 W. Park St.
Livingston, MT 59047
406-222-1350
www.murrayhotel.com

DINING
The Grand Hotel
(See above.)
Reservations highly recommended for the Livingston restaurants, below:

2nd Street Bistro
123 N. 2nd St.
Livingston, MT 59047
406-222-9463
www.secondstreetbistro.com
(fine dining)

Gil's Goods
207 W. Park St.
Livingston, MT 59047
406-222-9463
www.gilsgoods.com

Montana's Rib and Chop House
305 E. Park St.
Livingston, MT 59047
406-222-9200
www.ribandchophouse.com

The Sport Bar & Grill
114 S. Main
Livingston, MT 59047

LIBATIONS
The Grand Hotel saloon
(See above.)

Holly's Road Kill Saloon
1557 Main Boulder Rd.
McLeod, MT 59052
406-932-6174
(15½ miles south of Big Timber on MT 298 South)

The Murray Bar
201 W. Park St.
Livingston, MT 59047
406-222-6433
www.themurraybar.com

Neptune's Brewery
119 N L St.
Livingston MT 59047

Katabatic Brewery
117 W Park St.
Livingston, MT 59047

The Mint Bar & Grill
102 N Main
Livingston, MT 59047

The Owl Lounge
110 N 2nd St.
Livingston, MT 59047

EMERGENCY MEDICAL HELP
Livingston Memorial Hospital
1104 E. Park St.
Livingston, MT 59047
406-222-3011

CELL PHONE SERVICE
Cell service is good in Livingston and Big Timber. Outside these two towns, reception is spotty.

STREAM ACCESSIBILITY
3

WADING CHALLENGE
5

WILDLIFE ALERT
Bears—carry bear spray

BOZEMAN

GALLATIN RIVER

EAST GALLATIN RIVER

HYALITE CREEK

RUBY RIVER

LOWER MADISON RIVER—
BEAR TRAP CANYON

▶ **Location:** The perfect central hub for a Montana fly fishing excursion, Bozeman is a fantastic place for anglers and non-anglers alike to spend several days. Surrounded by five mountain ranges—Big Belt, Bridger, Gallatin, Madison, and the Tobacco Roots—Bozeman boasts stunning scenery! Downtown Main Street has kept its historic charm, with flowers hanging from every lamppost, benches for resting, unique shops, restaurants, and art galleries.

Weekly summer activities include Music on Main Street and a farmers' market at Lindley Park. Bozeman's Museum of the Rockies has one of the finest dinosaur exhibits in the world, and Montana State University (founded in 1893, with a current enrollment of more than 15,000) is a distinguished Carnegie research institution. John M. Bozeman established the Bozeman Trail and founded Bozeman in 1864. Bozeman has great history, even hosting a visit from the Lewis and Clark Expedition in 1805. Simms Fishing Products is based in Bozeman.

The Missouri River Headwaters State Park is 30 miles west of Bozeman and well worth a side trip. For additional day trips, consider a jaunt to Big Sky Ski Resort or Yellowstone National Park.

Downtown Bozeman.
www.downtownbozeman.org

REGION

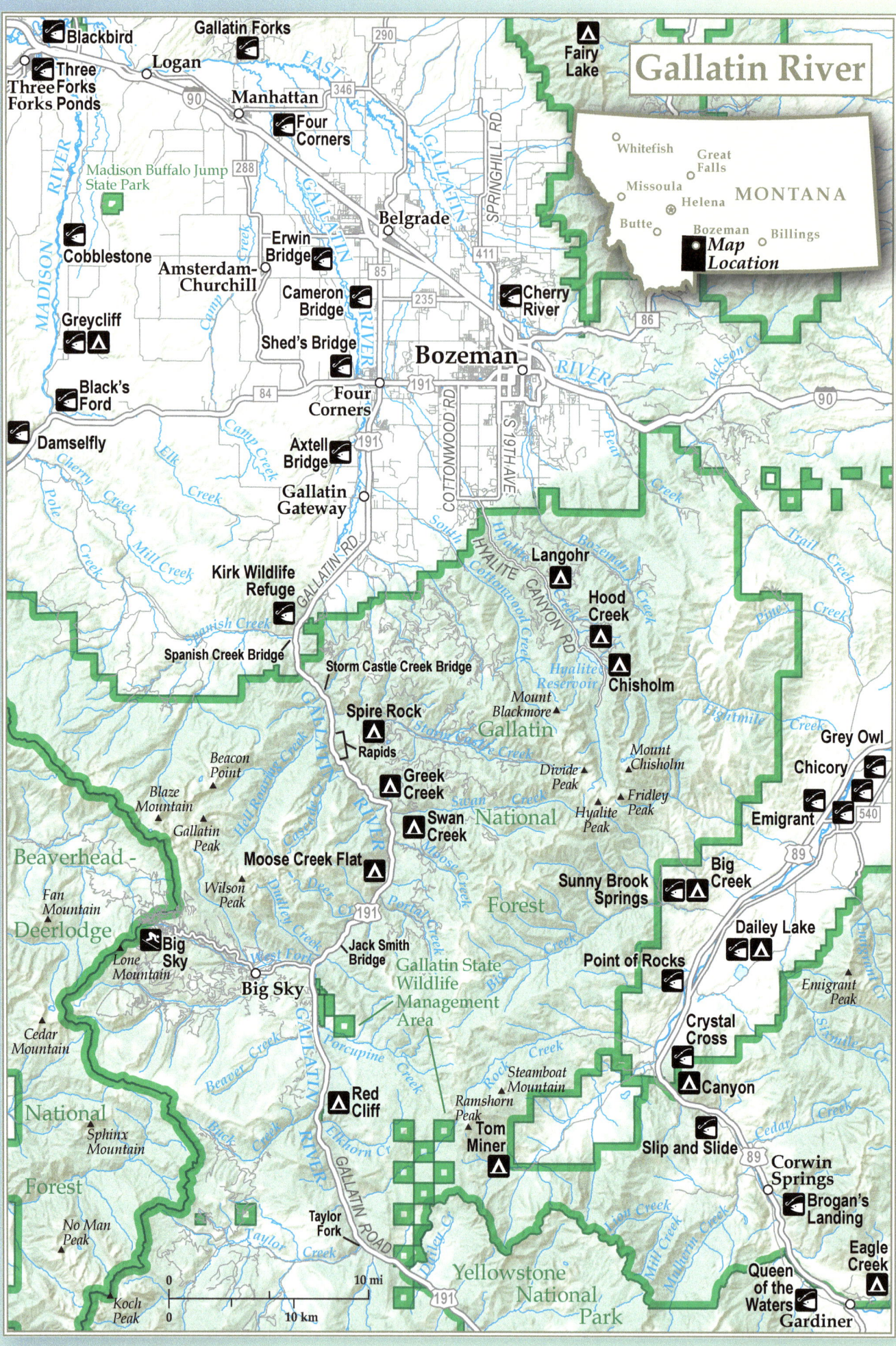

6 · Gallatin River

▶ **Location:** From Bozeman, drive west on Main Street/US 191. Turn south on Gallatin Road/US 191. This intersection is referred to as "Four Corners."

Flowing north from Yellowstone National Park (YNP), the Gallatin River travels 97 miles and then joins the Jefferson and Madison Rivers to form the Missouri River at the Missouri Headwaters State Park in Three Forks, Montana.

My overall impression of the Gallatin River is its outstanding diversity in both scenery and river character. As the river leaves Yellowstone National Park it curves through river brush and meadows before dropping into the canyon section south of Big Sky. After the canyon section it flows through the Gallatin valley as it heads toward Bozeman and beyond. Access is easy and the fish numbers are high. If you are willing to be adventuresome and leave the popular points of access behind, an even better fishing experience will result.

Dave Alvin, known locally as "Super Dave," has been fishing the Gallatin River since 1989. He and his wife, Katie, own East Slope Outdoors. Dave described the Gallatin as a "phenomenal resource, due to the diverse water type, diverse species, and available trout numbers." The river's character alternates from fast-flowing canyons to open riffles to meadows. Every angler, whether beginner or more advanced, can find a fishing situation on the Gallatin that fits his or her needs, be it easy wading or more strenuous water challenges. The only drawback to the river is the highway corridor, with its noisy traffic, large trucks, and the occasional bighorn sheep. Do follow the speed limit and be cautious.

The upper section near YNP is beautiful. The grassy meadows, willow-lined banks, and braided gravel runs make for easy wading and fun casting. If you have a YNP fishing permit, you can go upriver into the park as well. The fish are much less numerous here compared with the lower canyon, but the majestic scenery makes up for it. From YNP to Taylor Creek, also known as Taylor Fork, is a good place to be if Taylor Creek is dumping silt into the river from spring runoff or summer rains.

The water above Taylor Creek has some nice pools with convenient access. Do keep a quick pace, moving from one holding area to another. Taylor Creek does add volume to the river from where it dumps into the Gallatin. If Taylor Creek is turning the Gallatin off-color, the fishing will be poor; if the river is clearing, the fishing can be good. The Montana rule of thumb is 18 inches of water visibility or better for productive fishing. However, when the river is clearing, that rule can be bent to something less than 18 inches.

Taylor Creek to the Big Sky turnoff has the Red Cliff Campground with good access, Porcupine Creek (which adds water), and the Gallatin State Wildlife Management Area.

Downstream of Big Sky. Molly Semenik

Big Sky to the mouth of the canyon has the highest fish count. (Estimated at 3,500 to 4,000 fish per mile!) Jack Smith Bridge has nice access, as does Moose Creek Campground. There are several small tributaries that feed into the Gallatin that can be fun to fish as well, such as Swan and West Fork.

Several bridges in this section can serve as access points. From Big Sky to Storm Castle Creek, you share the river with whitewater rafters and kayakers. Fish early or late to avoid them. Spanish Creek Road is another good access point.

Keep an eye out for moose. Molly Semenik

Horses keeping their eyes on the moose. Molly Semenik

Guide Interview
Austin Trayser is a 20-year veteran of the Gallatin River—at the age of 28! Austin told me, "I caught my first fish on a fly on the Gallatin." Austin speaks of the Gallatin with great emotion, calling it a "gorgeous river, very romantic—one that as you drive through the canyon you can't keep your eyes off. " Austin learned how to fish as a young boy on the many tributaries that feed into the Gallatin River. Portal Creek is one branch that taught him the fundamentals. Austin recommends you "drive up and down, look at the obvious pullouts, and don't stop there." Austin has been a fly fishing guide, professional videographer, and photographer since 2008 (www.traysermediagroup.com, Austin@traysermediagroup.com).

Three river access sites can be found from the mouth of the canyon to the Four Corners area: Gallatin Gateway Bridge (turn left on Mill Street at the Gallatin Gateway Inn), Axtell Bridge, and Sheds Bridge (turn west on MT 84 and travel a few miles to the bridge crossing).

The East Gallatin meets the Gallatin at Gallatin Forks access. The Gallatin flows increase and boats can be launched from that point. If you're walk-wading, the only way to legally access the water there is from bridges. From there to the Missouri, rainbows and browns are common, with the possibility of very large browns in that section. Successfully fishing for them will depend on water temperatures and flows, as that stretch can be affected by irrigation demands and summer heat.

Brook trout can be found in the Gallatin's tributaries. Westslope and Yellowstone cutthroat are occasionally caught, with mountain whitefish occurring throughout. The fish range from 11 to 12 inches with some browns as big as 15 and 19 inches.

▶ **Hatches:** The Montana Hatch Chart applies, but if you'd like to fine-tune your kit on the Gallatin, consider the following:
- Winter fishing a Stonefly Nymph, Birch Creek, or Girdle Bug (#10–12)
- BWOs March through April
- Midges in spring and fall (below Big Sky, where the water is warmer)
- Caddis during May pre-runoff if there's enough water clarity; then great caddis hatches throughout the summer at dusk
- Golden Stones starting in mid-June, if water flow and clarity are acceptable
- Yellow Sally stoneflies in July
- Spruce moths flutter out of the pine trees into the water during late July and August—look for conifer-lined locations in the canyon section
- Small Beadhead Nymphs and soft-hackles in the upper section, near YNP.

▶ **Fishing regulations:** This Central District, Region 3 river is open the entire year. The combined limit for trout (browns and rainbows included) is five daily, and in possession, only one over 18 inches. All grayling and cutthroat trout must be released immediately.

▶ **Tackle and strategy:** In the upper section's smaller water, cast a 3-weight fly rod paired with a 7½-foot 4X leader. As you move downriver where the flow increases or if wind is present, a 5-weight rod will be in order.

Fish the pocketwater, riffles, seam lines, and around rocks. A great Gallatin technique is to use a dry top fly and a 2- to 3-foot 4X tippet section tied to the bend of the hook; to the attached tippet section, tie on the appropriate nymph or larva, depending on the time of year. This two-fly technique (one dry and one wet) is a great rig when trying to pin down what the fish are eating.

FLY SHOPS AND OUTFITTERS
East Slope Outdoors
32 Town Center Ave.
Big Sky, MT 59716
406-995-4369
www.eastslopeoutdoors.com

Fins & Feathers of Bozeman
81801 Gallatin Rd.
Bozeman, MT 59718
877-790-5303
www.finsandfeathersonline.com

Gallatin River Guides
47430 Gallatin Rd. (US 191)
Gallatin Gateway, MT 59716
406-995-2290
www.gallatinriverguides.com

Greater Yellowstone Flyfishers
29 Pioneer Way
Bozeman MT 59718
406-585-5321
www.gyflyfishers.com

Grizzly Outfitters
11 Lone Peak Dr., Suite 101
Big Sky, MT 59716
406-995-2939 or 888-807-9452
www.grizzlyoutfitters.com

The River's Edge West Fly Shop
59 North Star Ln.
Bozeman MT 59718
406-284-2401
www.theriversedge.com

Wild Trout Outfitters & Guide Service
¼ mile south of Big Sky on US 191
406-995-2975 or 800-423-4742
www.wildtroutoutfitters.com

LODGES
320 Ranch
205 Buffalo Horn Creek
Gallatin Gateway, MT 59730
800-243-0320
www.320ranch.com

Cinnamon Lodge
37090 Gallatin Rd.
Gallatin Gateway, MT 59730
406-995-4253
www.cinnamonlodgeadventures.com

The Covered Wagon Ranch
34035 Gallatin Rd.
Gallatin Gateway, MT 59730
800-995-4237
www.coveredwagonranch.com

Gallatin River Lodge
9105 Thorpe Rd.
Bozeman, MT 59718
888-387-0148 or 406-388-0148
www.grlodge.com

Lone Mountain Ranch
750 Lone Mountain Ranch
Big Sky, MT 59716
800-514-4644 or 406-995-4644
www.lonemountainranch.com

Rainbow Ranch Lodge
42950 Gallatin Rd.
Gallatin Gateway, MT 59730
800-937-4132 or 406-995-4132
www.rainbowranchbigsky.com

CAMPGROUNDS
Bozeman KOA (Bozeman Hot Springs)
81123 Gallatin Rd. (US 191)
Bozeman, MT 59718
406-587-3030
www.KOA.com

Find additional campgrounds along the Gallatin River: www.recreation.gov

DINING
Mama Mac Bakery and Sandwich shop
81809 Gallatin Rd. (Four Corners)
Bozeman, MT 59718
406-522-8690
www.mamamacs.com
(amazing breakfasts and lunches to go; hours: 6 a.m.–3 p.m.)

Corral Bar, Steakhouse & Motel
US 191, 5 miles south of Big Sky turnoff
888-995-4249
www.corralbar.com
(breakfast, lunch, and dinner)
The town of Big Sky has numerous restaurant offerings.

LIBATIONS
Corral Bar
Lone Peak Brewery
48 Market Pl.
Big Sky, MT 59716
406-995-3939
www.lonepeakbrewery.com

EMERGENCY MEDICAL HELP
Medical Clinic of Big Sky
11 Lone Peak Dr., Suite 202
Big Sky, MT 59716
406-993-2797
(hours: 10 a.m.–4:30 p.m.)

Near Bozeman:
Bozeman Deaconess Hospital
915 Highland Blvd.
Bozeman, MT 59715
406-585-5000
www.bozemandeaconess.org

Bozeman Urgent Care
1006 W. Main St.
Bozeman, MT 59715
406-586-8711
www.bozemanurgentcare.org

CELL PHONE SERVICE
Good reception near Big Sky; otherwise, spotty.

STREAM ACCESSIBILITY
2

WADING CHALLENGE
3 to 4 (cleats and staff recommended)

WILDLIFE ALERTS
Bear, moose

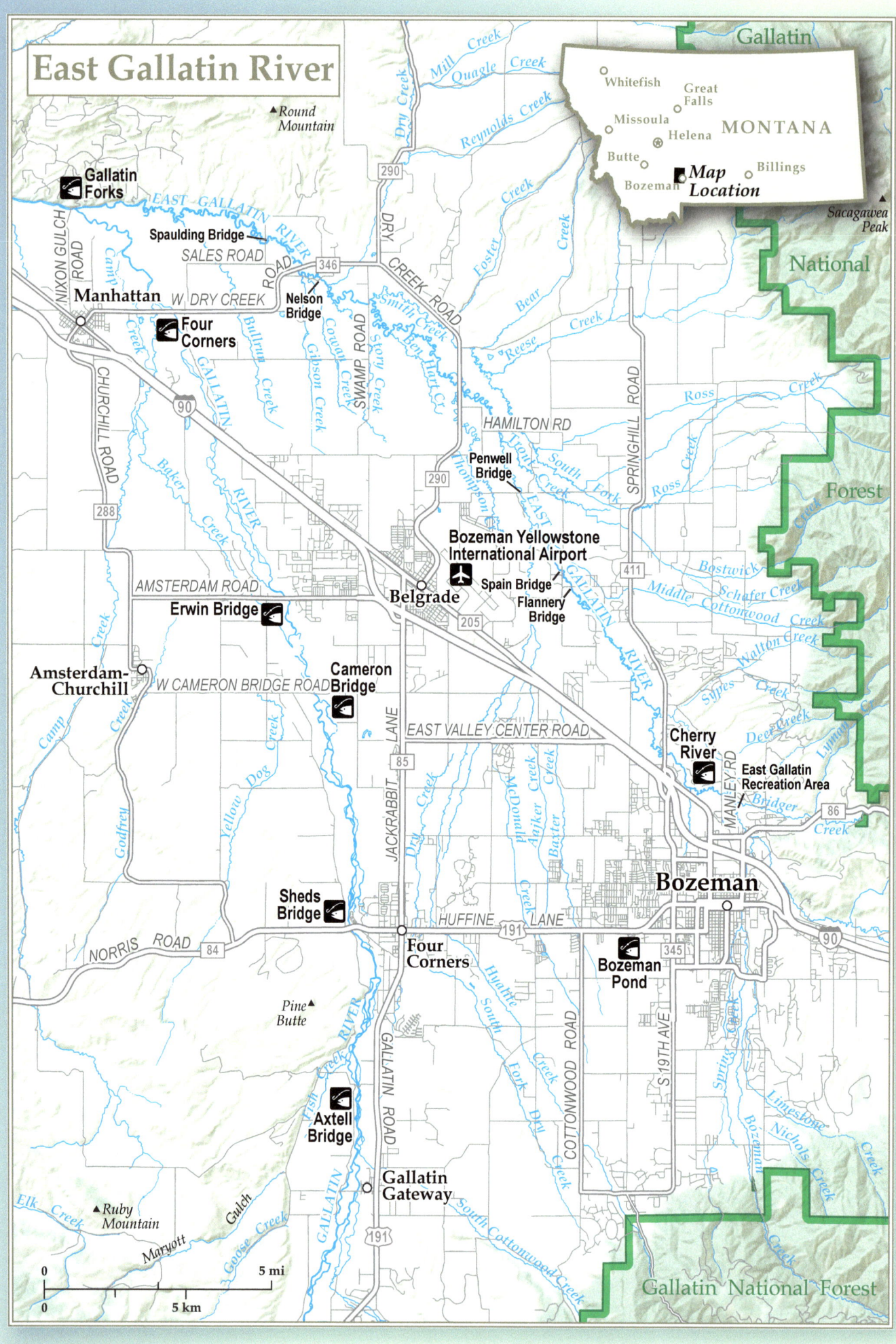

7 · East Gallatin River

▶ **Location:** The East Gallatin is north of Bozeman and flows northwest for 42 miles until it meets the Gallatin River at Gallatin Forks. If you wish to fish its upper reaches, take Main Street in Bozeman to Rouse Avenue; then turn right, or north. Go under the interstate, and turn left on Griffin Drive. Turn right—again, north—on Manley Road. Drive past the East Gallatin Recreation Area, and park after ¼ mile. You will come to a bridge crossing.

The East Gallatin is a local fishery that folks generally fish for a few hours when the weather and hatches are at their best. The river flows through residential neighborhoods, a golf course, and agricultural lands. It is small, with meandering oxbows, deep pools, and undercut banks.

The East Gallatin River's headwaters, Rock Creek and a few other small streams, are just east of Bozeman. Several spring creeks add water and nutrients to the East, including Ben Hart and Thompson Spring creeks. The East Gallatin is nutrient rich, so when hatches occur, they are prolific. During the heat of summer, the water recedes because of irrigation demands, and when the water warms up, the fish get sluggish. During the fall, water temperatures cool, irrigation demands lessen, and river volume increases.

The East Gallatin can be accessed via nine county bridges. Start either at Gallatin Forks Fishing Access Site (FAS) and head east, or at Manley Road and head west. A good county road map will guide you along. Follow the river and jump in at the bridges. Stay below the high-water mark and respect other anglers. If more than one car is parked at a bridge, you may wish to move on to the next bridge.

When traveling east on MT 346 just outside Manhattan, you will come to Four Corners FAS, which is actually on the Gallatin River; if time allows, stop and fish. If you continue east another few miles, you will pass Sales Road; keep heading east on MT 346 until the road crosses the East Gallatin.

The Gallatin Forks FAS, mentioned earlier, is located north of Manhattan, Montana. Take Broadway north out of town, turn left on Railroad Avenue, and drive for 2½ miles. Just downriver of the white metal bridge is where the East Gallatin and the Gallatin merge.

Brown and rainbow trout occur on the East Gallatin, along with mountain whitefish. The fish are a good size: 12 to 16 inches, with a few pushing 20 inches.

▶ **Hatches:** Consult the Montana Hatch Chart. Winter midge and Blue-winged Olive fishing can be epic if the weather cooperates. Once the water begins to clear in June, the caddis fishing is excellent. Yellow Sally stoneflies come off end of June and into July. August Tricos can be amazing, but always a challenge.

▶ **Fishing regulations:** A Central District, Region 3 stream, the East Gallatin is open year-round downstream from the mouth of Bozeman (Sourdough Creek). The combined catch limit for trout (including browns and rainbows) is five daily, and in possession only one, over 18 inches.

Fall on the East Gallatin. Molly Semenik

Top. Fall on the East Gallatin. Molly Semenik

Inset. Brown trout. Bill Toone

Above. Close to confluence of Gallatin. Molly Semenik

▶ **Tackle and strategy:** Your rigging for this river is the same as on the Gallatin.

If you're fishing undercut banks for browns, use a 7½-foot 3X leader. Try to get the streamer under the bank—and expect to get caught up in the bank from time to time. If a hatch is not present, fishing with two nymphs can be effective. The top fly should be the same size as or larger than the dropper (bottom) fly. For example, the top fly could be a size 14 Beadhead Pheasant Tail with a size 16 or 18 dropper—maybe a Zebra Midge, for example.

Here's another excellent method, especially during a caddis hatch: the top fly could be a size 16 caddis tied to a 4X leader, with a 5X piece of tippet tied to a caddis soft-hackle for the dropper. Swing the flies through the rising fish. (Review the basics of the Leisenring Lift if desired, as described in the chapter titled "Fly Fishing Strategies for Small Streams.") Caddis emerge quickly; therefore, swinging soft-hackles or emergers can be very effective on the trout. Cast across stream, and then let the flies drift down to the point where the leader straightens. Continue the drift, swinging until the leader is straight down from you. As you lift to recast, the flies will rise in the water column; this maneuver can instigate a grab, so be ready!

FLY SHOPS

Bozeman Angler
23 E. Main St.
Bozeman, MT 59715
406-587-9111
www.bozemanangler.com

The River's Edge
2012 N. 7th Ave.
Bozeman, MT 59715
406-586-5373
www.theriversedge.com

Montana Troutfitters
1716 W. Main St.
Bozeman, MT 59715
406-587-4707 or 800-646-7847
www.troutfitters.com

LODGE

Gallatin River Lodge
9105 Thorpe Rd.
Bozeman, MT 59718
888-387-0148 or 406-388-0148
www.grlodge.com

CAMPGROUNDS

Bozeman KOA
(Bozeman Hot Springs)
81123 Gallatin Rd. (US 191)
Bozeman, MT 59718
406-587-3030
www.KOA.com

Sunrise Campground
31842 Frontage Rd.
Bozeman, MT 59718
406-587-4797
www.sunriservcampground.com

LODGING

Best Western Plus GranTree Inn
1325 N. Seventh Ave.
Bozeman, MT 59718
406-587-5261
www.bestwesternmontana.com

All major hotel and motel chains may be found in Bozeman.

DINING

The Nova Café
312 E. Main St.
Bozeman, MT 59718
406-587-3973
www.thenovacafe.com
(breakfast daily, lunch on weekdays)

Main Street Overeasy
9 E. Main St., Suite E
Bozeman, MT 59718
406-587-3205
www.mainstreetovereasy.com
(breakfast and lunch)

Dave's Sushi
115 N. Bozeman Ave.
Bozeman, MT 59718
406-556-1351
www.davessushi.com

Montana Ale Works
611 E. Main St.
Bozeman, MT 59718
406-587-7700
www.montanaaleworks.com
(reservations recommended)

MacKenzie River Pizza
232 E. Main St.
Bozeman, MT 59718
406-587-0055

The Garage Soup Shack and Mesquite Grill
451 E. Main St.
Bozeman, MT 59718
406-585-8558

LIBATIONS

Montana Ale Works
(see above)

Bacchus Pub
105 W. Main St.
Bozeman, MT 59718
406-522-0079
www.thebaxterhotel.com

Plonk
29 E. Main St.
Bozeman, MT 59718
406-587-2170
www.plonkwine.com

EMERGENCY MEDICAL HELP

Bozeman Deaconess Hospital
915 Highland Blvd.
Bozeman, MT 59715
406-585-5000
www.bozemandeaconess.org

Bozeman Urgent Care
1006 W. Main St.
Bozeman, MT 59715
406-586-8711
www.bozemanurgentcare.org

CELL PHONE SERVICE
Good reception

STREAM ACCESSIBILITY
3

WADING CHALLENGE
2

WILDLIFE ALERT
General safety precautions for outdoor recreation in Montana

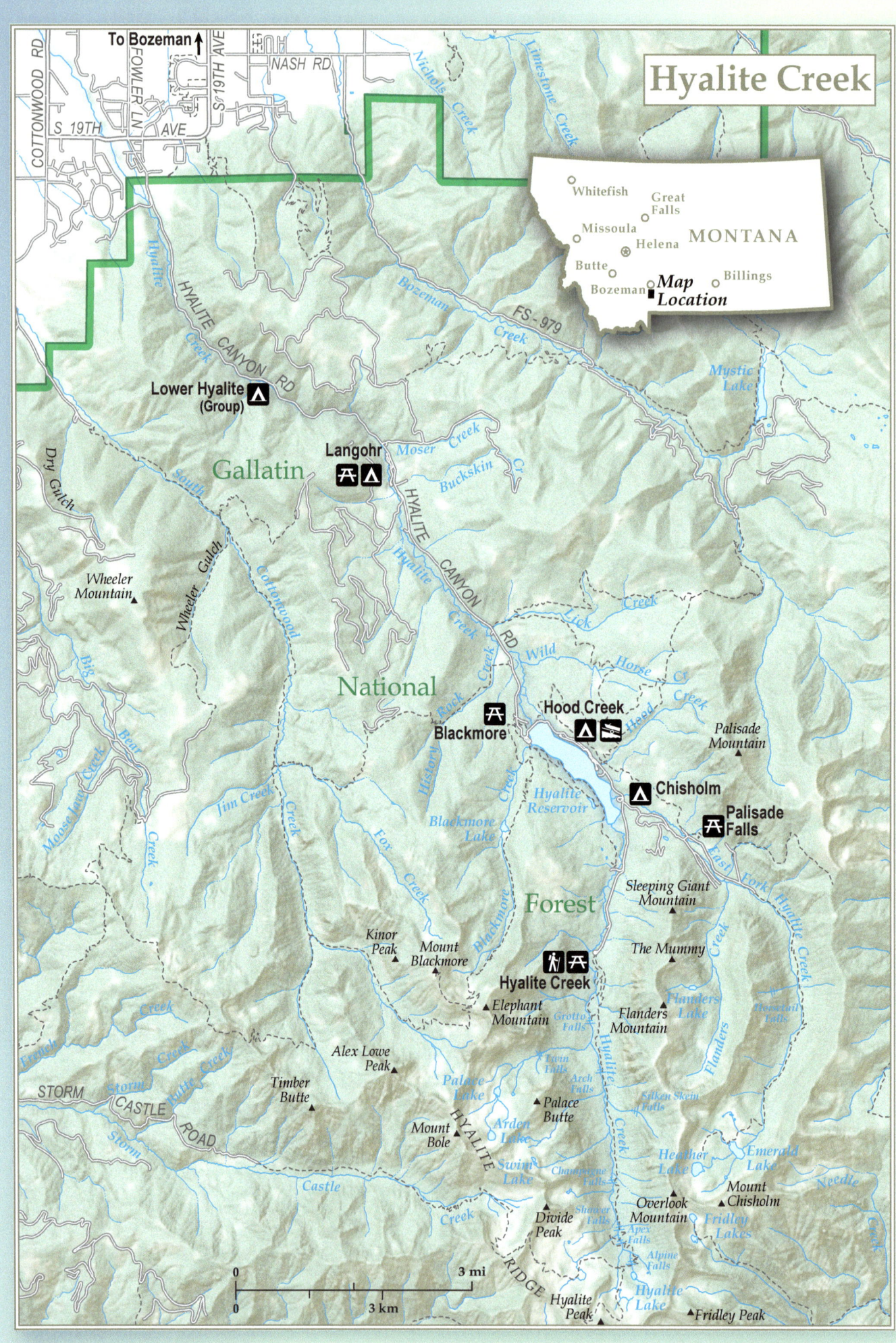

8 · Hyalite Creek

➤ **Location:** From Bozeman's Main Street, turn south onto South 19th Avenue/MT 345 S, and drive 7.1 miles. Turn left on Hyalite Canyon Road, and drive a short distance to the Hyalite orientation site, where you will find historical information and a good map of the canyon.

The Hyalite is a small creek, and perfect for families and beginners. Its scenery and proximity to Bozeman make for an enjoyable day of easy fishing. Hyalite Creek originates in the Gallatin Range and flows for 35.2 miles until it reaches the East Gallatin River. The most popular recreational destination in Montana, Hyalite Canyon was named after a rare translucent opal discovered there over a century ago.

The 250-acre Hyalite Reservoir was built in the 1940s and provides drinking water for Bozeman and irrigation water for local ranchers. Along with the fishing and boating activities on the reservoir, there are numerous hiking trails in the canyon as well. Hyalite trailhead is about two miles past the reservoir. The hike to 10,299-foot Hyalite Peak is just over seven miles, one way. Several waterfalls can be reached from the trail.

Just upstream from where Hyalite Creek enters the reservoir is a beautiful stretch for angling—fun for anyone who likes to catch brook trout or grayling, with Yellowstone cutthroat a possibility as well. For its first mile, the creek is small, heavily forested, and full of pools created by downed woodfall. To reach this section, park just past the reservoir at the large boulders designating the parking area. Cross the meadow in the direction of the creek. This stretch has special regulations to protect the spawning of cutthroat and grayling. Above this mile-long section, the creek gets too small to be productive for fishing

Above the reservoir, the stream opens July 15, and anytime after that is also good for fishing the reservoir itself. The fish are larger there compared with those in the creek, and more diverse: rainbow, Yellowstone cutthroat, and brook trout, Arctic grayling. Use a slow strip with a Beadhead Hare's-ear, Prince Nymph, or Leech when fishing the still waters of Hyalite Reservoir. Hopefully an evening caddis hatch will give you the opportunity to target rising fish.

Below the reservoir, the catch will be mostly rainbow trout averaging around 10 inches. Stream access is easy, thanks to a road that edges the creek for 8 or so miles out from the reservoir. You'll have many pull-offs to choose from. Langohr Campground has a fishing access trail running along its entire length.

Hyalite just below the dam. Molly Semenik

Above. Two anglers fishing Hyalite reservoir. Molly Semenik

Inset. Brook trout above reservoir Molly Semenik

Facing. Map of the canyon. Molly Semenik

▶ **Hatches:** Consult the Montana Hatch Chart when preparing your fly box for Hyalite Creek. For Hyalite Reservoir, you'll want Woolly Buggers, leeches, and *Callibaetis* mayfly imitations (both nymphs and drys). Check in with your local fly shop to find out how the lake is fishing.

▶ **Fishing regulations:** Hyalite Creek is in the Central District, Region 3. Above the Hyalite Reservoir, it's open July 15 through November 30. The combined catch limit for trout includes cutthroat trout: five daily and in possession, only one over 18 inches. All grayling must be released immediately.

Below Hyalite Reservoir, the creek opens on the third Saturday in May and goes until November 30. Catch-and-release is mandatory for cutthroat trout. In the reservoir, grayling must be put back, too.

Pre-season runoff may allow for some fishing if water temperatures are favorable. The best time to fish the creek would be after runoff, around the middle of July.

Check with the local fly shops regarding the status of Hyalite Reservoir. Water temperature and the presence of ice on the lake determine when spring fishing begins. Winter ice fishing is popular on this reservoir.

Bill Toone fishing above reservoir. Molly Semenik

▶ **Tackle and strategy:** Above and below the reservoir, the creek is small enough that a 3- or 4- weight fly rod with a 7½-foot 4X or 5X leader is sufficient. If you're using a dropper fly, I suggest taking tippet size to 5X on the dropper.

For lake fishing, lengthen your leader to 9 feet. Match the tippet size to the heft of your pattern and the clarity of the water. For Woolly Buggers, a 3X is recommended; with 4X or smaller tippets when you're casting small dry flies.

Fishing above the reservoir will require short casts and roll casts. The bow-and-arrow cast will come in handy, too.

FLY SHOPS, OUTFITTERS, LODGES
See the Bozeman region listings on page 000.

CAMPGROUNDS
Langohr Campground
(on Hyalite Creek)

Hood Creek Campground
(on Hyalite Reservoir)

HOTELS, DINING, LIBATIONS
See the Bozeman listings on page 000.

EMERGENCY MEDICAL HELP
Bozeman Deaconess Hospital
915 Highland Blvd.
Bozeman, MT 59715
406-585-5000
www.bozemandeaconess.org

Bozeman Urgent Care
1006 W. Main St.
Bozeman, MT 59715
406-586-8711
www.bozemanurgentcare.org

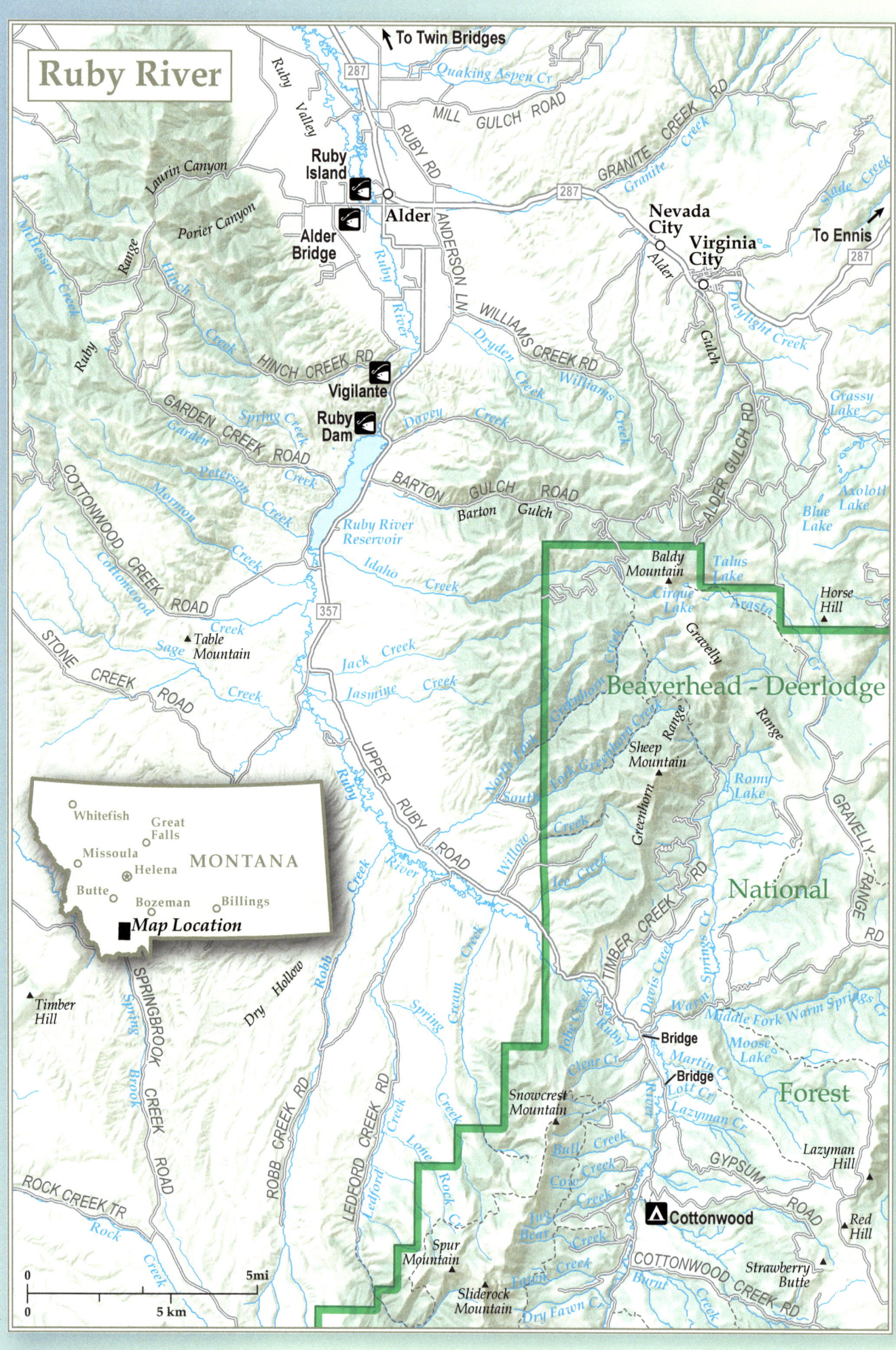

9 · Ruby River

➤ **Location:** The Ruby River can be accessed from the town of Twin Bridges along US 287 or from Ennis on US 287 heading west toward Alder. From Ennis to Alder is 27 miles. From Bozeman to Ennis is 57 miles. If you fish above the reservoir, the drive from Bozeman takes over two hours.

Originating in the Beaverhead-Deerlodge National Forest, the Ruby flows for 97.2 miles until it joins the Beaverhead River just south of Twin Bridges. Above the Ruby Reservoir, the river's upper reaches, are small and easy to fish. This section is upwards of 40 miles from Alder, and much of the travel is on well-maintained dirt roads. Fishing pressure on the remote watercourse is very low. For me, the solitude and beautiful scenery are well worth the extra effort.

The Cottonwood Campground fishing access is a good place to park and fish. Cottonwood Campground is a 30-minute drive south of Alder (it is a primitive campground with an outhouse.) The farther you walk from the parking area, the better the fishing. Downstream, some very nice bends with cliffs create deep, enticing holes. The westslope cutthroat, rainbow cutthroat, and mountain whitefish in this stretch average 9 inches but run up to 11 inches. Arctic grayling, a more recently introduced species, can grow to an impressive 12 inches!

Farther downstream, the trout get larger. Access the river by means of several bridge crossings from the Forest Service to the reservoir. (Landowners can get snippy on the Ruby, but remember—accessing the river from public bridges is perfectly legal.)

The Ruby Reservoir turns the lower Ruby into a tailwater fishery where brown trout dominate, with lesser populations of rainbow trout and whitefish represented. Take advantage of two convenient public access sites in the canyon section—the Ruby Dam and Vigilante Fishing Access Site. The riverbanks are lined with brush, so expect to do some walking through the stream when you move from one place to another. Be careful not to spook the fish with aggressive and splashy wading.

South of Vigilante, the landscape changes to open, arid agricultural land. Alder is another good place to fly fish. From the Alder Bridge FAS, you can head both upstream and downstream. Downstream, a landowner's gate (it's posted) can be used to get to the river. Ruby Island FAS is the second access point in Alder.

Vigilante trailhead. Molly Semenik

The next 40 miles or so below Alder, stream accessibility is a challenge. Landowners in that section are known for their unfriendliness toward anglers accessing the river—even at county bridges, where it is legal. Twenty miles up from the Beaverhead River, there is one public access: Silver Springs Bridge.

➤ **Hatches:** The waters below Ruby Reservoir flow through agricultural land, great for fishing during grasshopper season! In addition, the numerous good-sized browns in this area are susceptible to streamers. Early spring fishing on these tailwaters can be very good, and not so vulnerable to spring runoff as the above reservoir. Consult the Montana Hatch Chart on page xiv for more selections,

➤ **Fishing regulations:** Upstream from Ruby Reservoir, the combined catch limit for trout is five daily and, in possession, only one over 18 inches, including cutthroat. All Grayling must be released immediately. Downstream of and just below Ruby Dam, the river is closed year-round. (The protected area begins at the river's confluence with the Ruby Dam outlet channel and ends at the dam, and includes the outlet channel itself.) An extended season for mountain whitefish and trout (catch-and-release) opens December 1 and runs till the third Saturday in May. Below the Ruby Dam, (not including the closure area near the confluence

Above, Bill Toone and inset, Grayling, both near Cottonwood Camp. Molly Semenik

of the Ruby River and the Ruby Dam and outlet channel) it is five daily and, in possession, only one over 18 inches. All grayling must be released.

▶ **Tackle and strategy:** Either a 3- or 5-weight rod can handle this small stream. Above Ruby Reservoir, a 3 would be great; below it, you may prefer the 5. Fishing above the reservoir, use shorter leaders—7½ feet 4X or 5X tippet. The larger fish below the reservoir call for 4X. (You'll want to lengthen the leader a bit as well.)

For nymphing above the reservoir, try a size 16 Beadhead Pheasant Tail or Gold-ribbed Hare's-ear as the top fly, with a soft-hackle dropper. The small, hungry fish in this section are not choosy. Drys might include the size 16 Parachute Adams, Royal Wulff, Stimulator, or caddis.

Below the reservoir, where the larger browns are found, rigging is different; consider switching to a 4- or 5-weight. A 7½-foot 3X leader is in order when casting streamers. Nymphs and drys are best paired with a 9-foot 4X leader.

Here's a good nymph rig: a size 10 Prince Nymph with a size 16 Beadhead Pheasant Tail dropper. When fishing the deeper pools or runs, be sure there's enough weight to get the flies down to the fish. The browns will be finning under the banks, too, and at the ends of tailouts.

On a clear, hot summer day, sluggish fish can be difficult to catch. With water and sky clear, they are also more apt to notice your leaders, casting movements, and shadows. Going to a longer and lighter leader might help; however, you risk a broken leader and a lost fish.

Inset. Bill Toone near alder. Molly Semenik   *Near Cottonwood Camp. Molly Semenik*

FLY SHOPS AND OUTFITTERS
Four Rivers Fishing Company
201 Main St.
Twin Bridges, MT 59754
406-684-5651
www.4riversmontana.com
(cabin rentals available)

Flatline Outfitters Fly Shop
307 S. Main St.
Twin Bridges, MT 59754
406-684-5639
www.kingsflatline.com

Stonefly Inn & Fly Shop
409 N. Main St.
Twin Bridges, MT 59754
406-684-5648
www.thestoneflyinn.com

LODGE
Big Hole C4 Lodge
80 Utley Ln.
Twin Bridges, MT 59754
406-684-5760
www.bigholeC4lodge.com

Healing Waters Lodge
270 Tuke Ln.
Twin Bridges, MT 59754
406-684-5960
www.hwlodge.com

Ruby Valley Lodge
310 S. Main St.
Sheridan, MT 59749
406-842-7473
www.rubyvalleylodge.com

CAMPGROUNDS
Alder KOA
2280 US 287
Alder, MT 59710
406-842-5677
www.Koa.com

Two small primitive campgrounds, Canyon and Cottonwood, Camp are on the Ruby above the reservoir.

DINING
Old Hotel
101 E. Fifth Ave.
Twin Bridges, MT 59754
406-684-5959
www.theoldhotel.com
(fine dining—reservations recommended)

Wagon Wheel
207 N. Main St.
Twin Bridges, MT 59754
406-684-5099

LIBATIONS
Blue Anchor Bar
210 Main St.
Twin Bridges, MT 59754
406-684-5655

EMERGENCY MEDICAL HELP
Ruby Valley Hospital
220 E. Crofoot St.
Sheridan, MT 59749
406-842-5453
www.rubyvalleyhospital.com

CELL PHONE SERVICE
Ennis and Twin Bridges have cell phone reception

STREAM ACCESSIBILITY
2

WADING CHALLENGE
2

WILDLIFE ALERTS
Moose, bear

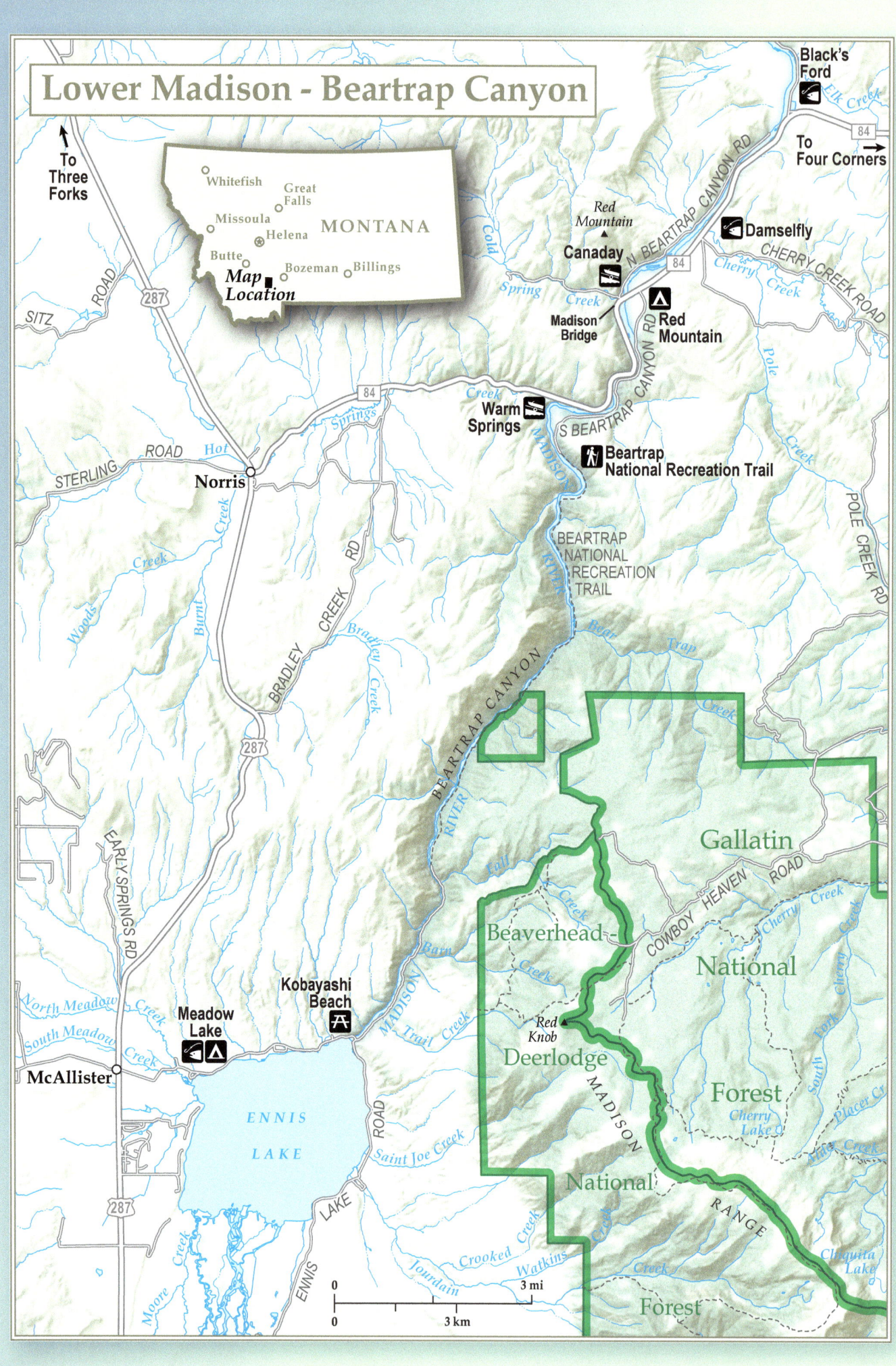

10 · Lower Madison–Bear Trap Canyon

➤ **Location:** The east side of the river can be reached from MT 84. From MT 84 just before the Madison bridge crossing and across from Red Mountain Campground turn south/left on Bear Trap Road, which is a gravel road. Access to the river along this road to its end in three miles is excellent. At the end of the road is the Bear Trap National Recreation Trailhead. From the parking area, hike upriver as far as you like. There is plenty of fishing in the first few miles so a long hike is not necessary. Beware of rattlesnakes during warm weather!

On the West side of the river, park at the Warm Springs boat launch, which is five miles beyond the bridge that crosses the river near the Canaday Boat Ramp. From the parking lot take the trail that heads upriver for about two miles or so. Large boulders mark good fishing, as do any large foam lines.

Montana's Madison River is designated a Blue Ribbon river. A Blue Ribbon fishery is a designation made by the U.S. government identifying a river of extremely high quality. Established criteria for Blue Ribbon status includes: water quality and quantity, accessibility to the public, a sustainable fishery, water that can sustain angling pressure, and selection based on a specific species.

The Madison River is one of Montana's premier large rivers. Even though the Madison is a river and not a stream, I included the lower section below Ennis Lake in Bear Trap Canyon because it looks and acts more like a medium-size stream. And due to there being very little boat traffic, the river can provide a quiet and peaceful experience. The river flows for 38 miles from Ennis Lake to the Missouri River. This area is one of my favorite places to fish because of the beauty, good fishing, and easy access from either side of the river. Unfortunately, a fire started by humans in the summer of 2012 greatly affected the landscape. Burned trees are now prominent and will be for many years to come. While affecting the aesthetics of the area, it hasn't impacted the fishing. The upper section of Bear Trap Canyon has Class III and Class IV rapids. Only very experienced rafters should undertake floating this section.

Ennis Lake is a shallow lake that warms up during the summer months. The water that comes out of the lake and travels down the lower Madison warms to a point where the water is not fishable. During this time, (July–August) the locals often refer to the great "raft hatch," a time when the locals enjoy the warmth and easygoing nature of the river. Not until mid-September do the pleasure rafters disappear and the anglers return. The Lower Madison is a tailwater fishery, and stays clear most of the time. Two major occurrences can muddy up the lower Madison. One is when there are strong winds on the lake, which can mix it up and turn it off-color. A second occurrence is lake turnover. During most of the year the lake has different temperature layers. In the spring and fall, the temperatures even out and the lake mixes up, causing a muddying effect. This generally occurs in April and mid-October to mid-November. It would be best to check with a local fly shop on water clarity during these times.

Lee Metcalf Wilderness Bear Trap Canyon. Molly Semenik

➤ **Fishing regulations:** Central District. Region 3. Open entire year. Combined trout includes brown and rainbow, with five daily and, in possession, only one over 18 inches. All grayling must be released immediately.

The lower Madison is a spring and fall fishery. The season begins in February and lasts through the middle of June. Fishing resumes, as the days grow shorter and the nights get colder, typically the middle of September.

➤ **What to catch:** Mostly brown trout, with some rainbow and whitefish. Size can range from 12 to 16 inches with a few browns close to 20 inches.

Foam lines offer good fishing. Molly Semenik

▶ **Hatches:** Refer to the Montana Hatch Chart

Special Mention: During the winter months midge fishing can be very good when the weather permits. A Griffith's Gnat #18, a Beadhead Black Zebra Midge #18 and maybe a size #16 Renegade is all that is needed. March through early April Blue-winged Olives will be hatching. The most famous hatch on the entire Madison is the caddis hatch. Caddis of all sizes and colors begin to hatch mid April. The evening caddis hatch is legendary. Salmonflies and Golden Stones start to hatch in Bear Trap Canyon and work their way up the Madison, usually traveling about two miles a day. The hatch begins in mid-June in Bear Trap and continues upriver into July. Golden Stone nymphs or rubber legs work year round. Mayflies follow along with terrestrials. Another worthy mention is not to overlook San Juan Worms and Crayfish. The crayfish patterns are smaller and lighter than most patterns found outside of Montana. Shop your local retailer for the crayfish patterns that work on the lower Madison.

▶ **Tackle and strategy:** Riggings: A 5-weight, 9-foot rod is a good all-around rod for the lower Madison. Leaders are typically 9-foot, 4X when fishing drys or 7.5-foot, 2X when fishing streamers.

Spring caddis hatch can be epic. Molly Semenik

Fishing Strategies: The lower Madison is full of large healthy weed beds. The fish hang out in and along the edges of these weed beds looking for food and cover. Crayfish patterns, tan Clouser Crayfish #8, can be fished along the weed beds and even along the top if they are not too heavy. Small beadhead nymphs or soft hackles can be used as a dropper fly. Streamers can be fished alongside the weed beds, patterns such as Olive Zonkers #6, rubber legs #6, or JJ Special #6. When boulders are present, fish around them and along any foam lines.

Above. William van der Vorst fishing the river's west side during a fall BWO hatch. Molly Semenik

Left. Gate with no fence. Molly Semenik

CLOSEST FLYSHOP/OUTFITTER
Four corners area (intersection of Highways 191 & 84), Bozeman

The River's Edge West Fly Shop
59 North Star Ln.
Bozeman, MT 59718
406-284-2401
www.theriversedge.com

Fins & Feathers of Bozeman
81801 Gallatin Rd.
Bozeman, MT 59718
877-790-5303
www.finsandfeathersonline.com

Greater Yellowstone Flyfishers
29 Pioneer Way
Bozeman, MT 59718
406-585-5321
www.gyflyfishers.com

Ennis

Madison River Fishing Company
109 Main St.
Ennis, MT 59729
800-227-7127
www.mrfc.com

The Tackle Shop
127 E. Main St.
Ennis, MT 59729
406-682-4263
www.thetackleshop.com

Thompson's Angling Adventures
208 Comley Way
Ennis, MT 59729
406-682-7509
www.thompsonsangling.com

CLOSEST CAMPGROUND
Many campgrounds can be found near the lower Madison and in Ennis. I have stayed at both of the sites below.

Red Mountain Campground BLM Public Land
(alongside the Lower Madison)
Restrooms and RV hookups
This campground is quite primitive, operated by the BLM.

Ennis RV Village (full service)
15 Geyser St.
Ennis, MT 59729
866-682-5272

BEST HOTEL
See Bozeman or Ruby (Ennis)

CLOSEST RESTAURANT & BEST RESTAURANT
See Bozeman or Ruby (Ennis)

CLOSEST & BEST GOOD DRINK:
See Bozeman or Ruby (Ennis)

NEAREST HOSPITAL/ URGENT TREATMENT CENTER:
See Bozeman or Ruby (Ennis)

WIRELESS AND CELL SERVICE
Bozeman

ACCESSIBILITY
2

WADING DIFFICULTY
2

WILDLIFE ALERT
Rattlesnakes and poison ivy

WHITEFISH REGION

NORTH FORK OF THE FLATHEAD
MIDDLE FORK OF THE FLATHEAD
SWIFT CREEK

LAKE CREEK
THOMPSON RIVER

With Glacier National Park as a backdrop, Whitefish offers spectacular scenery. The town is charming, with flower baskets hanging on every lamppost. There are shops and restaurants and, like all of Montana, plenty of locations for a cold drink. Having grown up in a Great Lakes state, an early evening swim is a real treat—no better place than the public beach on Whitefish Lake. Glacier National Park is 25 miles away and certainly worth including in your schedule while in the Whitefish area. Glacier National Park has a million acres of pristine wilderness, with some mountain peaks reaching 10,000 feet.

➤ **Location:** Whitefish can be reached by car, driving north on highway 93, or by air with the closest airport being Glacier Park International Airport (FCA) in Kalispell, 11 miles to the south. Whitefish has held steady with its population at 6,357 (2010). Keep in mind that Whitefish is a tourist town and summer numbers increase the population three fold. Rooms can be hard to find, especially on a weekend, so make room reservations early. If you have a golfer in the group, the Whitefish Lake Golf Club is the most requested 36-hole golf venue in Montana.

A noteworthy mention is the Bob Marshall Wilderness. Both the Middle and South Fork of the Flathead Rivers can be

Whitefish. Peter Lami

fished in the Bob Marshall Wilderness. The South Fork deep in the Bob Marshall is Montana's most inaccessible river. Native westslope cutthroat trout will easily take a dry fly in a setting that would provide a once-in-a-lifetime experience. My recommendation for lodging is the Spotted Bear Ranch, (800) 223-4333. www.spottedbear.com.

The first three streams for the Whitefish region, North Fork and Middle Fork of the Flathead River and Swift Creek, are all within easy reach from Whitefish.

FLY SHOPS/OUTFITTERS IN WHITEFISH

Lakestream Outfitters
334 Central Ave.
Whitefish, MT 59937
406-862-1298
www.Lakestream.com

Stumptown Anglers
5790 Hwy. 93 S.
Whitefish, MT 59937
Toll Free 877- 906-9949
406- 862-4554
www.stumptownangler.com

LODGES

For a full listing of lodging and dining please visit:
www.explorewhitefish.com
Note that during the weekends of peak season chain hotels book weeks in advance. Local non-chain lodge recommendations:

Good Medicine Lodge
537 Wisconsin Ave.
Whitefish, MT 59937
406-862-5488
www.goodmedicinelodge.com

Grouse Mountain Lodge
2 Fairway Dr.
Whitefish, MT 59937
800-321-8822
www.grousemountainlodge.com

CAMPGROUNDS

Koa Campgrounds of Whitefish
5121 US Hwy. 93 S.
Whitefish, MT
(406) 862-4242
www.koa.com

Whitefish RV Park
6400 US Hwy. 93 S.
Whitefish, MT
(406) 862-7275
www.whitefishrvpark.com

Mountain Meadow RV Park
9125 US Hwy. 2 E.
Hungry Horse, MT
(406) 387-9125
www.mmrvpark.com

Glacier Campground
12400 US 2.
West Glacier, MT 59936
(406) 387-5689
www.glaciercampground.com

Montana State Parks
1615 W. Lakeshore Dr.
Whitefish, MT
(406) 862-3991

HOTELS

Pine Lodge
920 Spokane Ave.
Whitefish, MT 59937
800-305-7463
406-862-7600
www.thepinelodge.com

Downtowner Inn
224 Spokane Ave.
Whitefish, MT 59937
406-862-2535
www.downtownermotel.cc

RESTAURANTS

Amazing Crepes & Catering
123 Central Ave.
Whitefish, MT 59937
406-862-6001
www.amazingcrepes.com

Buffalo Café (breakfast, lunch, and dinner)
2013 voted "Best of the Best"
514 3rd St. E.
Whitefish, MT 59937
406-862-2833
www.buffalocafewhitefish.com

Jersey Boys Pizza
550 1st St.
Whitefish, MT 59937
406-862-2212
www.jerseyboyspizzeria.net

BEST LOCAL BAR

The Palace Bar
(local favorite the "PBR Pounder")
125 Central Ave.
Whitefish, MT 59937
406-862-2428

Great Northern Bar & Grill
27 Central Ave.
Whitefish, MT 59937
406-862-2816
www.greatnorthernbar.com

Great Northern Brewing
2 Central Ave.
Whitefish, MT 59937
406-863-1000
www.blackstarbeer.com

HOSPITAL

North Valley Hospital
1600 Hospital Way
Whitefish, MT
406-863-3500
www.nvhosp.org

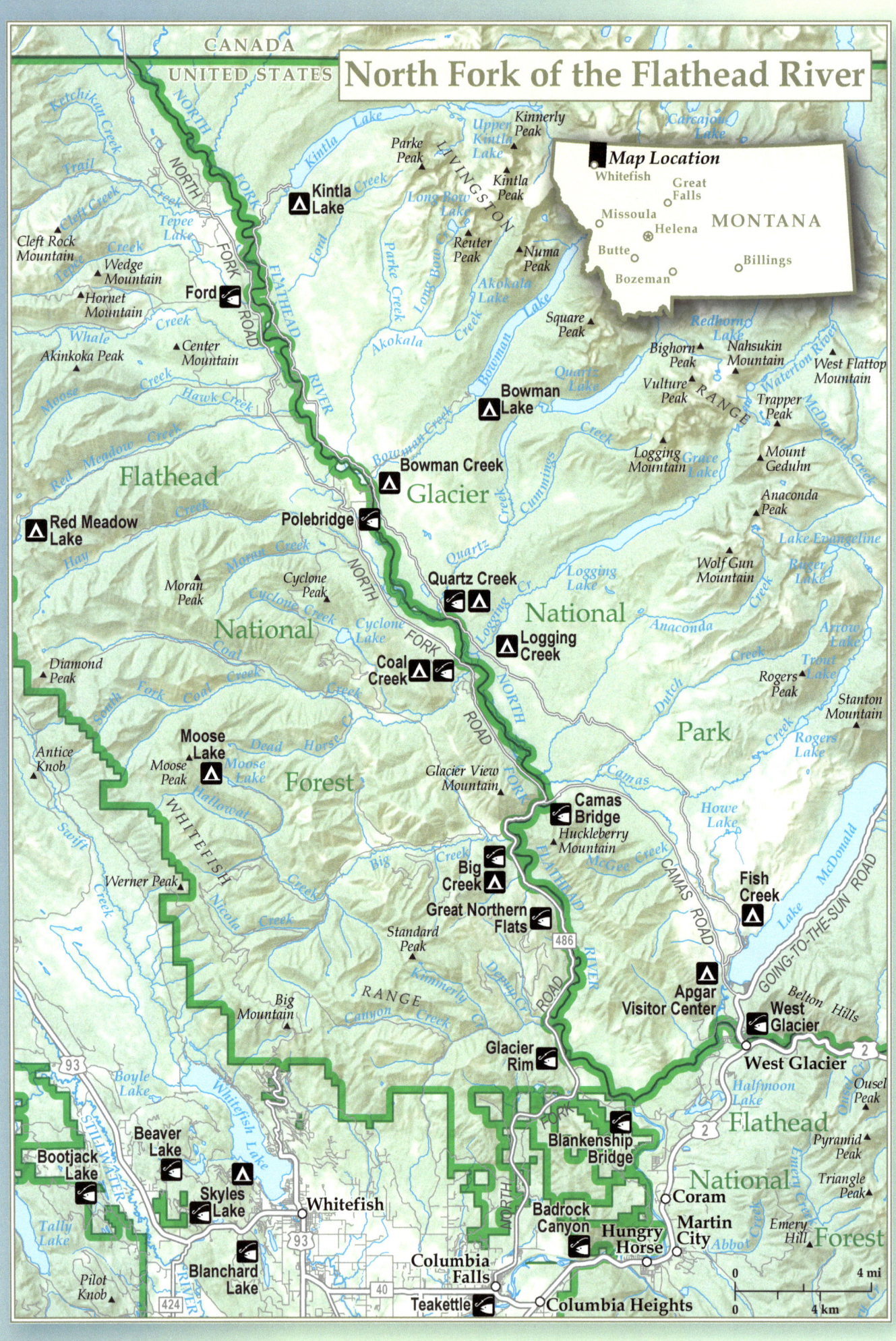

11 · North Fork of the Flathead River

▶ **Location:** From Columbia Falls turn north on Nucleus Avenue off of Highway 2. Turn east on Railroad Street, which then turns into North Fork Road after the railroad overpass. Continue northeast on North Fork Road. You will come to Blankenship Road to your east; stay left and continue on until you are within sight of the river. The pavement turns to dirt with dust and bumps for the remainder of your journey. Good tires are essential. The North Fork is approximately 22 miles north of Columbia Falls.

The North Fork of the Flathead River begins its journey in the McDonald Mountains in British Columbia, Canada. The North Fork flows south for approximately 45 miles until it reaches the Montana border. It then flows an additional 58 miles along the western edge of Glacier National Park until it meets the Middle Fork to form the Flathead River. There is more to this river than the size and number of trout. This river is stunning. Water clarity, color and natural beauty are great descriptors of not only the North Fork but all three forks of the Flathead River. The trout in the North Fork average 8-12 inches with some larger. The smaller size is a direct result of cold water and a limited food supply. Understanding where and how to fish this river will directly affect one's success. Exploring and taking in the beauty of this river is every bit as wonderful as the trout. Cutthroat and bull trout travel up from Flathead Lake to spawn in the North Fork River and its tributaries—cutthroat in the spring and bull trout in the fall. Some cutthroat have been tagged and found all the way north into Canada. Resident trout do exist in the North Fork throughout the season. The North Fork is designated a Wild and Scenic river from the border south to Big Creek Campground.

▶ **Fishing regulations:**
Western District, Region 1
Closed to angling June 1 through September 30 within a 150-yard radius of the Big Creek stream mouth.
Extended season for whitefish and catch-and-release for trout open December 1 to third Saturday in May.
Catch-and-release for cutthroat trout.
Combined Trout: 5 daily and in possession.
Note: Montana/Glacier National Park boundary is the middle of the river.

Above Camas Bridge. Peter Lami

Generally the best time to fish is from July through the end of August. However, pre-runoff and fishing into October can be good.

▶ **What to catch:**
Arctic grayling, bull trout, rainbow, westslope cutthroat, and cutbow.

▶ **Hatches:** Refer to the Montana Hatch Chart
Special Mention: Fly patterns are the same as the Middle Fork.
Pre-runoff: stonefly nymphs, egg patterns, worms.
Late March: Midges and Blue-winged Olives
March/April: March Browns, Grey and Brown Drakes, Black stonefly and attractor patterns.

Run-off: Sometimes during run-off there may be a drop in the river; if there is 2–4 feet of visibility you can fish.

June/July: Green Drakes, Golden Stones, Yellow Sallies

Mid July: PMD's (dries, emergers & cripples), caddis

End of July: spruce moth, nocturnal golden stoneflies

July/August: attractors (10–12), hoppers, 18–20 flying ants (tricos can imitate them), and beetles

September/October: streamers that imitate small fish. Blue-winged Olives, Mahogany Duns, October caddis, nocturnal golden stones. October fishing is good; a new group of fish come up the river preparing to spawn.

➤ **Tackle and strategy:** When fishing riffles, use a large foam pattern fly (10–12) with a 3X or possibly 4X, 9-foot leader. When fishing the slower water, a smaller fly with two feet of 4X tippet for the dropper fly. When fishing the deep pools for larger fish, a 9-foot 3X leader with sink tip fly line may be needed. A 4- or 5-weight rod will be enough for the North Fork. If windy, use a 5-weight. I spent some time visiting with Dave Brown of Stumptown Anglers. Dave said, "It is paramount to learn to use a fly-first presentation." What Dave means by this is to mend the fly line or cast the fly in such a way that the fly is presented to the trout first, rather than fly line. Dave suggested 5X tippet when using small flies or dead bug imitations. While I was visiting Dave's shop, a local man named Lou came in to drop off some of his homemade flies. I seized the moment and bought several of his flies tied for the local waters. It is always a treat to have flies in your box tied by your guides or locals from the region.

Following Dave's advice; be proactive with mending using either water mends or aerial mends. When prospecting, fish the deepest spots or pools, foam lines, along the edge and off shelves that precede a drop-off, boulders, and shoreline drop-offs.

Popular sections include Polebridge to Coal Creek with logjams and boulders. Park at Camas Bridge and hike downriver on the east side of the river. If you fish the river on a weekend, the upper half-mile will have lots of water craft; keep moving down river and fish the banks, foam lines and boulders. Remember the North Fork can be accessed from the park side, and you will need a proper park fishing license.

Just before Coal Creek Bridge there is a turnoff on the right side of the road. This is a nice place to fish with a few side channels. The Polebridge Mercantile general store is a fun place to visit, and Bowman Creek Campground is just a mile north of Polebridge.

Top. Below Camas Bridge. Peter Lami

Bottom. Molly fishing a drop off. Peter Lami

Above Camas Bridge. Peter Lami
Inset. Golden Stonefly. Peter Lami

CLOSEST FLY SHOP/OUTFITTER
In addition to the information listed under Whitefish:
The River Otter
5516 Old Hwy. 93
Florence, MT 59833
406-273-4858
www.riverotterflyfishing.com

CAMPING AND CABINS
Ford, Schnaus, and Ben Rover cabins are for rent from the U.S. Forest Service. www.Recreation.gov or call the Hungry Horse District office at (406) 387-3800. Campgrounds include: Bowman Creek, Quartz Creek, Logging Creek, Coal Creek, and Big Creek. Big Creek Campground has RV sites and a dump station.

LODGING, FOOD AND DRINK
See also Whitefish

Gentry River Ranch
(Located on the Flathead)
62 Gentry Way
Columbia Falls, MT 59912
406-892-1464
www.gentryriverranch.com

NEAREST HOSPITAL/URGENT CARE
Emergency Medical Help Center
Columbia Falls Clinic
1850 9th St. W. (US Hwy. 2)
Columbia Falls, MT 59912
406-892-3206
M–F 9:00–4:30

North Valley Hospital
1600 Hospital Way
Whitefish, MT 59937
406-863-3500
www.nvhosp.org

WIRELESS/CELL SERVICE: Columbia Falls

ACCESSIBILITY
3

WADING DIFFICULTY
5
The North Fork is very slippery; cleats and walking staffs are advised. Have an extra change of clothes for both the North Fork and the Middle Fork due to the water temperature.

WILDLIFE ALERTS
Bear, moose, and mountain lion. Have bear spray when hiking through brush.

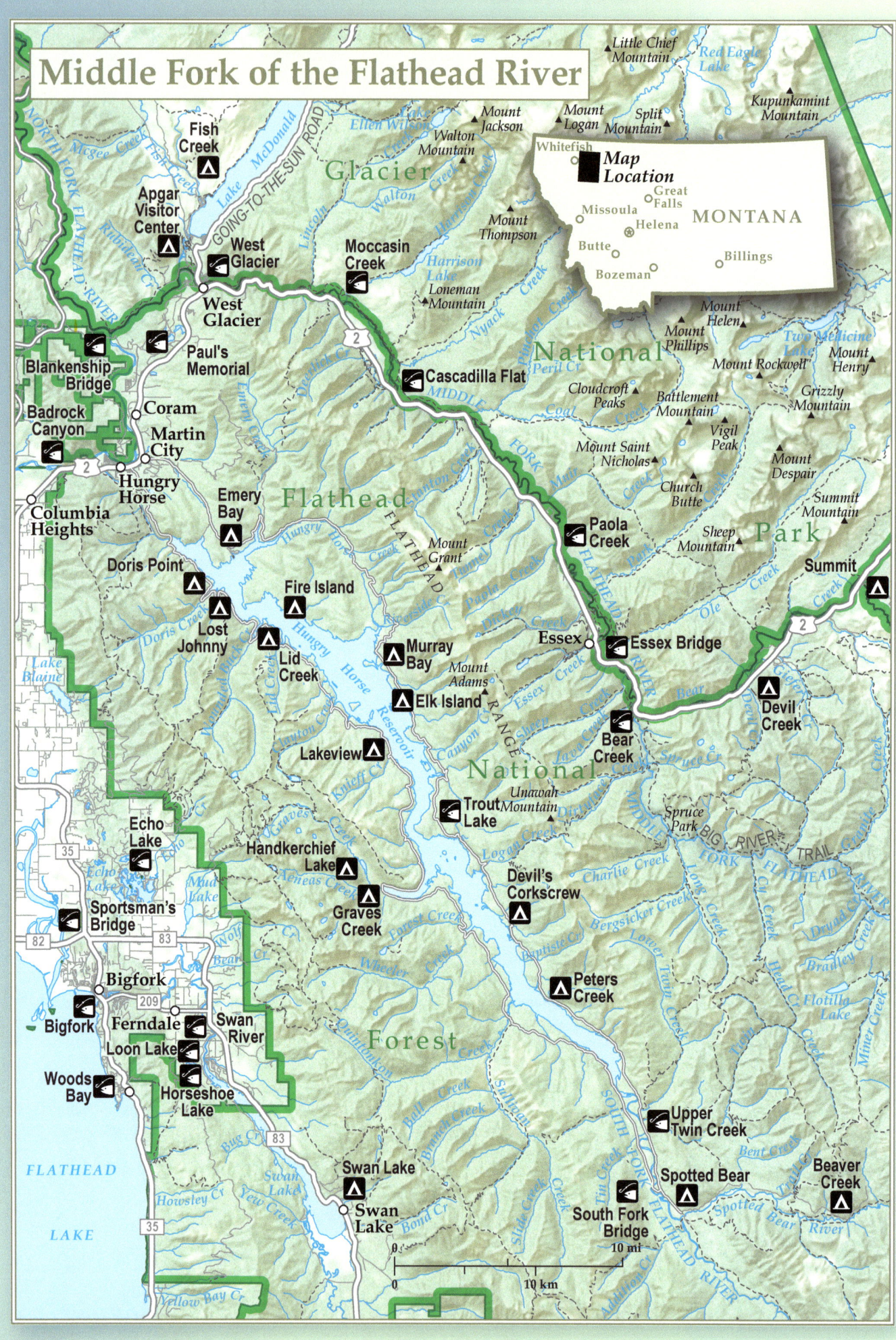

12 · Middle Fork of the Flathead River

➤ **Location:** From the town of West Glacier take Highway 2 east until Highway 2 leaves the river at Bear Creek Access. From this point a hiking trail will take you further upriver.

The headwaters of the Middle Fork begin with Bowl and Strawberry creeks in the Great Bear Wilderness. The river flows northwest from the headwaters for over 87.2 miles until it meets up with the Flathead River. From its headwaters to the Bear Creek Access (the point at which Highway 2 leaves the river), this area is designated Wild and Scenic. This upper 40 miles is reachable only by hiking or horse packing. Schafer Meadows, located in this upper reach, does have a landing strip for those that wish to fly in and hike or float downstream.

The remainder of the river from Bear Creek to the Blankenship Bridge is easily accessed via the fishing access points or campgrounds. This section is comprised of heavily forested canyons with moss-covered rock ledges and huge boulders. It is hard to imagine the magnificent clarity of the water. Trout at depths of fifteen feet can be seen. The color of the water is similar to the Caribbean Sea—emerald blues, deep greens, and turquoise. This section of the river is one for which you may want to consider hiring a guide and floating. By floating, you are able to access more prime water, which in turn will certainly boost the number of fish caught in a day; besides, the beauty of the river is reason enough for the expense. After Labor Day, another good access point is from Moccasin Access downstream. It is best after Labor Day because rafts are no longer launching from this site.

Guide Interview

Rob Weiker, assistant manager and guide for Lakestream Fly Shop in Whitefish, guided a friend and myself on the Middle Fork from Essex to Paola. Rob is a marvel at the oars; he got us to every spot a trout could be and often the same spot more than once. Rob is known as "row around Rob." Rob made the point of saying "mends are your friend, mends catch fish, not casts," and catch we did. What is important to note, is how the fish fight. It is hard to really estimate the size due to the power and excitement of the fight.

➤ **Fishing regulations:** Western District, Region 1
All streams within the wilderness:
- Combined Trout: three daily and, in possession, none over 12 inches in rivers and streams.

Non-wilderness:
- Combined Trout: five daily in possession
- Closed to angling June 1 through September 30 within a 150-yard radius of the Bear Creek stream mouth.

Breathtaking canyon walls. Peter Lami

Rob Weiker managing the boulders. Peter Lami

- Extended whitefish season and catch-and-release for trout open December 1 to the third Saturday in May with artificial lures.
- Catch-and-release for cutthroat trout.
- Note: Montana/Glacier National Park boundary is the ordinary high water mark on the park side of the river.

The Middle Fork of the Flathead can clear up before the Flathead River. Generally the season runs from July through August. However, pre-runoff fishing can be good, as well as September and October.

➤ **What to catch:** Rainbow, cutthroat and cutbows averaging 8 to 10 inches, many 12 to 14, and a trophy would be 17 inches. Rainbows are not as abundant in the lower 45 miles as they are higher up the river. Westslope cutthroat are found throughout the river but are most prominent in the upper 40 miles. Bull trout are found throughout, as are mountain whitefish. Bull trout start to migrate into the tributaries of the North Fork to spawn in the fall. Bull trout are off limits; they cannot be targeted and if accidently caught must be released immediately.

➤ **What to use:** Pre-runoff (March–April): stonefly nymphs, egg patterns, worms, midges and Blue-winged Olives.

March/April: March Browns, Grey and Brown Drakes, Black stonefly, and attractor patterns.

Runoff: Sometimes during runoff there may be a drop in the river, if there is 2-4' of visibility fishing can be productive.

June/July: Green Drakes, Golden Stones, Yellow Sallies
Mid-July: PMD's (dries, emergers & cripples), caddis
End of July: Spruce moth, nocturnal Golden Stoneflies
July/August: Attractors (10–12), hoppers, 18–20 Flying Ants (tricos can imitate them), and beetles

September/October: Streamers that imitate small fish. Blue-winged Olives, Mahogany Duns, October caddis, nocturnal Golden Stones. October fishing is good. A new group of fish come upriver preparing to spawn.

➤ **Patterns:**
#10 Para Green Drake
Beadhead Pheasant Tail
Prince Nymph
Beadhead Hare's Ear
Copper John

➤ **Tackle and strategy:** Mending continuously is key when fishing both the North Fork and Middle Fork of the Flathead River. There are many currents of varying speeds and careful adjustments must be made throughout the entire drift. A 9-foot, 4X leader with a 4X dropper is ideal. The deep pools hold the larger fish while the shoreline tends to hold smaller fish. Shelves dropping into pools are key spots as are foam lines, boulders, and the shoreline

Below. Large red dry attractors. Peter Lami
Left. Rob and author noting the clarity of the water. Peter Lami.

Above. Boulder field. Peter Lami
Inset. Molly taking in the scenery. Peter Lami

with 2–3 feet of depth. Across and downstream presentations will be most commonly used. Cutthroat trout have poor memories and are willing to go a second or third round so if you are walk wading, take the time to stop fishing and rest the hole for 10 minutes or so. You might have another opportunity at that nice fish you put down or lost. The season for these fish to grow is short and the food supply is not ample, so the trout will eat when the opportunity shows itself. If walk wading, I would start by walking at least 100 yards up or down from Essex access. If you are fishing a deep pool with split shot and/or a sink tip, you may catch some nice sized rainbows. If you see a bull trout you may not intentionally target it since it is protected by law.

CLOSEST FLY SHOP /OUTFITTER
Glacier Anglers Fly Shop

Glacier Outdoor Center
12400 Hwy. 2 E.
West Glacier, MT 59936
800-235-6781
www.glacierraftco.com

CLOSEST LODGE
Cabin rentals at Glacier Outdoor Center

Glacier Guides Lodge
120 Highline Blvd.
West Glacier, MT 59936
406-387-5555
www.glacierguides.com

Belton Chalet / Grill and Tap Room
12575 Hwy. 2 E.
West Glacier, MT 59936
888-235-8665
www.beltonchalet.com

CLOSEST CAMPGROUND
Many camping facilities are available from West Glacier to Columbia Falls

FOOD AND DRINK:
I did not find anything worth mentioning

NEAREST HOSPITAL/URGENT TREATMENT CENTER
Columbia Falls Clinic
1850 Ninth St. W. (US Hwy. 2)
Columbia Falls, MT 59912
406-892-3206
M–F 9:00–4:30

North Valley Hospital
1600 Hospital Way
Whitefish, MT 59937
406-863-3500
www.nvhosp.org

WIRELESS
No cell service while in the canyon

ACCESSIBILITY
2

Access at the public access points is easy. Outside of public access or venturing from the access points gets more difficult.

WADING DIFFICULTY
4

This really depends on how far you go from the access.

WILDLIFE ALERT
Black bear, Grizzly bear, and mountain lion

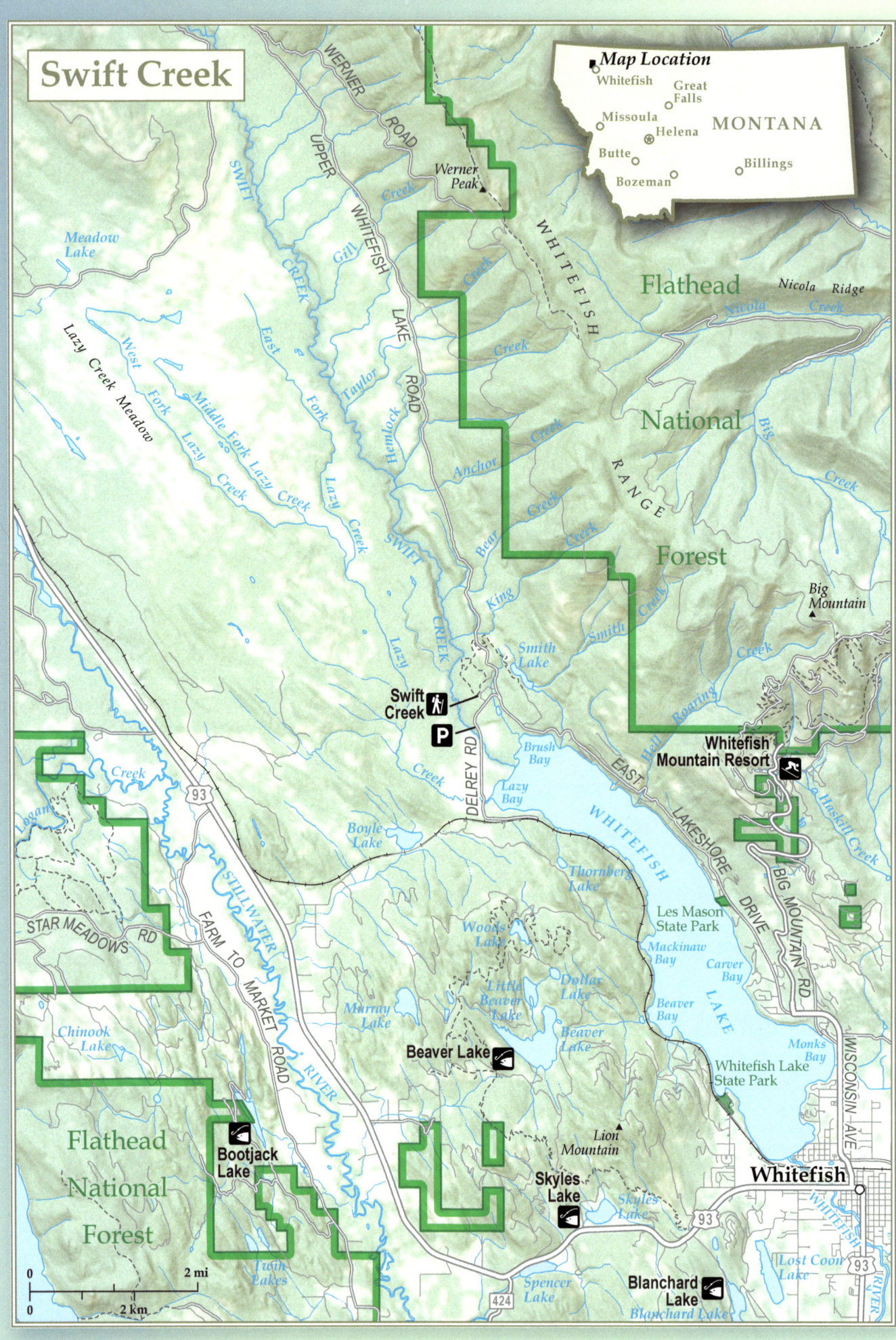

13 · Swift Creek

▶ **Location:** Swift Creek flows into Whitefish Lake at the north end of the lake. From the town of Whitefish, take Wisconsin Avenue north along the eastern side of the lake. Wisconsin will turn into East Lakeshore Drive. Continue to travel north; Swift Creek is 6.8 miles past The Lodge at Whitefish Lake. A quarter of a mile before you reach Swift Creek, you will see a Swift Creek Trailhead sign; turn right and park at the trailhead information panel. The hike to Swift Creek overview is about one mile. If you are up for a short hike, it takes under 30 minutes with nice scenery, ending with an overview of Swift Creek. There is no trail to Swift Creek from the overview. Return to your car to continue on to the creek. In ¼ mile, just before the Swift Creek Bridge, you will see a place to park on the right side of the road. Fish up river for as far as you wish to go. The property on either side of the creek from the lake to just ⅛ mile past the bridge is private. Approximately ⅛ mile upstream of the bridge, the land is public for at least 18 miles or until you reach Upper Whitefish Lake.

Swift Creek takes me back to my Brothers Grimm fairy tale days as a kid (with out the scariness). This stream has classic small-creek character. Fallen logs, bends, drops into pools, shadow-laden banks. This is not a stream to visit if you are looking for large trout. It is a stream for kids, beginners and anglers that, like me, find it fun to fish these small, beautiful creeks. The trout in these waters will average 6 to 8 inches with a few 10-inch trout. This creek is close enough to Whitefish that it can be a half-day adventure. The creek flows for 16.6 miles. The first four miles are the most productive and easiest to reach.

▶ **Fishing regulations:** Brook trout, 20 daily in possession. Cutthroat trout, three daily and in possession, none over 10 inches. Bull trout off limits.

Open third Saturday in May to November 30. This creek is one that would best be fished after run-off and at a time when the wading is safe and enjoyable. Check with a local fly shop for water conditions.

▶ **What to catch:** Brook trout are abundant in the first four miles. Westslope cutthroat and bull trout are found throughout the creek.

▶ **Hatches:** Refer to the Montana Hatch Chart.

Special Note: caddis larva blanket the rocks. Small drys size 16, caddis, Parachute Adams, or a Royal Wulff is all that is needed. Nymphs may include size 16 Beadhead Pheasant tail or Hare's ear. Caddis larva of any color.

Walking Swift Creek trail. Peter Lami

Above. View of Swift Creek from trail. Peter Lami
Inset. Trailhead sign. Peter Lami
Below. Fishing to deadwood. Peter Lami

➤ Tackle and strategy:

Small creeks require short leaders. The water is very clear; a 7.5-foot, 5X leader is perfect. This would be a creek where a 7.5- or 8-foot, 3-weight rod would be fun. Young children really benefit from using these smaller, lighter rods. A dropper can be attached to the dry fly, 18 inches of 5X. Allow the dropper fly to swing under tree fall, quickly pulling it out before catching any wood. Brook trout will charge out from under the wood fall to grab the wet fly. Any beadhead pattern would work as well as soft hackles. I would begin by using a single dry fly and add a dropper if necessary. Small terrestrials will work, particularly a size 16 Flying Ant. Casting across and down worked best on this small stream. If fishing small tight runs, use a high-stick presentation. Roll casts would work well, eliminating the possibility of back cast snags. This creek meanders through a forest, so be prepared for multiple creek crossings and slow travel upstream.

Handle with care. Peter Lami

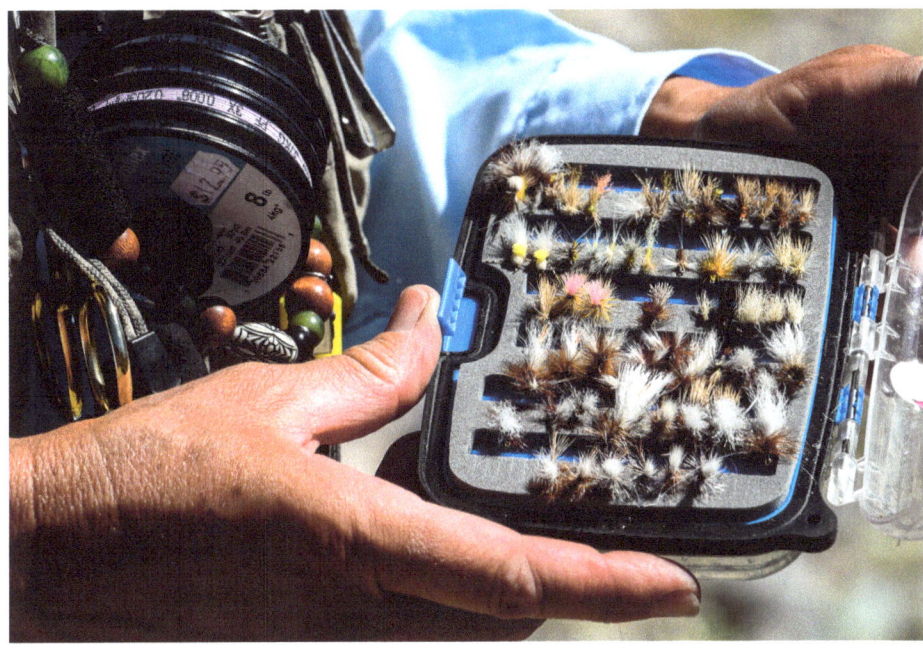

Drys are all you need. Peter Lami

CLOSEST FLY SHOP /OUTFITTER
The town of Whitefish (see introduction to Whitefish)

CLOSEST LODGE
The Lodge at Whitefish Lake
1380 Wisconsin Ave.
Whitefish, MT 59937
877-887-4026
www.lodgeatwhitefishlake.com

CLOSEST CAMPGROUND
Whitefish Lake State Park, one mile west of Whitefish.
www.montanastateparks.reserveamerica.com

WIRELESS AND CELL SERVICE
In Whitefish

ACCESSIBILITY
1

WADING DIFFICULTY
1

WILDLIFE ALERT
General safety regarding bear and moose

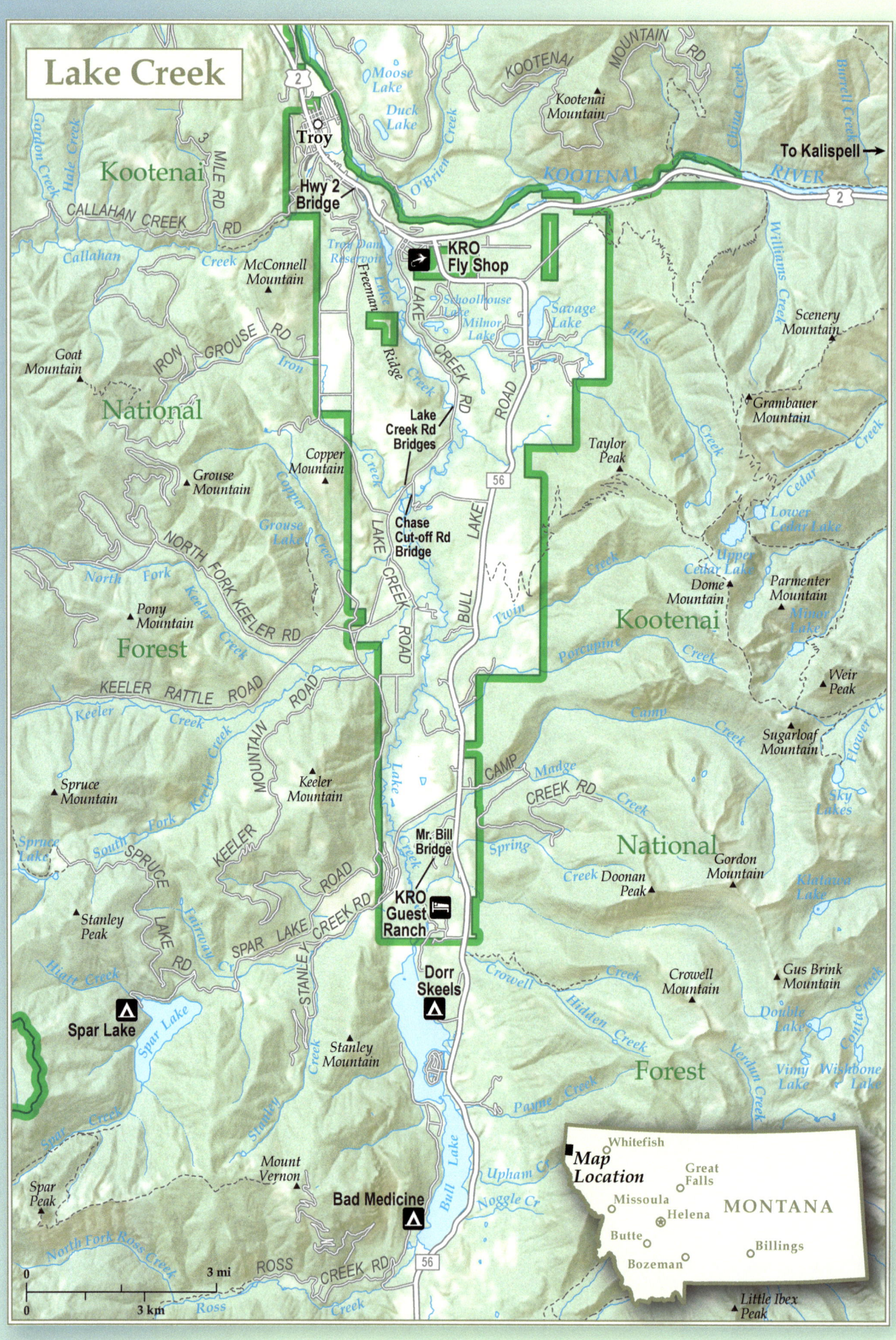

14 · Lake Creek

➤ **Location:** From Whitefish, the drive is just over two hours. Travel Highway 2 west for approximately 105 miles to Highway 56 and the KRO Fly Shop. To access Lake Creek, continue west on Highway 2 toward the town of Troy. Lake Creek flows into the Kootenai River on the eastern edge of Troy.

Lake Creek is a gem of a creek, worthy of a day or two of fishing. Lake Creek is a convenient stop if Thompson River is the next destination point. From Thompson Falls, Missoula is 102 miles and Whitefish is 124 miles. This is the only stream in the book in which I cover public access and private access.

A word on safety—Lake Creek is a walk-and-wade creek. Too many dangerous obstacles, logjams and sweepers can get a floater into trouble. Lake Creek is small and clear. The first cast needs to be a good one. Multiple casts will spook the fish and announce your presence. Some holes are easier for the angler, while others are more challenging. For the more skilled angler, the diversity is intriguing. For the beginner angler, snags and limited room for backcasts can be a challenge.

Several public access points do exist. The Highway 2 bridge that crosses Lake Creek just on the eastern border of Troy is one. Several more can be found on Lake Creek Road. Lake Creek Road can be reached from Highway 2, a half mile west of the KRO Fly Shop. Between Highway 2 and the Chase Cutoff Road Bridge are two additional bridges and a few obvious pull-offs. Chase Cut Off Road Bridge is another access. From here, I would drive east back to Highway 56. If you are adventuresome, more access can be found further upstream if you are willing to bushwhack and explore.

Private access to Lake Creek can be arranged with Robert Winstrom, owner of KRO-Kootenai River Outfitters and KRO Fly Shop. Robert is great to work with and not only offers guiding on Lake Creek and on the nearby Kootenai, but also provides other fishing experiences on the Bull River, the Yaak and less-typical, pike fishing on the many surrounding lakes. The KRO Ranch property has three cabins on Lake Creek. If you are renting a cabin from KRO, it is not required to have a guide to fish Lake Creek.

The two-mile or so section of Lake Creek that flows through KRO's property is gorgeous. The creek is gin clear. A spring creek feeds the creek along with mountain run-off that flows into Bull Lake from which Lake Creek begins. Lake Creek

Looking upstream of Cabin #1 toward Bull Lake. Molly Semenik

KRO cabin on Lake Creek. Molly Semenik

flows for 22.9 miles until it meets the Kootenai River just east of Troy. The Cabinet Mountains provide the backdrop. The best fishing is from Mr. Bill Bridge near Cabin 1, downstream for about two miles, passing cabins 2 and 3 along the way. A very large fallen tree crosses the creek just past Cabin 3. Robert said, "Past the tree is a bit tougher wading, but it is very wade accessible and there's still another mile plus of fantastic water. Some of the best water is below the tree." The river bottom is sand and cobble with a few deep holes. Brush and

Below Mr. Bill Bridge. Molly Semenik
Inset. Westslope cutthroat. Molly Semenik

grassy banks line the creek. Careful wading is mandatory, not only for safety, but to ensure your presence not be known to the fish. Pack water and food because you will venture far from your cabin. The forest, creek, and mountains make for stunning scenery in a very private atmosphere.

All three of the KRO cabins are modern, spacious and privately situated on the water with gorgeous views of the high peaks and creek. All the cabins have full-size covered decks with grills. Bring your own meal fixings; the cabins have fully equipped kitchens, a full bath, wood and /or propane stoves, propane heaters, power, and phones. Washers and dryers are available in each cabin. All of the guest cabins sleep 2 to 6 comfortably with a separate queen bedroom downstairs and either a queen an/ or two or three twin beds in the loft. Each has roughly 900 square feet on the main floor plus the loft. Along with access to Lake Creek, rowing or canoeing upstream to Bull Lake is a fun outing as well. A boat dock (supplied with a canoe or kayak) is near Cabin 1 and available for all renters. Guests are welcome to bring their own watercraft to head up stream to Bull Lake. After a full day, campfire rings and firewood are provided for a relaxing evening under the stars.

▶ **Fishing regulations:** KRO property is a catch-and-release, artificial single barbless hook fishery. Lake Creek fishes the end of May through early September. June through the middle of July offers the greatest variety of dry fly fishing. If you are interested in fishing the Kootenai, it is not generally ready to fish until July 1. Call KRO for water conditions.

▶ **What to catch:** west slope cutthroat trout, brook, brown, rainbow and bull trout, Columbia redband trout and whitefish. Hybrids such as brook and bull trout and redband and westslope cutthroat trout also exist. During my visit, I caught only westslope cutthroat all approximately 14 to 16 inches, with a few larger than 16 inches.

▶ **Hatches:** Refer to the Montana Hatch Chart.
Special Mention: June through mid-July, Green and Gray Drakes, Salmonflies and Golden Stones. July, caddis and PMD's, followed by terrestrials. Streamers can be effective under banks, and near logjams and deep pools. During August, small Flying Ants are very effective. If using a hard to see ant, try using it as a dropper off a small grasshopper or black cricket pattern.

Westslope cutthroat. Molly Semenik

▶ **Tackle and strategy:** Like most small streams, fishing the pools, grassy banks, and along deadfall will prove productive. All methods of casting can be utilized on the stream. This section of Lake Creek has a few special attributes. Upstream from Mr. Bill bridge is a flat, clear spring or creek-like slough with some very large trout; it is easy to see them and it is easy for them to see you. As Robert said to me, "Look like a heron, act like a heron." After you have worked the center flat, work over toward the fallen tree and your hooking odds will improve. I would not spend too much time here; much easier fishing is to be had. Below Mr. Bill Bridge is fabulous water for a little over two miles downstream on KRO property and another 20 miles to the Kootenai.

I used a 9-foot 5X leader and a 4-weight rod. If there is some wind, you may wish to go to a 5-weight. If nymphing, any size 16 beadhead nymph with an 18-inch long dropper will work. A soft hackle would be a good dropper pattern. Fish the deep pools, many fish seek these areas. Fallen trees are okay, but the grassy banks, in tight along foam lines, is most productive. Be mindful not to have too much slack, if you do and a fish bites, you may miss the set. Stay on top of the mending. Casting may include a few overhead casts (keeping them to a minimum), or the best bet, roll casts. A good roll cast that presents a fly within 6 inches of the grassy bank is not only fun to execute, but very efficient and effective!

CLOSEST FLY SHOP/OUTFITTER
KRO (Kootenai River Outfitters)
800-537-8288 or 406-295-9444
www.kroutfitters.com

Troy
Troy is 20 minutes away and offers all of the amenities that you might need. Groceries (open 6:00 A.M. until 11:00 P.M.), gas (24 hrs.), restaurants, and taverns. Libby, Montana is 30 minutes away.

NEAREST HOSPITAL
Saint John's Lutheran Hospital
350 Louisiana Ave.
Libby, MT 59923
406-293-0100

WIRELESS AND CELL SERVICE
Troy has a new cell tower that works for Verizon only. Libby has cell service. At the cabins, 1 and 2 bars on newer phones. Cabins 2 and 3 have WiFi for all to use.

STREAM DIFFICULTY
2

WADING DIFFICULTY
2

WILDLIFE ALERT
General Montana wildlife safety precautions

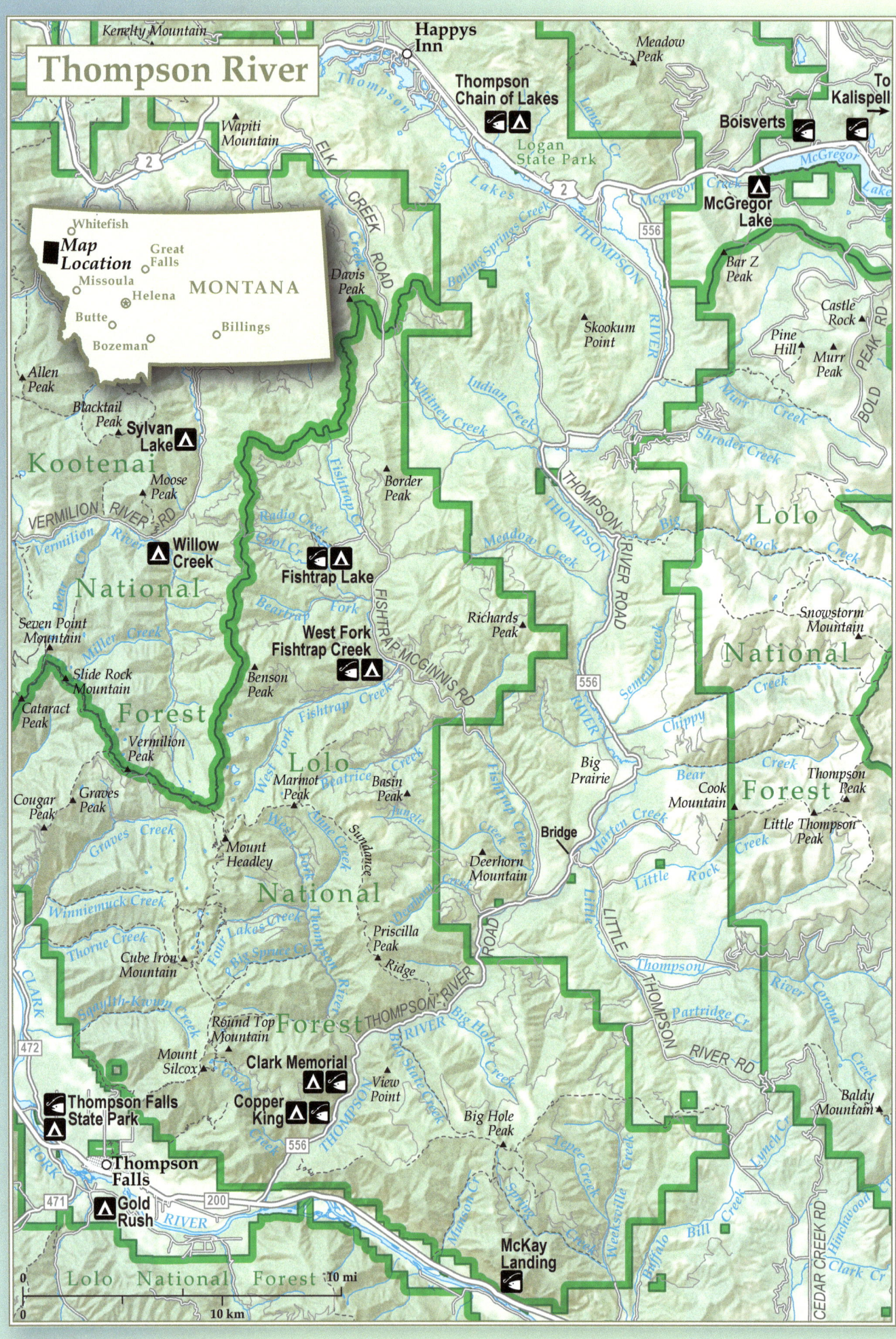

15 · Thompson River

▶ **Location:** The Thompson River is five miles east of Thompson Falls; turn north on Thompson River Road (MT-556). There is a dirt road on both sides of the river. Thompson River Road travels along the west side of the river and Plum Creek Road travels along the east side of the river. If you wish to make a loop, stay left on Thompson River Road, and travel upriver 18 miles to where the road crosses the river. Turn immediately right onto Plum Creek Road, and travel downriver back to where you started. The first few miles of Plum Creek Road is full of pot holes but the road smooths out as you get further along.

The Thompson River flows south from the Thompson Lake chain of lakes for 55.2 miles to where it meets the Clark Fork River. A dirt road travels along side the river from Highway 200 north for 43 miles to Highway 2. The road is open year-round, weather permitting, and is in relatively good shape. However, a four-wheel-drive vehicle is recommended when the road is muddy. The road is a result of logging activity, which has left its mark. Today the logging business is not as active as years past.

Access is excellent due to the paralleling road. The scenery, forest, and clear water make this a very nice river to fish. Fishing pressure can be high, especially on the weekends. Park or walk away from the obvious access sites, and fish water that requires a walk through the woods to get to areas less pressured. The river is isolated, with no services along the 43 miles of road. The Thompson River has all the features of a good trout stream. Boulder fields, long runs, pools, and grassy banks make for plentiful fish-holding water. Fishing regulations have changed considerably over the last few years. The Thompson River has a reputation for being a catch and eat fishery. A few years back Fish, Wildlife and Parks initiated a regulation that required all trout between 10 and

East side with many pools to fish. Molly Semenik

West side fish can hold in deep water. Molly Semenik

Rising trout love small red ants. West side. Molly Semenik

18 inches must be released. Today, the entire river is catch-and-release. It seems from local reports, that the fish size has increased and the fish numbers are stable and in good shape. The Thompson River is a great river to fish for both the beginner and experienced angler. With all the access, finding good water and solitude is not difficult.

▶ **Fishing regulations:** Western District, Region 1
Entire River:
- Catch-and-release for cutthroat trout and rainbow trout
- Brown trout: three daily and in possession, any size.
- Artificial lures only, except anglers 14 years of age or younger may use bait.

Upstream from mouth of the Little Thompson River (where Blanchard's Corner Road intersects with 556):
- The Thompson River clears up before most other large rivers in Montana. Fishing begins mid-May and fishes well into November. The Salmonflies are out early June, and the river is fishable at this time. If weather permits, a good time to pursue large trout would be late December through March below Little Thompson River.
- Closed to fishing December 1 to third Saturday in May

Mouth of the Little Thompson River to the confluence with the Clark Fork River:
- Extended season for whitefish and catch-and-release for trout open December 1 to the third Saturday in May with artificial lures only

▶ **What to catch:** Brook trout can be found in the upper 40 miles. Brown trout are found throughout the river. Bull trout inhabit the lower 15 miles along with whitefish. Rainbow trout and cutthroat are throughout the river. In the lower stretch, the trout size ranges from 10 to 14 inches with some 16 to 18 inches. In the upper reaches the fish size is smaller.

▶ **Hatches:** Refer to the Montana Hatch Chart

Skwala and Salmonflies. Good river for dry flies: Parachute Adams, caddis, and terrestrials. Streamers and stonefly nymphs including the always-effective Prince Nymph.

▶ **Tackle and strategy:** When fishing small dry flies, a 9-foot 5x leader is sufficient. Dropper systems work well using a mayfly nymph or caddis larva. If fishing larger patterns, such as stoneflies, shorten the leader to 7.5 feet 3x leaders. The deep pools can hold some large trout. All the basic Montana flies exist on the Thompson River. The structure of the river is classic and the general strategies and rigging work well. If you locate a riffle shelf that drops into a pool, use a size 6 rubber leg stonefly nymph with a good amount of weight to get down to the bottom of the pool. All casting techniques can be used on the Thompson River.

Brown trout found throughout river. Molly Semenik

CLOSEST FLY SHOP/ OUTFITTER
Thompson Falls has one sporting goods store called **S & S Sports**. A fishing license can be purchased there along with a limited supply of fishing tackle. The store is on the east end of town on 4 Airport Road, 406-827-2950.

CLOSEST CAMPGROUNDS
Lolo National Forest: Cooper King Campground (four miles from Hwy. 200, five sites, no available water) and Clark Memorial Camping, both on the west side of the river.

Thompson Falls State Park. Between mile markers 64 and 65 on Highway 200, turn north on Blue Slide Rd.

Best Hotel
Falls Motel-WiFi
112 S. Gallatin St.
Thompson Falls, MT 59873
800-521-2184 or 406-827-3559
www.thompsonfallslodging.com

River Front
4907 Hwy. 200
Thompson Falls, MT 59873
406-827-3460
www.riverfrontlodging.com

CLOSEST RESTAURANT
Minnie's Montana Café (great breakfast)
921 Main St.
Thompson Falls, MT 59873
406-827-3747

Thompson Grill
105 Broad St.
Thompson Falls, MT 59873
406-827-4900

Mother Lode Casino and Crystal Room Restaurant
809 Main St.
Thompson Falls, MT 59873
406-827-9523

Subway and Harvest Foods
grocery east end of town

CLOSEST BEST GOOD DRINK
Mother Lode Casino and Crystal Room Restaurant (see above)

NEAREST HOSPITAL/URGENT TREATMENT CENTER
Thompson Falls Family Medicine
120 Pond St.
Thompson Falls, MT 59873
406-827-4442

St. Patrick Hospital
500 W Broadway St.
Missoula, MT 59802
406-543-7271
www.saintpatrick.org

Missoula Urgent Care
500 W Broadway St.
Missoula, MT 59802
406-329-7500

WIRELESS AND CELL PHONE SERVICE
Cell service in Thompson Falls

ACCESSIBILITY
1

WADING DIFFICULTY
2

WILDLIFE ALERT
General Montana wildlife safety precautions

HELENA REGION

BOULDER RIVER NEAR CARDWELL
LITTLE PRICKLY PEAR CREEK
NORTH FORK OF THE BLACKFOOT

MONTURE CREEK
LITTLE BLACKFOOT

➤ **Location:** Helena is in western Montana centrally located along interstate 15.

I always enjoy spending time in Helena. There is quite a bit of history, fine dining, and many interesting sites to visit. Today, Helena has nearly 30,000 residents. Gold was discovered in Last Chance Gulch in 1864, and in today's dollars, an estimated 3.6 billion dollars' worth of gold was produced in a 20-year period. By 1888, an estimated 50 millionaires lived in Helena. After having read several books about the mining history of Butte, Anaconda, and Helena, all the money in the world would still not ease the harshness of living in these areas in the mid-nineteenth century. Air pollution, poor mine conditions and extreme cold lead to a very harsh environment.

A visit to the state capitol building is worth the effort. The capitol reflects the American Renaissance of the late mid-nineteenth century with a dome made of Montana copper. Inside you will find beautiful themed murals painted by famous Western artists including Charles M. Russell and Edgar S. Paxson. Other sites include the Cathedral of St. Helena, the Montana Historical Society Museum and the downtown mall. If you are visiting in late summer, try to catch the Last Chance Community Pow Wow.

Cutthroat. Peter Lami

CLOSEST FLY SHOP
Cross Currents Orvis Fly Shop
326 Jackson St.
Helena, MT 59601
406-449-2292
www.crosscurrents.net

Montana Fly Goods Company
3180 Dredge Dr., Suite A
Helena, MT 59602
406-442-2630
800-466-9589
mfg@montanaflygoods.com

CLOSEST OUTFITTER
Montana Fishing Outfitter
Helena, MT 59602
406-431-5089
www.montanafishingoutfitters.com

Montana Fly Goods Company—Big Sky Expeditions
(Same as above)

Osprey Expeditions
Helena, MT 59624
406-465-3339
www.osprey-expeditions.com

PRO Outfitters
Helena, MT 59604
pro@prooutfitters.com
800-858-3497
406-442-5489
www.prooutfitters.com

CLOSEST CAMPGROUND
RV Parks and Campgrounds can be located by going to http://www.rvparkreviews.com/regions/Montana/Helena.html

BEST HOTEL
A local favorite
Jorgenson's Inn & Suites
1714 11th Ave.
Helena, MT 59601
406-442-1770
www.jorgensonsinn.com

Most motel/hotel chains are located in Helena

RESTAURANTS
Steve's Café "Original"
(6:30 A.M.–2:30 P.M.)
1225 East Custer Ave.
Helena, MT 59601
406-444-5010

The New Steve's Café
630 N. Montana Ave.
Helena, MT 59601
406-449-6666
www.stevescafemt.com

Park Avenue Bakery
(breakfast & lunch)
44 South Park Ave.
Helena, MT 59601
406-449-8424
www.parkavenuebakery.com

Benny's Bistro
108 E. 6th Ave.
Helena, MT 59601
406-443-0105
www.bennysbistro.com

Brewhouse Pub & Grill
939 ½ Getchell St.
Helena, MT 59601
406-459-9390
www.atthebrewhouse.com

MacKenzie River Pizza Company
1110 Road Runner Dr.
Helena, MT 59602
406-443-0033
www.mackenzieriverpizza.com

Mediterranean Grill
42 South Park Ave.
Helena, MT 59601
406-495-1212
www.mediterraneangrillhelena.com

CLOSEST GOOD DRINK
York Bar
7500 York Rd.
Helena, MT 59602
406-475-3751

Brewhouse Pub & Grill
939½ Getchell St.
Helena, MT 59602
406-459-9390
www.atthebrewhouse.com

NEAREST HOSPITAL/URGENT TREATMENT CENTER
St. Peter's Hospital
2475 Broadway St.
Helena, MT 59601
406-442-2480

Helena Urgent Care
33 Neill Ave., Suite 208
Helena, MT 59601
406-443-5354
urgentcare@mt.net

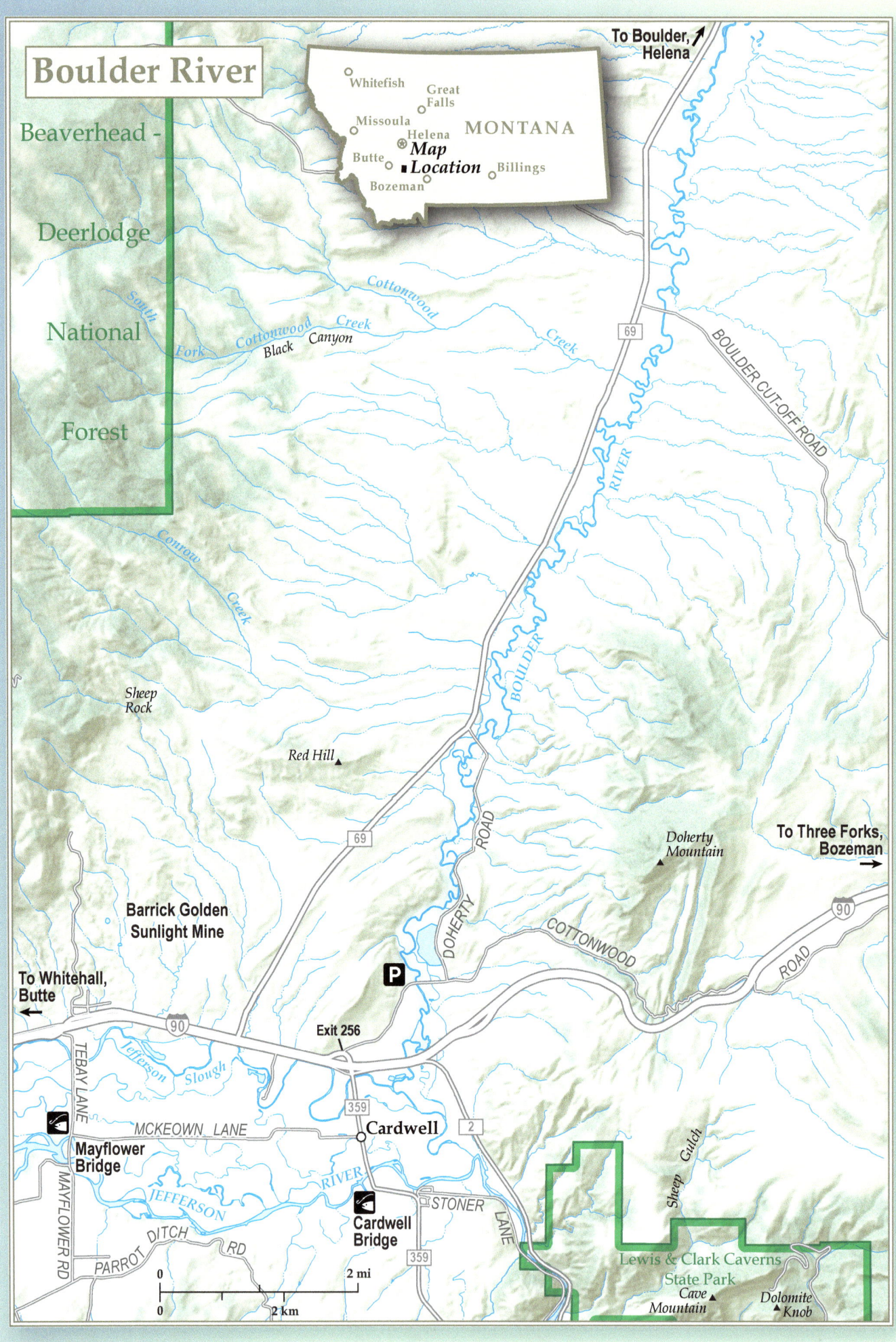

16 · Boulder River

▶ **Location:** The mouth of the Boulder River can be reached from Helena (59 miles) or from Bozeman (50 miles). If traveling I-90 from Bozeman, make a stop at Wheat Montana, near Three Forks for great pastries and sandwiches. From I-90 take exit 256 and turn north and go 0.2 miles to Cottonwood Road, turning right onto the dirt road. In one mile, a small bridge crosses the river; park before the bridge in the parking area on the left. The sign-in box is for hunters during the hunting season. This area is called the Barrick Golden Sunlight Mine. Access the river at the bridge, and fish upstream or downstream. When heading upstream, it will be necessary to cross the stream several times as you work your way upriver. The river has a classic character of bends, riffles, and pools along with undercut banks. Brown trout are abundant in this section. After three to four bends, an irrigation dam creates a wonderful, deep pool. Upstream of the dam, a slow, shallow stretch makes for spooky fish and challenging fishing. Once above the slow water, the river returns to its natural, classic character. Access to the river will be dependent on the time of year as the Boulder River is affected by spring run-off.

Another access option is to drive across the bridge and take your first left and follow the river upstream. You are still on mine property. Drive until the road becomes impassable due to poor conditions. Park at any of the pull-offs and follow the pathway to the river. A person could easily spend an entire day fishing in this few miles of river.

Montana has two Boulder Rivers, one that is well known and flows into the Yellowstone River at the town of Big Timber, and the "other" Boulder River, which flows into the Jefferson River near Cardwell. This section is about the Boulder River near Cardwell. The headwaters of the Boulder River divide Silver Bow and Jefferson Counties just east of the continental divide. The river flows north then turns east toward the town of Boulder. Once it leaves Boulder, it turns south toward the Jefferson River.

While my focus will be on the lower few miles of the river, the upper section, west of Bernice on Boulder River Road, is an area worth exploring as well. Travel along Boulder River Road using the pull-offs next to the road until the river gets too small to fish. Fish the meadow areas and any beaver ponds that you come across. The section from Bernice to Boulder is straight, fast, and is affected by old mine seepage and tailings. The section from Boulder to one mile south of Boulder Cut-off Road is mostly silted in with sand and often de-watered during the summer growing season. One mile below the Boulder Cut-off road is a natural spring

River access by crossing bridge and turning left on road, following river upstream. Molly Semenik

on private property. The spring pumps over 50 cubic feet per second of water into the Boulder River. This spring is why the fishing is so good from this point down. However, the only access is the public access that the Barrick Golden Sunlight Mine provides.

If you are one that likes soaking in hot springs, Boulder Hot Springs has a co-ed outdoor hot pool and indoor hot pool for men and for women an indoor hot pool and cold plunge. Day use is provided.

Above bridge and below spillway. Molly Semenik

Inset. Photo taken from the bridge at the sign for Barrick Golden Sunlight Mine. Molly Semenik

➤ **Fishing regulations:** Central District, Region 3

From the mouth to the bridge on Boulder Cut-off Road (mile marker 14.4), open third Saturday in May through September 30; above the Boulder Cut-off Road, third Saturday in May through November 30.

The best time to fish this section from the Barrick Mine is after runoff, generally the middle of July through closing, September 30.

➤ **What to catch:** From the headwaters for approximately 20 miles downstream, brook trout are the predominant fish from 6-12 inches. The middle section of the river has mostly rainbow. From the mouth of the Jefferson upstream for the next eleven or so miles, brown trout are abundant. The brown trout average 14 inches with a few reaching 18 inches. Whitefish can be found throughout.

➤ **Hatches:** Refer to the Montana Hatch Chart

Due to the brown trout population, streamers are always a good option.

➤ **Tackle and strategy:**

Rigging: A 5-weight fly rod would be best. With no detectable hatch, a good go-to rig is a 9-foot, 4 or 5X leader with an 18-inch 4X or 5X dropper. A good top fly choice could be a size #10 Beadhead Prince Nymph with a bottom fly size #16 Pheasant Tail. Place the strike indicator 5 feet up from the bottom fly. Streamers are always a good option due to the predominance of brown trout.

Fishing Strategies: This stream is wide enough for across-stream presentations. When nymphing in narrow sections, the high-sticking method would be a good choice. If fishing near the irrigation dam, cast upstream as far as possible, stripping in slack at the same pace as the waters flow; be ready for a grab—the trout in the deep plunge pool are a good size.

Deep pool below spillway. Molly Semenik

Brown trout outnumber rainbows. Molly Semenik

CLOSEST FLY SHOP /OUTFITTER
Bozeman or Helena

CLOSEST CAMPGROUND
Closest campgrounds would be in the town of Whitehall

BEST HOTEL, RESTAURANTS AND BARS
Bozeman or Helena

NEAREST HOSPITAL/URGENT TREATMENT CENTER
Boulder Medical Clinic
214 S. Main St.
Boulder, MT 59632
406-225-4201

WIRELESS AND CELLULAR: in Cardwell

ACCESSIBILITY
3

WADING DIFFICULTY
3

WILDLIFE SAFETY
General Montana safety precautions

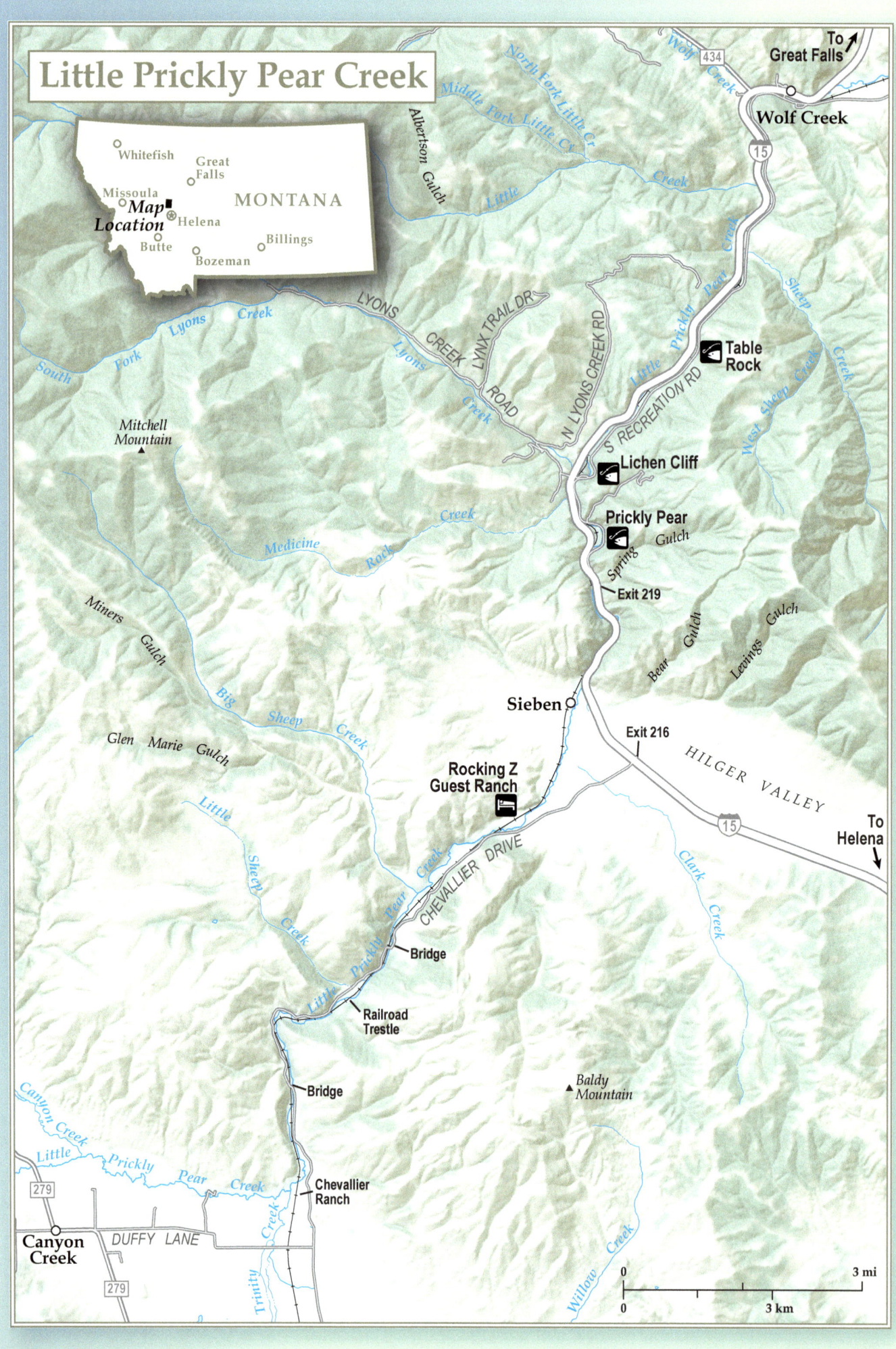

17 · Little Prickly Pear Creek

▶ **Location:** For this writing I will divide the creek into two sections: north of Sieben and west of Sieben. From north of Sieben, Little Prickly Pear can be fished to the town of Wolf Creek. If driving from Helena, travel 26 miles to the Spring Creek exit 219. There are three Fish, Wildlife and Parks Fishing Access Sites (FAS). To reach the first, travel three miles north on recreation road to the Prickly Pear FAS. Travel another mile to reach the second, Lichen Cliff FAS. At Lichen Cliff, turn left onto Lyons Creek Road and park before going under the overpass. Continue along the river to reach the third FAS, Table Rock. There are multiple areas to pull off in this stretch. All three of the fishing access sites provide good fishing. I recommend having lunch at The Frenchman and Me, which serves breakfast, lunch, and dinner with a full bar.

The second section of the Little Prickly Pear is accessed from the Sieben exit 216. Head west on Chevallier Drive. The first few miles of road travel through private ranch land. Beyond the ranchlands, access points include: the first bridge crossing the creek, state owned land (which is marked), the railroad trestle, and the block land management area just past the state owned land access. The next good access is in another half mile where the creek runs close to the road, park at any pull off along the road. The last access point is at a metal bridge with the river on the right side of the road.

Lastly, you will come to the historic Chevallier Ranch. Drive to the top of the hill, park, and step out and enjoy the view, a classic Big Sky Country view!

Heading back to Helena, continue on Chevallier Drive to Silver City. From Silver City access Highway 279 continue south to Interstate 15 and back to Helena. A local favorite is the Maryville House Bar and Restaurant (great chicken, steak, and bar). You can try your hand at horseshoes while your meal is being prepared. Hours: Wednesday through Sunday. Bar opens at 4:00 and restaurant at 5:00. You can reach Marysville one of two ways: From Chevallier Ranch turn west on Duffy Lane to Long Gulch Road. Turn south on Long Gulch Road to Marysville. Or, from Chevallier Ranch, continue south on Chevallier Drive to Silver City, then west on Marysville Road to Marysville.

It is important not to confuse Little Prickly Pear Creek with the Prickly Pear Creek; they are different creeks in different locations. Little Prickly Pear originates in the Helena National Forest west of Canyon Creek. Three creeks act as the headwaters: North Fork and South Fork of Little Prickly Pear and Lost Horse Creek. The creek flows for 36 miles to where it meets the Missouri River northeast of Wolf Creek. The Little Prickly Pear Creek has had a difficult past but has managed to continue to thrive despite its history. I stopped in for a visit with Zack Wirth, owner of the Rocking Z Guest Ranch on Chevallier Drive. Zack's family has been on the ranch property for five generations. He told me how through the years the Little Prickly Pear Creek has been diverted and its flow contained due to the building of both the railroad

Map of area north of Sieben. Molly Semenik

Above. Near Wolf Creek. Molly Semenik
Left. West of Sieben. Molly Semenik

and Interstate 15. However, even with all the challenges, the creek remains clear and beautiful. Access is good for both the section north of Sieben on Interstate 15 and west of Sieben toward the headwaters.

▶ **Fishing regulations:** Central District, Region 4

Downstream from the most southerly I-15 bridge over Little Prickly Pear Creek (1.9 miles north of Sieben Interchange, exit 216), open third Saturday in May through Labor Day. The remainder of the creek, general regulations.

▶ **What to catch:** Throughout the 36 miles of creek, brown trout are common and rainbow are abundant. Brook trout and mountain whitefish are rare. Like all mountain streams, the closer to the mouth, the larger the fish, and the closer to the headwaters the smaller the fish. During the spawn, rainbows and browns will travel up from the Missouri River, at which time this section is closed to fishing.

▶ **Hatches:** Refer to the Montana Hatch Chart

➤ **Tackle and strategy:** The Little Prickly Pear is a small stream; a 3-weight rod would work well. Keep the leader short 7.5 feet. Tippet size can be 4X to 5X. Fish the pocketwater upstream and downstream of rocks, fish riffles and undercut banks.

Left. The Frenchman and Me. Molly Semenik
Above. Journey's end at Chevallier Ranch. Molly Semenik

CLOSEST FLY SHOP /OUTFITTER
Montana River Outfitters
Wolf Creek Fly Shop (Summer Only)
800-800-8218 (Wolf Creek Shop)
406-761-1677 (Great Falls Shop)
www.mt-river-outfitters.com

CLOSEST CAMPGROUND
All three FAS's offer a few campsites Primitive camping on Wood Siding Gulch Road. Exit 226 Wolf Creek follow Take exit 226 in Wolf Creek and follow Recreation Road south for about 8 miles. Turn east on Wood Siding Gulch Road (gravel) and go another 4 miles. This is located in Sleeping Giant Wilderness Area.

Campgrounds can also be located in nearby Craig.

CLOSEST RESTAURANT & BEST RESTAURANT
The Frenchman and Me
260 Wolf Creek Main St.
Wolf Creek, MT 59648
(turn left and go under Interstate to stop sign, turn right, and the restaurant is on the left-hand side of the street).
406-235-9991

CLOSEST GOOD DRINK
The Frenchman and Me

NEAREST HOSPITAL/URGENT TREATMENT CENTER
28 miles to Helena
St. Peter's Hospital
2475 Broadway St.
Helena, MT 59601
406-442-2480

Helena Urgent Care
33 Neill Ave., Suite 208
Helena, MT 59601
406-443-5354
urgentcare@mt.net

WIRELESS: in Wolf Creek

ACCESSIBILITY
3

WADING DIFFICULTY
3

WILDLIFE ALERT
Rattlesnakes

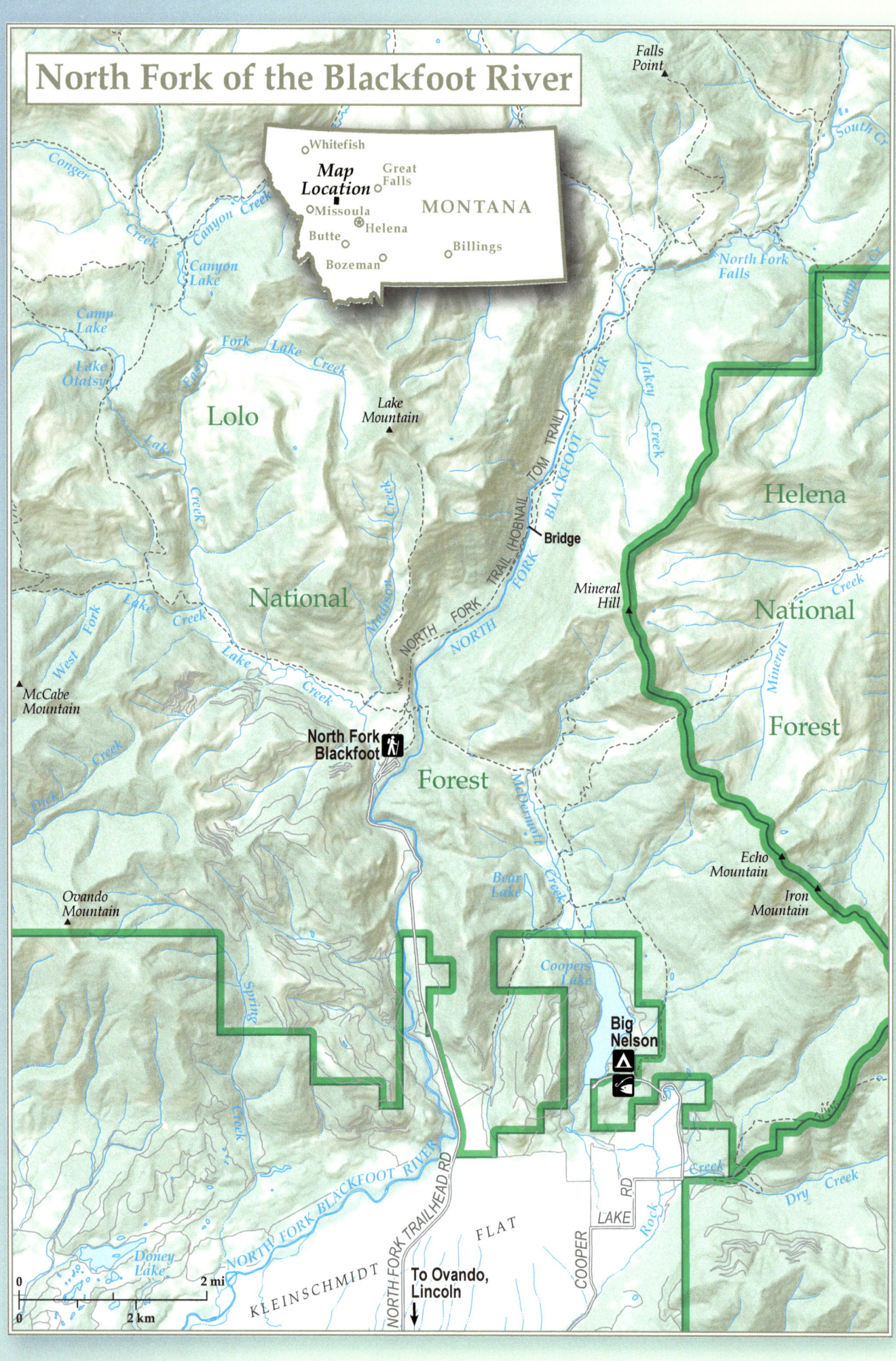

18 · North Fork of the Blackfoot River

➤ **Location:** If arriving from the west; from Clearwater Junction (Highway 200 and Highway 83) travel east on Highway 200 for 19.5 miles. Turn north on North Fork Blackfoot Road 550 (Kleinchimidt Flat Road). Drive two miles. Continue going north on North Fork Trail Head Road for 8.5 miles to the trailhead. Signs will guide you. I travelled from Helena taking Highway 279 over the Flesher Pass and on to Lincoln. This was a good road with great views of the valley. When traveling west on Highway 200, go 4.4 miles past the junction of Highway 141 and Highway 200.

The North Fork of the Blackfoot River begins near the continental divide in the Lolo National Forest and flows for 38.5 miles until it meets the Blackfoot River south of Ovando. The North Fork is the largest tributary to the Blackfoot River. It is an important spawning tributary and a critical one for the bull trout. During my last visit in mid-October, I was taken by a sight I have not witnessed before—the intense gold color of the Western Larch, a conifer that loses its needles in the fall. The trees (also called Tamarack) are found in the Northwest corner of Montana. Lodge pole pines are also present; many of them were burned in the Canyon Creek Fire of 1988. Today the forest is healthy and thriving with new growth and an amazing diversity of grasses, shrubs and trees. The trail from the trailhead is popular with hikers and horse packers. If you come across a horse train on the trail, you should step off the trail at least 10 feet so as not to spook the horses.

Once in the Lolo National Forest, the river can be accessed at any point. However, the river is quite a ways down into the canyon. Find a location that does not require too much of a steep decline. The river can also be accessed from the parking area at the trailhead or from a trail that follows the river upstream. I like to hike the trail for about a mile or so and take any path down to the river. If you are more adventurous you can go as far upstream as you wish.

The clarity of the North Fork of the Blackfoot reminded me of the Middle Fork of the Flathead River. Jewel-like colors are seen as you look to the river bottom; they shine through to even the deepest pools. The area of the river that I will focus on is the section in the Lolo National Forest.

➤ **Fishing regulations:** Western District, Region 4. Open third Saturday in May through November 30.

Combined trout: three daily and in possession. No rainbow over 12 inches, any size brown. Catch-and-release all cutthroat trout. No angling for bull trout.

After spring run-off beginning in late June. Water temperature is important—the water must be warm enough to fish. If fishing in June, get out later in the day after the water warms up. This is the same during the fall season.

Spring: Royal Wulff #10, Yellow Humpy #10

Summer (mid-July): Terrestrials (beetles, rusty ant), large attractors

Fall: Caddis, drakes, BWO's and streamers

One of many trails going down to river. Molly Semenik

Canyon view driving to parking area. Molly Semenik

Below. Molly with nice Westslope cutthroat. Molly Semenik

Bull trout sign. Molly Semenik

➤ **What to catch:** Brown trout and mountain whitefish are in the first six miles from the mouth. Bull trout are throughout the entire river but are protected and cannot be intentionally fished for. Rainbow trout are found in the first 24 miles. Westslope cutthroat are found throughout the entire river.

➤ **Hatches:**

Royal Wulff #10–14, Yellow Humpies #10–14, Stimulators #10–14
Parachute Adams #12–16
Elk hair Caddis #14
Madam X #10–12
Parachute Hoppers
Beetles and Rusty Ants
October Caddis or Orange Stimulator #12–14
Blue-winged Olives
Steamers

➤ **Tackle and strategy:**

Rigging: A 5-weight fly rod is best on the stream. 9-foot leaders with a tippet-size fitting for either drys, nymphs, or streamers.

Fishing Strategies: The Blackfoot and the North Fork of the Blackfoot are perfect rivers for large dry fly patterns. Not only are they easy to see, they work! Westslope cutthroat love to come up from the depths and eat a large dry. Look for hatches in the tailouts. Nymphing is effective as well. Fish the areas where there is slight chop, 2 feet of depth and foam lines. Also fish upriver and downriver of rocks. Seams are important as well. Note that bull trout are not to be targeted. If caught, release them immediately.

Large boulders and deep pools. Molly Semenik

Mark Ozog with a fish on! Molly Semenik

CLOSEST FLY SHOPS/OUTFITTERS
Blackfoot Angler and Supplies
401 Main St.
Ovando MT 59854
406-793-3474
www.blackfootangler.com

CLOSEST LODGE
Pro Outfitters' North Fork Crossing Lodge
328 North Fork Hill Rd.
Ovando, MT 59854
800-858-4397
406-439-9039
http://www.orvis.com/store/product
.aspx?pf_id=8C64&rdr=1

BEST HOTEL
Lincoln is the closest town and offers lodging and dining.

Sportsman Motel
416 Main St.
Lincoln, MT 59639
406-362-4481
http://www.ovandomontana.net/recreation/camping.php

Three Bears Motel
203 Main St.
Lincoln, MT 59639
406-362-4355
www.threebearsmotel.com

CLOSEST RESTAURANT AND BAR
Lambkins of Lincoln
(great breakfast)
200 Stemple Pass Rd.
Lincoln, MT 59639
(next to the Sportsman Motel)
406-367-4271

Trixi's Antler Saloon and Family Diner
(famous local spot, good food and drink)
Hwy. 200
Ovando, MT 59854
406-793-5611

Stray Bullet Café
Beer and wine available
Take-and-Bake casseroles to go
403 Main St.
Ovando, MT 59854
406-793-4030

* Be sure to visit "Sculpture in the Wild," just east of Lincoln on Highway 200.

NEAREST HOSPITAL/URGENT TREATMENT CENTER
Parker Medical Clinic
2363 West Hwy. 200
Lincoln, MT 59639
Emergencies dial 911
Medical Clinic M–F 8:00–5:00
406-362-4603
406-362-4617

For emergency room services, the closest hospital is in Helena.

St. Peter's Hospital
2475 Broadway St.
Helena, MT 59601
406-442-2480

WIRELESS: In Lincoln

ACCESSIBILITY
4

WADING DIFFICULTY
4

WILDLIFE ALERT
Grizzly and Black Bear, Moose
(bear spray a must)

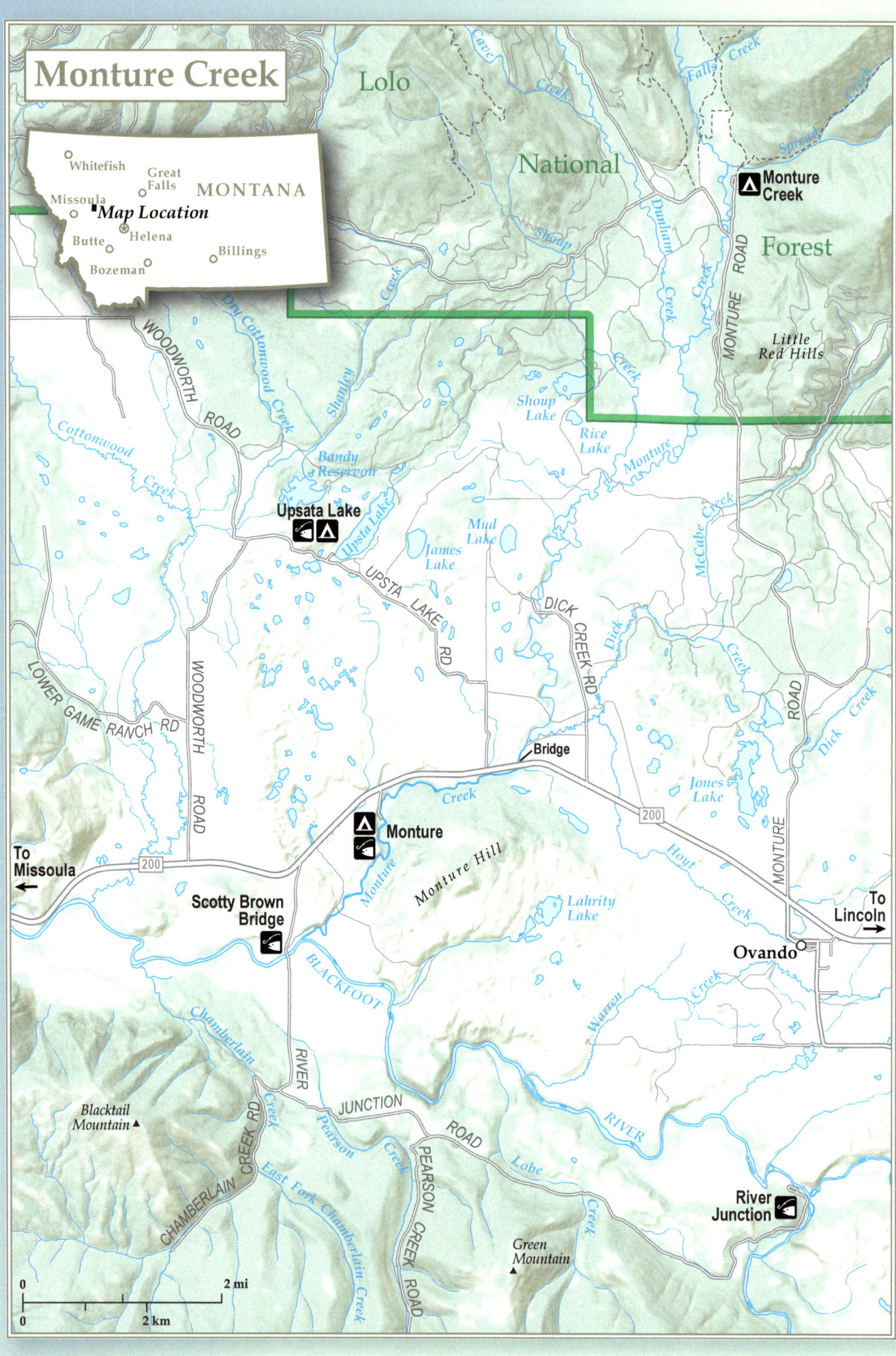

19 · Monture Creek

➤ **Location:** Monture Creek starts just south of the Bob Marshall Wilderness and flows for 29.4 miles through Lolo National Forest. It continues until it meets up with the Blackfoot River. Monture Creek can be reached via Highway 200.

I have had some very memorable days on the lower section of Monture Creek. This is an easy creek to wade and fun to fish. There are not many river miles to fish, but it is a nice creek to spend a day on. The wading is easy with sand, cobble, and some boulders. The upper section of Monture Creek is ridden with fallen trees and brush, and is very difficult to fish. In addition to the debris, the flows are low. There is a campground seven miles north on Monture Creek Road that is nice and close to the creek. You could give fishing a try but again, the going would consist of a great deal of climbing over fallen debris.

There are only three good access points to the lower river. One is at the Highway 200 Bridge that crosses the creek at mile marker 42. Park near the bridge and fish down river until you get close to the private land, which is about a mile downriver of the bridge. The second good access is at the Monture FAS. A great deal of restoration work has been done on the lower nine miles of the river with the intent of improving the spawning habitat for the bull trout. When you access the river from this site, fish downstream. The landowner upriver has placed a wire fence across the river to show where his property starts. Even though Montana law allows for anglers to access water below the high water mark, I would avoid this section of the river. Fish downstream to the campground. Once you reach the campground, access gets difficult to navigate through the thick brush. The third way to access the creek is from the Blackfoot River. Hike approximately a quarter mile upstream on the north side of the river from the Scotty Brown Bridge (FAS). Note the special parking restrictions at the access site.

➤ **Fishing regulations:** Spring and fall are the best times to fish Monture Creek. During the heat of the summer the water temperature gets too high. Late June would be a good time to fish. A call in to the Blackfoot Angler would be the best way to find out about water clarity and levels.

Western District, Region 2: Open third Saturday in May through November 30.

Combined trout: three daily and in possession. No rainbow over 12 inches, any size brown. Catch-and-release all cutthroat trout. No angling for bull trout.

➤ **What to catch:** Brook, brown, rainbow and westslope cutthroat trout.

➤ **Hatches:** Refer to the Montana Hatch Chart

Monture Creek has a good population of Green Drakes, Golden Stones, and Salmonflies. The Drakes start mid-June, as do the Salmonflies followed by the Golden Stones. The Golden Stonefly will start to hatch a few weeks into the Salmonfly hatch. Golden Stone patterns work well not only during the golden stonefly hatch, but for several weeks after as well.

Upper Monture. Molly Semenik

➤ **Tackle and strategy:**

Riggings: A 5-weight, 8.5- or 9-foot, 4X leader is sufficient. The best all-around rod size would be a 5-weight 9-foot rod. Monture Creek, like the Blackfoot, is a stream that fishes big bushy dry flies or mayflies such as a drake. A large

Above. Lower Monture. Molly Semenik
Below. Upper Monture. Molly Semenik

Trixi's family dining bar. Molly Semenik

dry fly by itself is the most enjoyable rig to use. If this is not effective, tie on 18 inches of 4X tippet with a nymph attached. An example might be a golden stone pattern for the top fly and an olive Hare's-ear to imitate a Green Drake Nymph for the dropper. If the Drakes are hatching, a Drake Cripple pattern will generally do the trick. A Drake Cripple could be tied off a large dry fly, a double dry fly rig (on a windless day). Monture Creek is big enough for across stream presentations and downstream presentations including the Leisenring Lift.

Above. Upper Monture. Molly Semenik
Inset. Downtown Ovando. Molly Semenik

CLOSEST FLY SHOPS/OUTFITTERS
Blackfoot Angler and Supplies
401 Main St.
Ovando MT 59854
406-793-3474
blackfootangler.com

Pro Outfitters' North Fork Crossing Lodge
328 North Fork Hill Rd.
Ovando, MT 59854
800-858-4397
406-439-9039
http://www.orvis.com/store/product
.aspx?pf_id=8C64&rdr=1

CLOSEST CAMPGROUND
Monture FAS has three primitive campsites.
http://www.ovandomontana.net/recreation/camping.php

LODGING, RESTAURANTS AND BARS
Located either in Lincoln or Missoula

NEAREST HOSPITAL/URGENT TREATMENT CENTER
Parker Medical Clinic
2363 West Hwy. 200
Lincoln, MT 59639
Emergencies dial 911
Medical Clinic M–F 8:00–5:00
406-362-4603
406-362-4617

For emergency room services, the closest hospital is in Helena.

St. Peter's Hospital
2475 Broadway St.
Helena, MT 59601
406-442-2480

WIRELESS
Spotty service in Ovando and along Hwy 200.

ACCESSIBILITY
3

WADING DIFFICULTY
2

WILDLIFE ALERT
Carry bear spray if fishing the upper reaches of the creek.

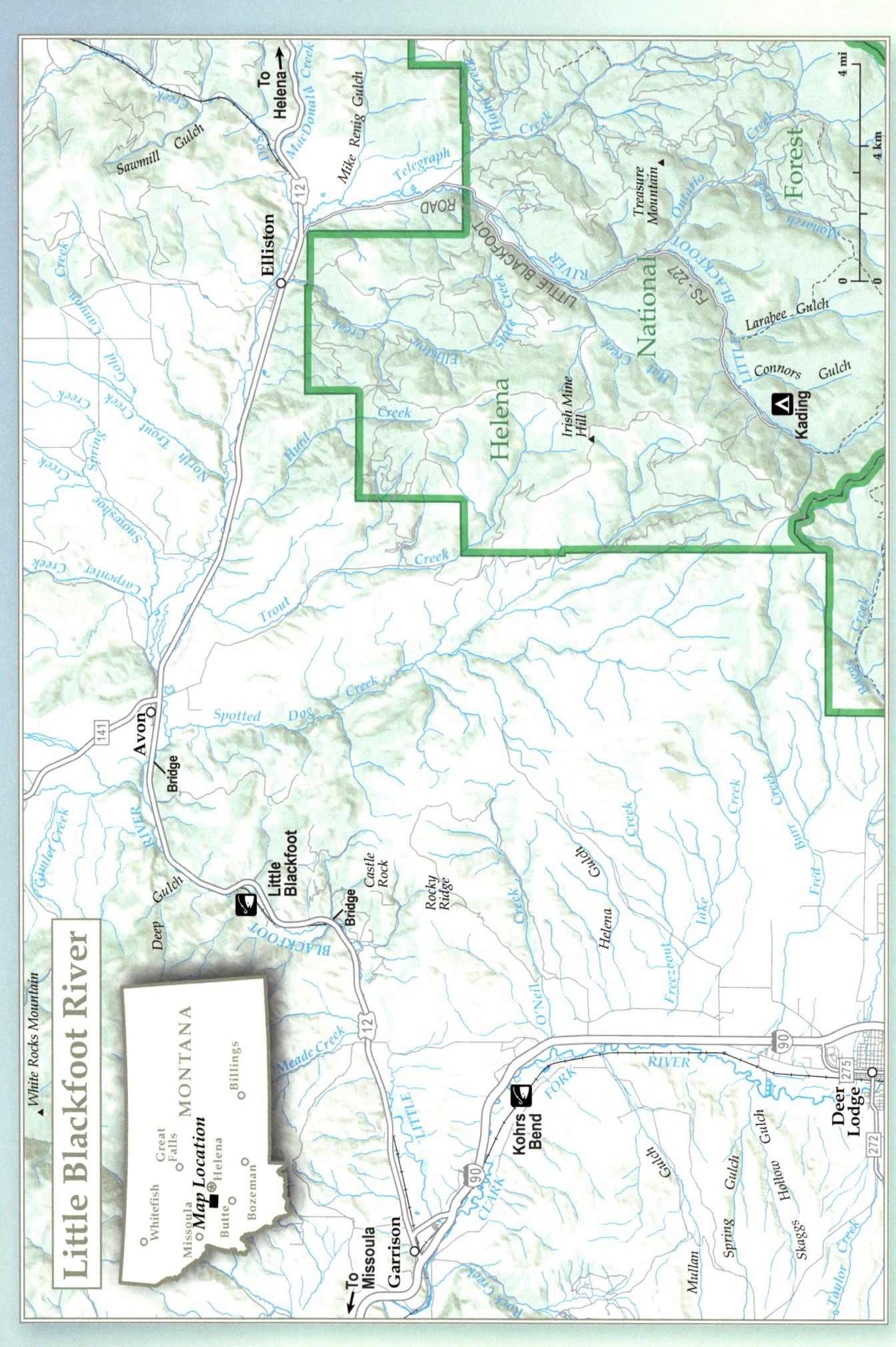

20 · Little Blackfoot River

➤ **Location:** From the north, take Highway 141 south to Highway 12. Travel on Highway 12 east from Garrison or west from Helena to the town of Elliston. Turn south on Little Blackfoot River Road (Forest Road 227), and follow the road for 13 miles. Return to Highway 12 and travel west to Garrison where the river meets up with the Clark Fork River. From Elliston it is 21 miles east to Helena.

The Little Blackfoot is a small stream up high in the National Forest. As it travels its length of 47 miles toward the Clark Fork River, it transforms into a meandering valley stream. The headwaters are in Helena National Forest, south of Elliston. It joins the Clark Fork River in the town of Garrison. The Little Blackfoot has many tributaries and springs that help keep the water temperature somewhat consistent. Therefore in the heat of the summer, the water temperatures are cooler than many of the rivers in the area. In addition, these springs allow the lower reaches to be fished in the winter months due to the waters being warmer.

From Elliston south, the river is a small mountain stream. This is where I spent most of my time during my October visit; the fall colors where at their peak and the daytime temperature where a cool 45 degrees. The prior evening, we had received a few inches of snow at the higher elevations, marking the approach of winter. As I gained elevation, patches of snow blanketed the ground. The river was small and beautiful. The river gently cascades over rocks, drops into pools, and flows through both forest and meadow. Access is easy because of a dirt road that follows the river until reaching the Kading Camp Campground. During October, like all small mountain streams in Montana, the best time to fish is during the warmest time of the day, 12:00–3:00. Seven miles

West of Avon. Molly Semenik

Little Blackfoot FAS eight miles east of Garrison. Molly Semenik

from Elliston the river access is good. Many pulloffs indicate parking and fishing access. The river alternates from forest to meadow and back to forest. Once past the road to Ontario Creek, the road climbs and the creek gets very small. Once again the area opens and turns to meadow before reaching the end at Kading Camp, a Helena National Forest Campground 14 miles from Elliston.

West of Elliston, the river flows through a beautiful valley until it reaches the Clark Fork River. Access on this section of river is more difficult. Anywhere Highway 12 crosses the river will allow access. There are several crossings; one in Avon and one just west of Avon with good parking. It is 12 miles from Avon to Garrison. East of Garrison between eight and ten miles, there are two good access points. One is near where the highway crosses the river; park down by the river under the overpass (approximately nine miles). The other is the Little Blackfoot FAS, eight miles east of Garrison. Check the current regulations, to confirm that this access site provides year-round fishing.

▶ **Fishing regulations:** Western District, Region 2.

Extended whitefish season and catch-and-release for trout open December 1 to the third Saturday in May. Third Saturday in May through November 30, catch-and-release for cutthroat trout.

The lower section of the Little Blackfoot offers good fishing pre-runoff. During March and April, Blue-winged Olives and Midges are the flies of choice and in April, caddis. Once spring run-off gets started fishing will not resume until early June. Through July mayfly and caddis fishing is good.

▶ **What to catch:** In the upper river south of Elliston brook trout and westslope cutthroat are common, with brook trout averaging 10 inches and cutthroat trout averaging 12 inches. West of Elliston or downriver, brown trout are common averaging 14 inches with some larger fish caught in the fall during their staging time prior to spawning. Whitefish are found throughout the entire river.

▶ **Hatches:** Refer to the Montana Hatch Chart

Pre-runoff in March and April: Skwala's, BWO's, Midges, and March Browns

After runoff, follow the Montana Hatch Chart.

One note: when fishing the valley section during the heat of the summer, grasshoppers can be great due to the valley vegetation lining the river.

▶ **Tackle and strategy:** During pre-runoff, 9-foot, 4 or 5X tippet. Size 18 Blue-winged Olives and Midges. After runoff, if the water is off-color a shorter and stouter leader

Above. Highway crossing east of Garrison. Molly Semenik
Left. South of Elliston near Kading Camp. Molly Semenik

can be used. As the water drops and clears, the leader will need to be lengthened. This of course depends on the section of the river you are fishing. At higher elevations where the stream is smaller, a shorter leader is best with short cast presentations. In the valley section, go to longer leaders with smaller tippets. Presentations will depend on the section of river fished.

CLOSEST FLY SHOPS/OUTFITTERS
See also Helena

The Stonefly Fly Shop
2205 Amherst Ave.
Butte, MT 59701
406-494-4218
www.thestonefly.com

CLOSEST CAMPGROUND
Kading Campground
www.travelmt.com/mt_sites_2187_Kading+Campground.html

Riverfront RV Park
115 Riverfront Ln.
Garrison, MT 59731
800-255-1318
www.riverfrontrvparkmt.com

BEST HOTEL
See also Helena

CLOSEST RESTAURANT & BEST RESTAURANT
Avon Family Café (excellent home cooking, breakfast, lunch, dinner)
13436 Hwy. 12 E.
Avon, MT 59713
406-492-6381

CLOSEST GOOD & BEST DRINK
See also Helena

NEAREST HOSPITAL/URGENT TREATMENT CENTER
St. Peter's Hospital
2475 Broadway St.
Helena, MT 59601
406-442-2480

Helena Urgent Care
33 Neill Ave., Suite 208
Helena, MT 59601
406-443-5354

Deer Lodge Medical Center
1100 Hollenback Ln.
Deer Lodge, MT 59722
406-846-2212
www.dlmed.org

WIRELESS AND CELLULAR:
Garrison, Helena, and Butte

ACCESSIBILITY
2

WADING DIFFICULTY
2

WILDLIFE ALERT
General Montana wildlife safety precautions

MISSOULA REGION

ROCK CREEK

EAST BITTERROOT

WEST BITTERROOT *BONUS CREEK, BLUE JOINT CREEK

SEYMOUR CREEK

WISE RIVER

The University of Montana, three major rivers—the Bitterroot, Blackfoot, and the Clark Fork of the Colombia—and an active downtown all make Missoula a great launching point for the angler and non-angler alike. The population of Missoula is close to 67,000. The city has everything you need including the very nice downtown Riverside Park. North Reserve Street has all the big-box stores and chain lodging; whereas downtown offers a college town atmosphere of restaurants, cafés, coffee houses and breweries. Fort Missoula, established in 1877, was one of the first military posts in Montana. It is now the Historical Museum of Fort Missoula. The Elk Country Visitor Center has trophy elk displays, a wildlife theater and walking trail. If visiting in the fall and you don't wish to go to a University of Montana Grizzlies' football game, the Paradise Falls sports bar has thirty televisions. If you enjoy local art, the Missoula Art Museum features contemporary works by Native American and regional artists.

Brennan's Wave, Caras Park (Downtown Missoula). Kim Dahl Photography

CLOSEST FLY SHOPS
Blackfoot River Outfitter
3055 North Reserve St., Suite A-1
Missoula, MT 59808
406-542-7411
www.blackfootriver.com

Grizzly Hackle
215 W Front St.
Missoula, MT 59802
406-721-8996
www.grizzlyhackle.com

The Kingfisher Fly Shop
926 E. Broadway
Missoula, MT 59802
406-721-6141
www.kingfisherflyshop.com

Missoulian Angler
802 South Higgins Ave.
406-728-7766
www.missoulianangler.com

OUTFITTERS
There are close to twenty outfitters in Missoula and the Bitterroot Valley.

CLOSEST CAMPGROUND
Jellystone Park RV Resort
9900 Jellystone Ave.
Missoula, MT 59808
406-543-9400
800-318-9644
www.campjellystonemt.com

Jim and Mary's RV Park
9800 Hwy. 93 N.
Missoula, MT 59808
406-549-4416
www.jimandmarys.com

Missoula KOA
3450 Tina Ave.
Missoula, MT 59808
406-549-0881 800-562-5366
www.missoulakoa.com

BEST HOTEL
Holiday Inn Missoula Downtown
200 South Pattee St.
Missoula, MT 59802
406-721-8550
800-399-0408
www.himissoula.com

You will find all the major chain hotels in Missoula

CLOSEST & BEST RESTAURANTS
Big Dipper Ice Cream
631 South Higgins Ave.
Missoula, MT 59801
406-543-5722
www.bigdippericecream.com

Bob Marshall's Biga Pizza
241 West Main St.
Missoula, MT 59802
406-728-2579
www.bigapizza.com

Caffe Dolce
500 Brooks St.
Missoula, MT 59801
406-830-3055
www.caffedolcemissoula.com

Depot Restaurant & Bar
201 Railroad St. W.
Missoula, MT 59802
406-728-7007
www.depotmissoula.com

Hob Nob (breakfast, lunch, & take-out)
531 S. Higgins Ave.
Missoula, MT 59801
406-541-4622
www.hobnobonhiggins.com

Pearl Café
231 E. Front St.
Missoula, MT 59802
406-541-0231
www.pearlcafe.us

Closest Good drink & Best Good drink
Iron Horse Brew
501 N. Higgins Ave.
Missoula, MT 59801
406-728-8866
www.ironhoursebrewpub.com

Plonk
322 N. Higgins Ave.
Missoula, MT 59802
406-926-1791
www.plonkwine.com

Nearest hospital/Urgent treatment center
St. Patrick Hospital
500 W. Broadway St.
Missoula, MT 59802
406-543-7271
www.saintpatrick.org

Missoula Urgent Care
500 W. Broadway St.
Missoula, MT 59802
406-329-7500

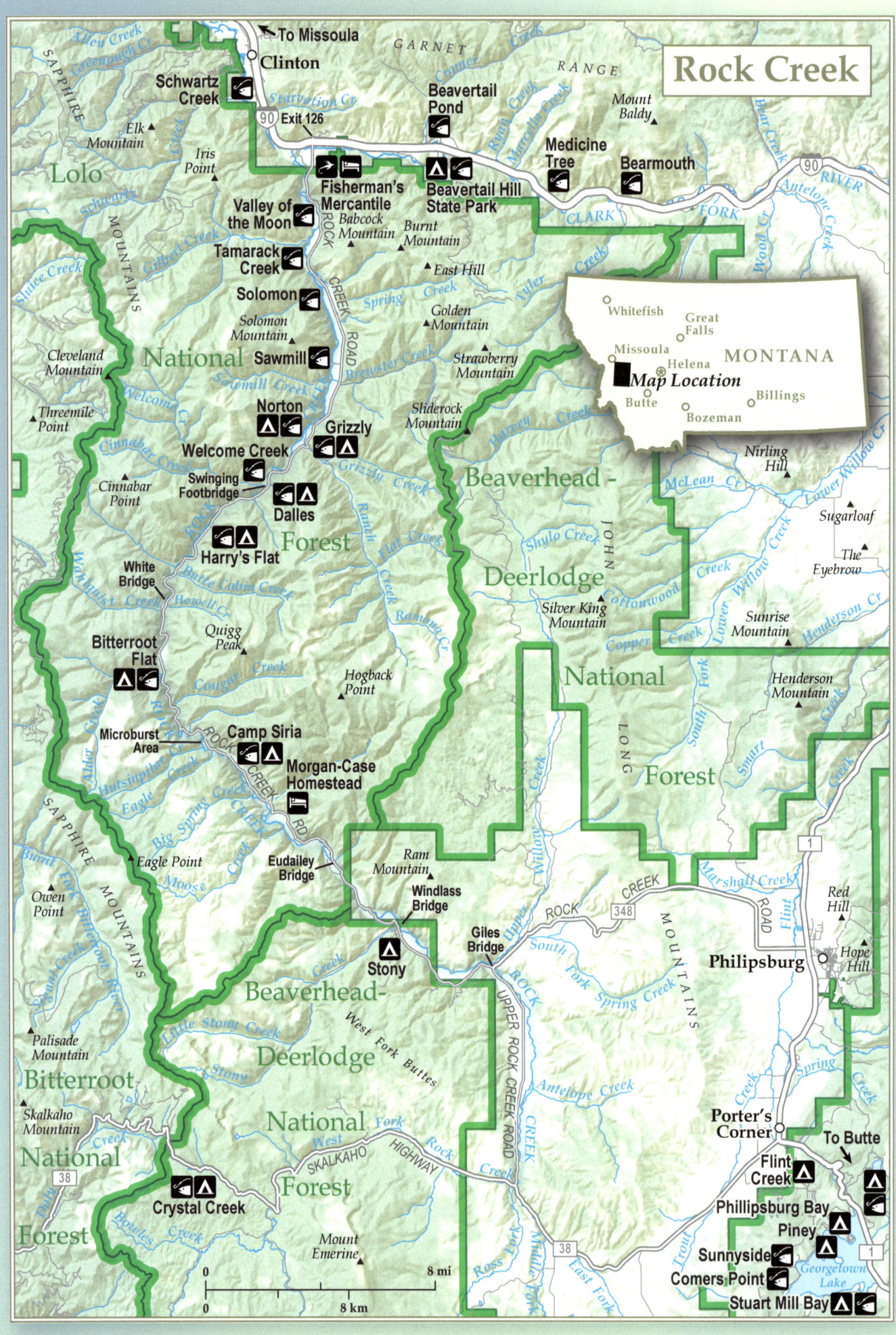

21 · Rock Creek

➤ **Location:** To access the lower river, drive on I-90 and take exit 126. The road for the first eleven miles is in good enough condition for RVs. If accessing the upper river, drive I-90 and take the Drummond exit 153 drive south on US-10A/MT-1 for approximately 23 miles (continue straight for two miles and you will arrive at Philipsburg). Turn west on Marshall Creek Road, and drive for 15 miles to Rock Creek Road; then turn.

Rock Creek is a fantastic, classic Montana river with a winding pothole-ridden dirt road running alongside the entire river. Rock Creek is easy to access and fun to fish, but the wading is tricky. This is a river where cleats and a wading staff are important not only for keeping you safe but also for helping you move from one place to another. The river is easy to read and of medium size. I can describe how to fish this river in two words, "keep moving." Look for the places where fish would be: seams, foam lines, and near rocks, deep runs or pools. If after four or five casts no fish show any interest, move on to the next fishy spot. There are many obvious pulloffs for access; I recommend finding a location where others don't travel. Take a walk through the woods or brush and look for spots that are not easily accessed.

Rock Creek gets its water from three streams: the West Fork, the Middle Fork, and the East Fork. The West Fork runs near Skalkaho Highway (MT 38), which you can drive to get to the Bitterroot Valley if you wanted to fish the West and East forks of the Bitterroot River after fishing Rock Creek. From where MT-38 meets Upper Rock Creek Road and MT-348 meets Rock Creek Road, access can be found on three bridge crossings. The fishing is not as good in this section as it is in the lower sections. From Gilles Bridge to Windlass/Concrete Bridge, there are a few places where the river flows near the road with pull-offs for parking. Be mindful of the high-water mark, as the river in this section flows through private property. Keep your eyes open for moose; this is a meadow area with nice brush and ponds for moose to visit. From Concrete Bridge to Morgan Case Homestead (30 miles from the mouth of the Clark Fork) are several great non-designated sites exist, some on the river requiring a hike from the car to the river site. Fishing access along this stretch is excellent, with pull-offs and bridge accesses. The Forest Service offers a historic cabin for rent near Morgan-Case Homestead, which can be found at the Lolo National Forest website. Between miles 26 and 29, access is more difficult due to the river leaving the road. This section has less pressure and is worthy if you are willing to hike. This area is known as

Long riffles are great for evening hatches. Molly Semenik

the microburst area. In 1989 a massive wind gust leveled hundreds of trees. Some anglers believe from this area up for the next ten miles, offers the best fishing on Rock Creek. From Gilles Bridge to Morgan Case is about 20 miles. From the confluence of the Clark Fork to Morgan Case is about 30 miles. One could spend a few days on the top end, then relocate nearer to the town of Clinton and work up river from the lower end of the creek. If pulling an RV, the middle section (microburst area) is too narrow and rough to navigate; at one point it is a single-lane road.

Jean Kahn fishing with nymphs. Molly Semenik

Canyon section. Molly Semenik

From Bitterroot Flat Campground to Dalles Campground the road is very narrow, and the fishing is good but it is hard to find a place to park. The Dalles area is known for deep pools and large boulders. This area is best fished using nymphs, streamers, and sink tips. A few more campgrounds—Grizzly, Norton, and Spring Creeks are located in this lower stretch. The Swinging Cable Bridge is near mile marker 11 and worth a visit. For the remainder of the river, browns lurk deep or hide undercover. Late season would be best for this section using streamers or nymphs or looking for risers. As you get closer to the interstate, the river is more heavily fished and as a result a bit harder to be successful. The Valley of the Moon is a braided area that later in the season can be a nice spot for BWO's. Between mile markers 3 and 5, you may have the opportunity to see bighorn sheep. Once you get to the town of Clinton, make sure to stop in at the Fisherman's Mercantile and Motel. Carolyn Persico has owned and operated this business since 1990 and has been fly fishing since 1965. A good map titled "Rock Creek Access Map #4" can be purchased at the Fisherman's Mercantile. For a list of locations that sell the map go to www.riverratmaps.com

➤ **Fishing regulations:** Western District, Region 2
• Extended season for whitefish and catch-and-release for trout open December 1 to third Saturday in May with artificial lures.
• Combined Trout: three brown trout daily and in possession; catch-and-release for rainbow and cutthroat trout.
• Closed to fishing from boats/vessels July 1–November 30.

The start of spring runoff can vary up to three weeks. Generally speaking, runoff occurs late May through mid-June. Before spring runoff, mid-March through April, March browns and Skwala stoneflies will be present. The mid-June Salmonfly hatch is epic as are the people it attracts, and it can last up to two weeks. The Golden Stoneflies start a week or so after the Salmonflies. The Golden Stonefly hatch, like on many Montana rivers, is more of a productive fishing hatch than the Salmonflies. Golden stonefly patterns can be fished even after the live Goldens have left the area. As July approaches, the angler numbers will start to subside. Along with your typical Montana mayflies, Pale Morning Duns are plentiful and last for a good part of the summer. During the heat of summer, fishing is best early with nymphs. Switch to drys when a hatch is present. Terrestrials such as hoppers and ants work well; the foam patterns will be the easiest to see. As the afternoon heats up, take a nap, eat an early dinner, and fish again from 4:00 pm to dark. Fall is the time to fish streamers, especially in the lower stretches of the creek.

➤ **What to catch:** Cutthroat, rainbow and brown trout; 8–18 inches. Bull trout do inhabit the waters but must be released immediately if caught and not intentionally targeted. Upriver of Gilles Bridge, the trout are smaller in size and consist of cutthroat, rainbow, and cutbow trout.

➤ **Hatches:** Refer to the Montana Hatch Chart

➤ **Tackle and strategy:** Pre-runoff is a great time to nymph. When nymphing, it is important to have enough weight, tungsten Beadhead patterns are good patterns for this water. A two-fly rig is best, with any attractor top fly such as a Hare's-ear or Prince nymph for the top fly and a stonefly dropper or rubber leg for the second fly. Add weight if the rig is not bumping the bottom from time to time. Cast upstream enough so that when it reaches the target area, it is deep in the zone. It is helpful to not cast too far—the speed and volume of the water will pull the flies up too high in the water column. The Leisenring Lift is a good strategy while nymphing. When a hatch is present, switch to a single dry. Watch your drift. It is better to cast a shorter distance and have a good drift than to try to cast far with a poor drift. Mending will be critical. This is a river that requires a great deal of mending, making fly rods with 9 feet of length preferable. Across and down presentations work well on Rock Creek.

CLOSEST FLY SHOP
Rock Creek
Fisherman's Mercantile & Motel (lower Rock Creek)
73 Rock Creek Rd.
Clinton, MT 59825
406-825-6440
www.rcmerc.com

Trout Bums Fly Shop (flies & tackle), coffee and cabins
824 Rock Creek Rd.
Clinton, MT 59825
406-825-6146
www.rockcreektroutbums.com

Philipsburg
Flint Creek Outdoors (upper Rock Creek)
116 Wt. Broadway
Philipsburg, MT 59858
406-859-9500
www.flintcreekoutdoors.com

HOTELS AND RESTAURANT
Rock Creek
Ekstrom's (restaurant, cabins & camping)
81 Rock Creek Rd.
Clinton, MT 59825
406-825-3183
www.ekstromstagestation.com

Philipsburg

Philipsburg Brewing Company
101 W. Broadway
Philipsburg, MT 59858
406-859-2739

Silver Mill Restaurant
128 E. Broadway
Philipsburg, MT 59858
406-859-7000
www.silvermillrestaurant.com

Sunshine Station
3830 Hwy. 1
Philipsburg, MT, 59858
406-859-3450

LODGING
Blue Damsel Lodge
1081 Rock Creek Rd.
Clinton, MT 59825
406-825-3077
888-875-9909
www.bluedamsel.com

Boulder Creek Lodge, cabins, RV tents, and restaurant
4 Boulder Creek Rd. (mm 49 on Hwy. 1 between Drummond and Philipsburg)
Hall, MT 59837
406-859-3190
www.newbouldercreeklodge.com

The Inn at Philipsburg RV Park
915 W Broadway
406-859-3959
www.theinn-philipsburg.com

Broadway Hotel
103 W. Broadway
Philipsburg, MT 59858
800-877-4436
www.broadwaymontana.com

B & B
Big Horn Bed and Breakfast
Host Ginny and Jerry Gallagher.
t406-859-3109.
Quigley Cottage
418 W Broadway
Philipsburg, MT 59858
406-859-3812
www.philipsburgbb.com

CAMPING
There are 15 undeveloped/primitive campsites along Rock Creek. Each site has a number 1–15. The following are developed campgrounds that can be found at www.fs.usda.gov within the Lolo National Forest. Norton Campground, Dalles Campground, Harry's Flat, Bitterroot Flat, and Siria Campground.

NEAREST HOSPITAL/URGENT TREATMENT CENTER
St. Patrick Hospital
500 W. Broadway St.
Missoula, MT 59858
406-543-7271
www.montana.providence.org

Granite County Medical Center
310 Sansome St.
Philipsburg, MT 59858
406-859-3271
www.gcmedcenter.org

WIRELESS/CELLULAR
Philipsburg and Rock Creek

ACCESSIBILITY
2

WADING DIFFICULTY
3

WILDLIFE ALERT
Watch for moose and keep your camp bear safe.

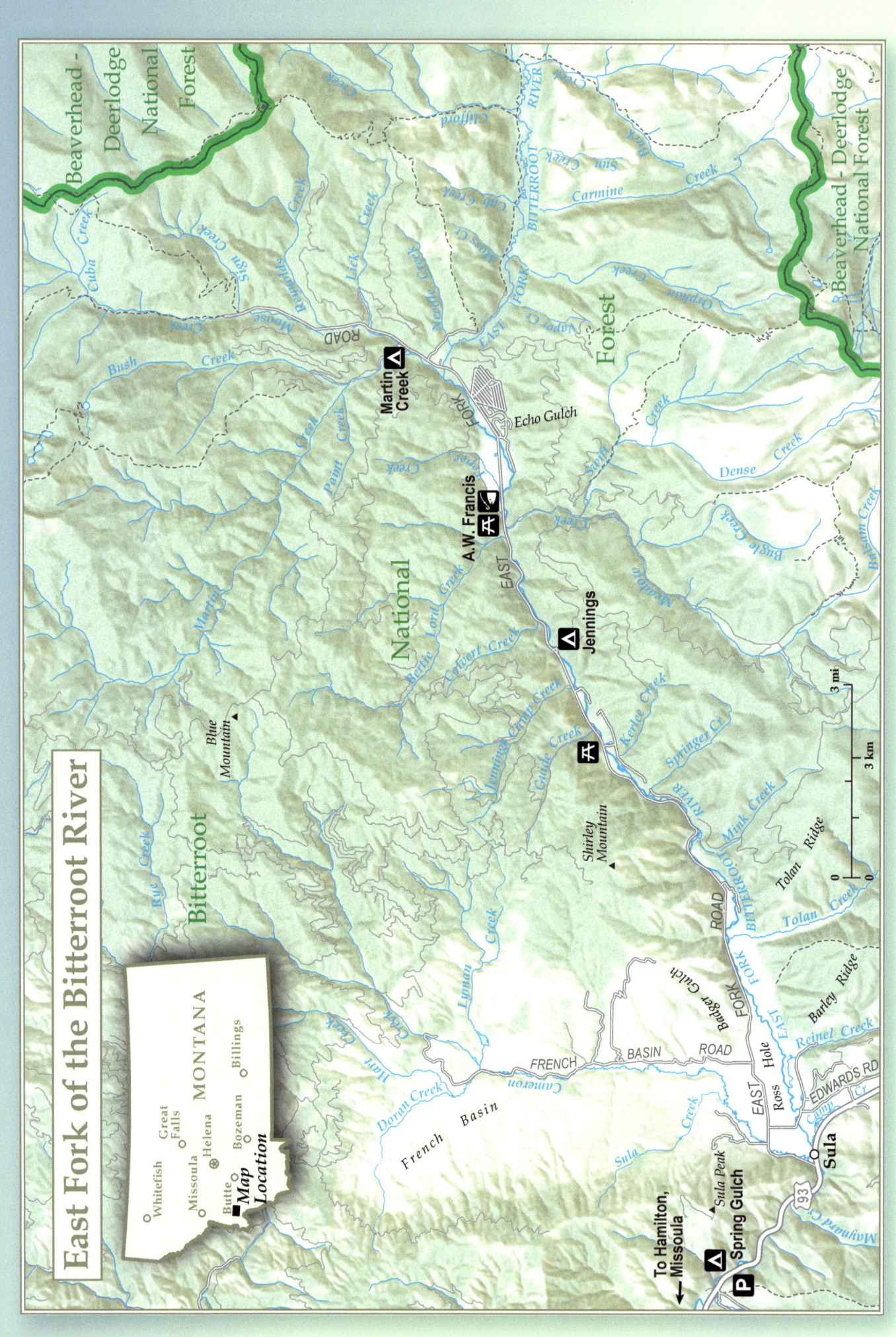

22 · East Fork of the Bitterroot River

➤ **Location:** Take Highway 93 south of Hamilton near the town of Conner. If traveling from Sula to the town of Wisdom (26 miles), there is no cell service. You will pass the Big Hole Battlefield along the way. Once in Wisdom, the Antler Saloon is a good place for a cold beverage.

The East Fork tributary of the Bitterroot River flows for 42 miles from the Anaconda-Pintler Wilderness to the Bitterroot River. From the mouth of the East Fork to East Fork Road, just north of Sula is approximately 15 miles. East Fork Road is approximately 15 miles, ending in a parking lot. From the parking lot to the headwaters is another 10 miles with a trail running alongside for most of the way. Fishing access is good from the mouth all the way to the end of East Fork Road.

During my last visit, my first stop was along Highway 93 traveling east toward Sula. Just past Spring Gulch, a few miles north of Sula, is a wide paved parking area just off the highway on the west side of the road. From the parking area, hike along the river and go under the overpass (Highway 93), following the river upstream. The fishing from here to where the creek runs alongside East Fork Road is excellent. Fish average 16 to 18 inches. The first section near the overpass has large boulders with deep runs. As you travel further upstream, the access gets a bit easier. Fish the runs between the rocks or along foam lines and seams.

Another great section is along East River Road all the way to where the road ends. The following mile marker locations were taken from *Fly Fishing the Bitterroot,* written and compiled by the Fly Fishers of the Bitterroot, www.flyfishersofthebitterroot.org.

Starting from the beginning of East Fork Road at Highway 93:
- mm 1.1 then 0.4 miles west on Edwards
- mm 10, Jennings Campground
- mm 12.9, A.W. Francis Picnic Area & Fishing Access

At the end of the road is a parking area. Access can be found from the parking area or while traveling up the trail for as far as you wish to venture.

➤ **Fishing regulations:** Western District, Region 2
Opens third Saturday in May through November 30th.

East Fork downstream from Star Falls: catch-and-release for cutthroat trout and rainbow trout. Brown trout: three daily and in possession.

West Fork downstream from Painted Rocks Dam: catch-and-release for cutthroat trout and rainbow trout. Brown trout: three daily and in possession.

Small pocketwater on the Upper East Fork. Molly Semenik

Below highway overpass. Molly Semenik
Inset. Large boulders line the stream. Molly Semenik

Both the East Fork and the West Fork clear up before the Bitterroot River. The Skwala hatch can occur anytime between mid-March and mid-April, depending on the winter. Runoff occurs in May, except on the West Fork, which is a dam-controlled fishery below the dam, and therefore less affected by runoff. Early June starts the Salmonfly hatch with the Golden Stoneflies arriving a few weeks later. It would be best to call a local fly shop to check on water conditions. Fishing remains good on the West Fork until mid-September. During the heat of the summer, the East Fork waters can get low and warm. It is best fished early in the season and then again after the hottest summer months.

▶ **What to catch:** Brown, rainbow, westslope cutthroat, bull trout, and whitefish.

▶ **Hatches:**
   February–early April: Blue-winged Olive, Midge
   Mid-March–mid-April: Skwala & March Brown, Brown Dun
   May–October: caddis
   Late May–early July: Salmonfly, best on the West Fork
   June–August: Golden Stones
   Late June–August: Green Drake
   July–August: Pale Morning Dun
   July–September: Yellow Sally & Terrestrials (June–October)
   Mid-August–late September: Tricos, Gray and Brown Drakes, Mahogany Duns
   Sept–October: BWO's and October caddis

▶ **Tackle and strategy:** A good nymph rig could be a 7.5-foot 4X leader with a size 8–12 Prince Nymph or Golden Stone as the top fly and an 18-inch dropper with a Lightning Bug or Pheasant Tail size 14–16. A BB split-shot may be needed to get to the deeper holes. Evenings bring on fantastic caddis and Yellow Sally hatches in late July, starting as late as 8:15 P.M. When imitating your Drakes or Pale Morning Duns, cripple patterns, Compara-duns, and parachute patterns work well. Attractor patterns such as your Royal Wulff, Purple Haze, or Yellow Stimulator (10–14) could all have a soft hackle, nymph, or hard-to-see ant (14–16) tied to the bend of the hook.

CLOSEST FLY SHOP / OUTFITTER

Angler's Roost
815 Hwy. 93
Hamilton, MT 59840
406-363-1268
www.anglersroost-montana.com

Chuck Stranahan's Flies and Guides
109 E. Main St.
Hamilton, MT 59840
406-363-4197 (summer)
www.chuck-stranahan.com

Fishaus Fly Fishing
702 N. 1st St.
Hamilton, MT 59840
406-363-6158

Montana Hunting and Fishing Adventures
(Outfitter)
870 Sleeping Child Rd.
Hamilton, MT 59840
406-363-3510 office, 406-360-7238 cell
www.montanahuntingandfishingadv.com

Osprey Outfitters Guide Service
1963 N. 1st St.
Hamilton, MT 59840
406-363-1000
www.ospreyoutfittersflyshop.com

Freestone Fly Shop
906 S. 1st St.
Hamilton, MT 59840
406-363-9099
www.freestoneflyshop.com

Bitterroot fly company
808 ½ N. Main St.
Darby, MT 59829
406-821-1624
www.bitterrootflycompany.com

CLOSEST LODGE

Angler's Lodge
815 B Hwy. 93 S.
Hamilton, MT 59840
406-363-0980
www.anglerslodgemt.com

Triple Creek Ranch
5551 W. Fork Rd.
Darby, MT 59829
800-654-2943
www.triplecreekranch.com

CLOSEST CAMPGROUND

Sula Country Store and Resort (RV, tents, and cabins)
7060 US Hwy. 93 S.
Sula, MT 59871
406-821-3364
www.bitterroot-montana.com

For a list of campgrounds on both the East Fork and West Fork of the Bitterroot visit: www.fs.usda.gov Bitterroot National Forest.

BEST HOTEL

Townhouse Inn Hamilton
1113 N. 1st St.
Hamilton
800-442-4667
www.townhouseinnhamilton.com

CLOSEST RESTAURANT AND DRINK:

Coffee Cup Café
500 N. 1st St.
Hamilton, MT 59840
406-363-3822

The Loft Café (breakfast & lunch)
217 W. Main
Hamilton
406-375-8624
www.thelofthamilton.com

Bradley O's Steakhouse and Saloon
1831 Hwy. 93 S.
Hamilton, MT 59840
406-375-1110
www.bradleyos.com

Bitter Root Brewing
101 Marcus St.
Hamilton, MT 59840
406-363-7468
www.bitterrootbrewing.com

Sleeping Child Farms and Farm Table Restaurant
1639 Sleeping Child Rd.
Hamilton, MT 59840
406-375-8765
www.sleepingchildfarms.com

Spice of Life Café and Catering
163 S. 2nd St.
Hamilton, MT 59840
406-363-4433
www.thespiceinhamilton.com

The Edge Restaurant & Sports Bar
140 Bitterroot Plaza Dr.
Hamilton, MT 59840
406-375-0007
www.theedgerestaurant.com

Sula Country Store
(cabin rentals and RV camping)
7060 US Hwy. 93 S.
Sula, MT 59871
406-821-3364
www.bitterroot-montana.com

NEAREST HOSPITAL/URGENT TREATMENT CENTER

Marcus Daly Memorial Hospital
1200 Westwood Dr.
Hamilton
406-363-2211
www.mdmh.org

WIRELESS AND CELLULAR

From Hamilton to Sula along Highway 93

ACCESSIBILITY
2

WADING DIFFICULTY
2

WILDLIFE ALERT
General Montana safety precautions

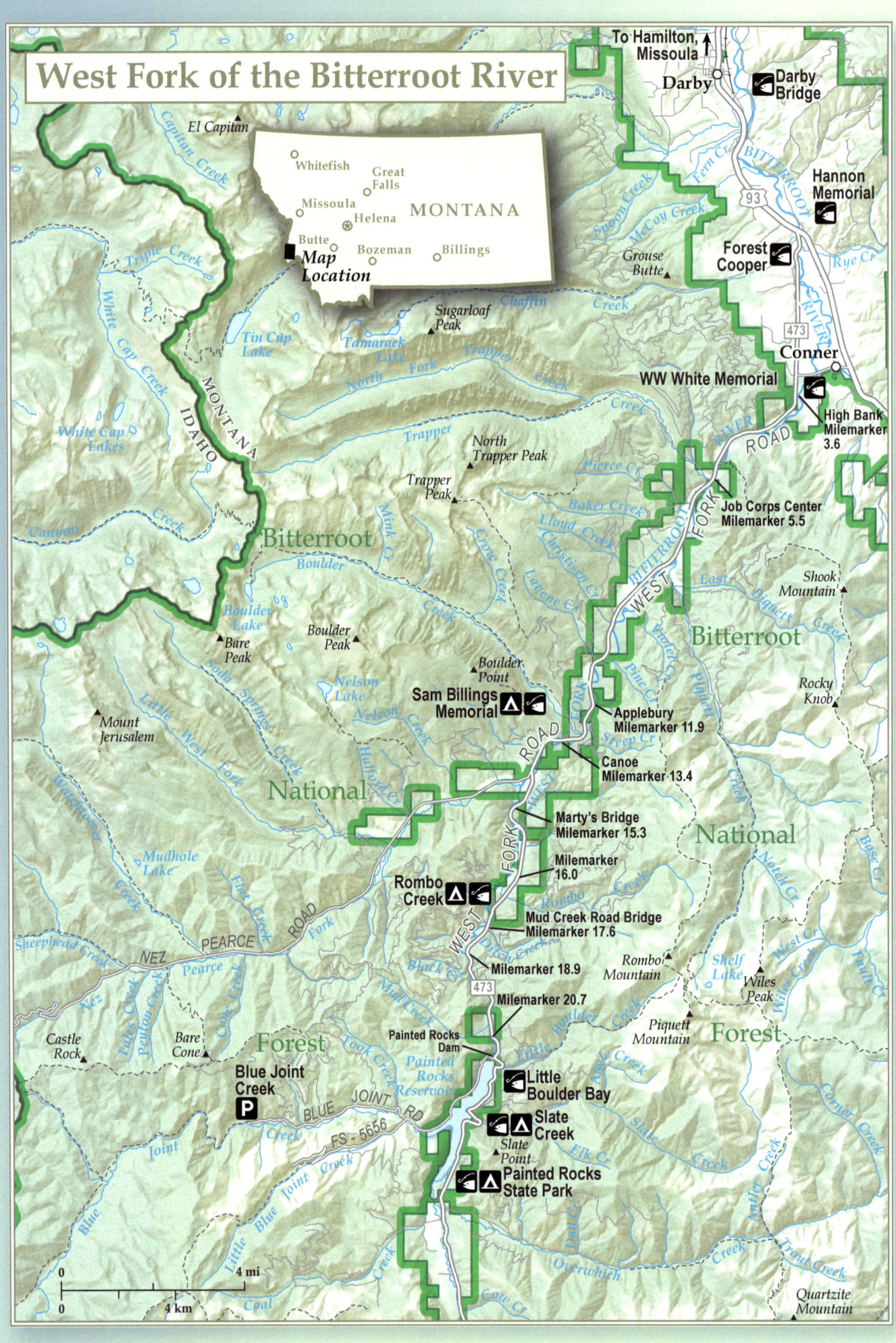

23 · West Fork Bitterroot River

➤ **Location:** Travel just south of Darby. Turn off of Highway 93 onto State Road 473/West Fork Road. West Fork Road turns into Horse Creek Pass Road, which will take you all the way into Idaho and to the Salmon River (for those great adventurers).

The headwaters for the West Bitterroot start near the border of Idaho in the Bitterroot National Forest. The headwaters to the man-made Painted Rocks Reservoir is about 15 miles. From Painted Rocks, the creek flows for approximately 35 miles to where it joins the East Fork of the Bitterroot. West Fork Road follows the river for most of its entirety, making for great river access. The waters above the reservoir are smaller with smaller trout. Below the reservoir conditions change considerably. The cool, clear water coming out of the Painted Rocks Dam provides for a healthy environment for trout and the foods they eat. The water is pulled near the bottom of the reservoir, keeping the flows steady and much cooler than most of the other waters in the surrounding area. The water clarity is excellent for most of the year, making this a good choice during runoff and during the hotter months. Below the dam the fish are larger as well. There are numerous access points from the reservoir to the Bitterroot. Just look for popular pull-offs. Listed access sites from the dam downriver taken from *Fly Fishing the Bitterroot,* written and compiled by the Fly Fishers of the Bitterroot www.flyfishersofthebitterroot.org.

- West Fork Road mm 20.7,
- West Fork Road mm 18.9.
- Mud Creek Road Bridge, West Fork Road mm 17.6.
- Rombo Campground, West Fork Road mm 17.9. (nice for RVs)
- West Fork Road mm 16.
- Marty's Bridge, West Fork Road mm 15.3.
- Canoe, West Fork Road mm 13.4.
- Applebury, West Fork Road mm 11.9.
- Job Corps Center or Trapper Creek, West Fork Road mm 5.5.
- High Bank, West Fork Road mm 3.6.

➤ ***Bonus Creek: Blue Joint Creek**

At the Painted Rocks Dam, follow the road over the dam; drive alongside the dam, passing Little Blue Joint Road. Continue to Blue Joint Road, and go, straight until you see Blue Joint Creek below to your left. Along Blue Joint Road, the Native American populations, including the Nez Pierce that once lived in the area, stripped the bark from the ponderosa pines, leaving a scar. They stripped the bark to expose and extract the trees' sweet cambium layer for food. Look for the scars in the forest to the right of the road. Blue Joint Creek has small cutthroat, brook, and bull trout. Use terrestrials or small Golden Stones. A 7.5-foot 5X leader is sufficient. The creek offers easy wading. Look for fallen trees and deeper runs. This creek is great fun and in a beautiful, remote location.

➤ **Season:** The West Fork can be fished as soon as the weather permits. Depending on the winter, the *Skwala* hatch can start anytime between mid-March to mid-May. The Salmonflies should start early June.

➤ **Hatches:** Refer to the Montana Hatch Chart
February-early April: Blue-winged Olive, Midge
Mid-March–mid-April: Skwala and March Brown, Brown Dun

Near the junction of 473 and Highway 93. Molly Semenik

Above. Evening fishing on the West Fork. Molly Semenik

Inset. Great evening hatch. Molly Semenik

May–October: Caddis
Late May–early July: Salmonfly, best on the West Fork
June–August: Golden Stones
Late June–August: Green Drake
July–August: Pale Morning Dun
July–September: Yellow Sally and terrestrials (June–October)
Mid-August–late September: Tricos, Gray and Brown Drakes, Mahogany Duns
September–October: BWOs and October caddis

▶ **Tackle and strategy:** The water above the reservoir is classic small stream water. Short leaders and dry flies are best. Roll-cast and high-sticking will be the best casting methods for this small stream. Below the reservoir deep pools and large boulders allow for weighted rigs using streamers and large nymphs that will get down deep in the water column. Large fish can be found in the deeper pools, some pushing 19 inches. A good nymph rig could be a 7.5-foot 4X leader with a size 8–12 Prince Nymph or Golden Stone as the top fly and an 18-inch dropper with a Lightning

Guide Interview: Jim Mitchell of Montana Hunting and Fishing Adventures.

Jim Mitchell's father, Bill, started outfitting in the Bitterroot Valley in 1969. Jim was born and raised in Hamilton and started guiding for his father in 2001. Jim took over the business in 2009. Jim spent a day showing me some of his favorite spots on the West Fork of the Bitterroot. He not only shared his knowledge of the fishery, but also his vast knowledge of the history of the area as well. I asked Jim what he liked about the West and East Forks and he said, "I like the tributaries because they both have lots of pocketwater; they are easier to fish than bigger water and they are great for walking and wading." I also asked Jim what he liked about guiding, and he replied, "I get to meet a lot of nice people and make new friends from all over the country. It feels good when you can help someone catch their first fish on a fly rod." Jim has added Tenkara fly rod fishing to his offerings. Tenkara fishing is a great match for the many small streams in the area. Jim has several forest service permits giving him access to many small streams in the area.

Below Painted Rocks. Molly Semenik

Yellow Sally hatch at 8 PM in mid-July. Molly Semenik

Bug or Pheasant Tail size 14–16. Evenings bring on fantastic caddis and Yellow Sally hatches in late July, starting as late as 8:15 P.M. When imitating your Drakes or Pale Morning Duns, cripple patterns, comparaduns and parachute patterns work well. Attractor patterns such as your Royal Wulff, Purple Haze, or Yellow Stimulator (10–14) could all have a soft hackle, nymph or hard-to-see Ant (14–16) tied to the bend of the hook.

CLOSEST FLY SHOP /OUTFITTER
See East Fork of the Bitterroot

CLOSEST LODGE
See East Fork of the Bitterroot

CLOSEST CAMPGROUND
See East Fork of the Bitterroot

WIRELESS AND CELL SERVICE
See East Fork of the Bitterroot

ACCESSIBILITY
2

WADING DIFFICULTY
2

WILDLIFE ALERT
General Montana wildlife safety precautions (no grizzly or black bear)

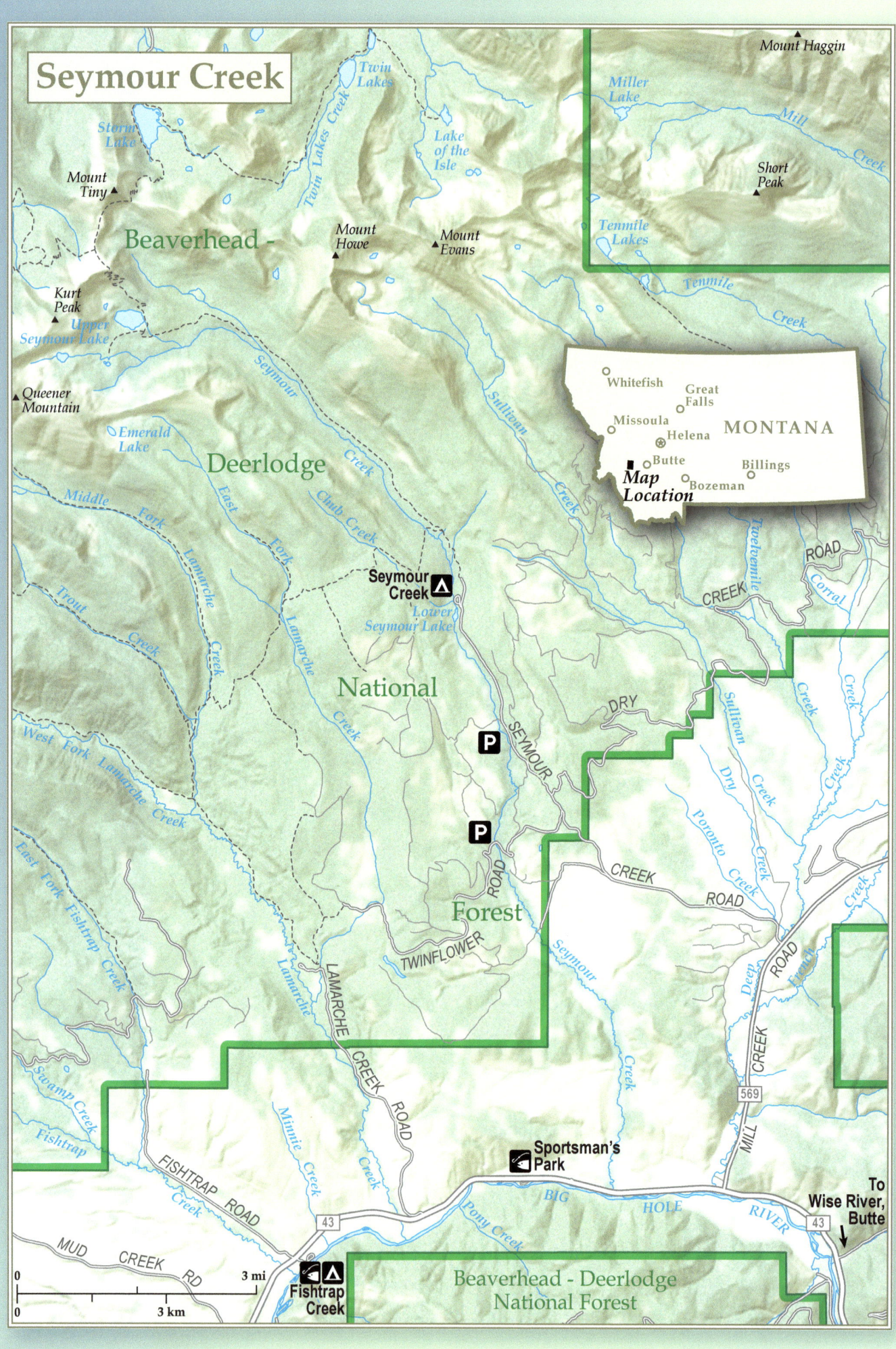

24 · Seymour Creek

➤ **Location:** From the town of Wise River, travel 11 miles west on Highway 43. Turn north on 569 toward Anaconda, and drive four miles. At Forest Road 934/Seymour Creek Road drive 8 miles to Seymour Creek Campground. Access below the lower lake can be found a few miles prior to the campground; two dirt roads on the left dip down toward the creek on the left side of the road.

Seymour Creek flows for 14 miles from Upper Seymour Lake near the continental divide to the Big Hole River. From the Seymour Creek Campground a trail follows the river for seven miles up to Upper Seymour Lake. The first 5.5 miles is gentle and well maintained. The trail meanders through lodgepole pine forests and meadows full of wildflowers. The next few miles gets more strenuous leading up to the last 1.5 miles which is a steady climb to the lake. The upper lake holds rainbows and cutthroats. The first few miles upriver from the campground offer plenty of fishing opportunities. The conditions are tight, requiring careful casting; primarily roll casting or the bow and arrow cast. The forest creates an atmosphere that is dark, with beams of light streaming through the trees creating a wonderfully peaceful and quiet setting. The brook trout are the predominant fish and they are eager to eat. They are not large, generally 10 inches maybe a few pushing 14 inches, but they are a beautiful. Fishing Seymour Creek can transform the angler into a fairy-tale-like setting that is unique and special.

Lower Seymour Lake can be reached from the edge of the campground. Walk out a ways from where the creek enters the lake and cast a dry fly to any unsuspecting trout. This is great fun and offers an easy casting scenario—no trees to catch a backcast. Fishing below the lake is good as well and a bit more open than the creek up from the campground.

➤ **Fishing regulations:** Central District, Region 3.

Third Saturday in May through November 30. Combined trout, five daily and, in possession, only one over 18 inches. All grayling and cutthroat must be released. The best time to visit would be toward the end of June and through early October.

➤ **What to catch:** Rainbow and brook trout averaging 10 inches, some 12–14 inches.

➤ **What to use and rigging:** This is as easy as it gets. Use a 6– to 7.5-foot 5X leader and as small a fly rod as you have, 2–4 weight rods would be excellent choices. A few dry fly options, size 14–16 Elk Hair Caddis, Royal Wulff, or Parachute Adams—pretty simple. I also suggest you have on hand a few terrestrials such as ants and beetles. If you are forced to use a dropper, tie on a small Hare's-ear or Pheasant Tail just 12 inches from the top fly, but be careful of snags. When fishing the lake, the leader can be lengthened to 9 feet. Along with drys, small streamers or leeches could be very effective.

Small pocketwater. Molly Semenik

Above. Lower Seymour Lake. Molly Semenik

Below. Jean Kahn fishing into a nice pool from tight quarters. Molly Semenik

When looking for holding water in the creek, the trout can be found in any deep pool, near grassy banks, or under woody structures. This is a time when a bow-and-arrow cast or short roll cast will be needed. If overhead casting, you will be mostly casting your leader and maybe a few feet of fly line. The fish hit fast, so be ready. Seymour Creek is a perfect family location. The campground is nestled in lodgepole pines and well maintained.

Beautiful brook trout. Molly Semenik

Seymour Creek as it enters Lower Seymour Lake. Molly Semenik

CLOSEST FLY SHOP/LODGING
See Wise River

CLOSEST CAMPGROUND
Seymour Creek Campground and Picnic Area
Travel 11 miles west from the town of Wise River on Highway 43.

BEST HOTEL, RESTAURANT, AND BAR
See Wise River

NEAREST HOSPITAL/URGENT TREATMENT CENTER
See Wise River

WIRELESS AND CELL PHONE SERVICE
See Wise River

ACCESSIBILITY
2

WADING DIFFICULTY
1

WILDLIFE ALERT
General Montana wildlife safety precautions

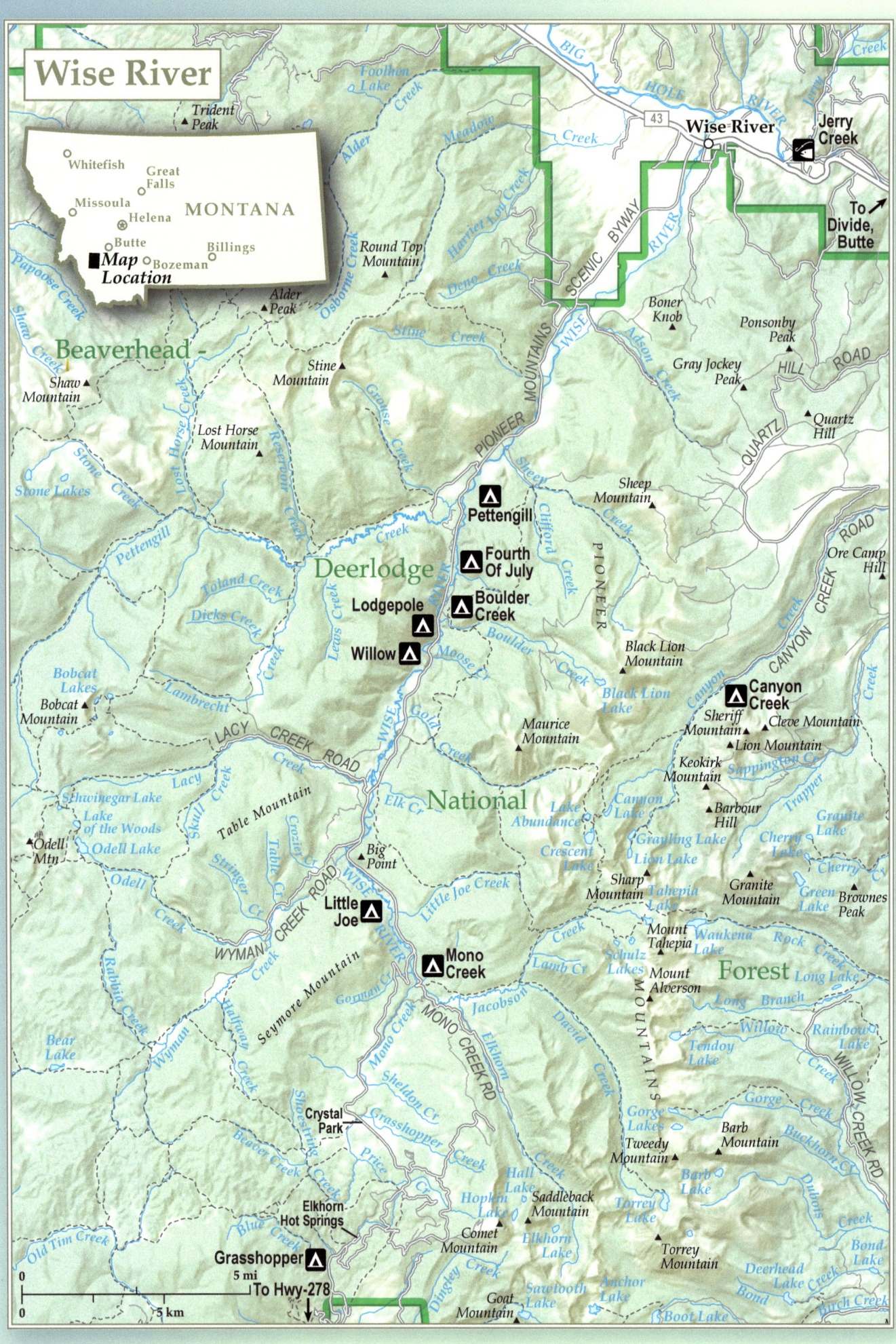

25 · Wise River

► **Location:** If traveling from Butte, take Interstate I-15 south to the town of Divide. Take exit I-15, and travel west on Highway 43 for 11 miles. The Wise River can be reached from the Scenic Byway 73 south out of the town of Wise River. If traveling from the Bitterroot Valley, 13 miles south of Sula is Highway 43. Take Highway 43 east over the Chief Joseph Pass to Wisdom; from Wisdom, travel north along the Big Hole River for 23 miles to Wise River.

The Wise River flows north from the headwaters near Mono Creek Campground to the Big Hole River near the town of Wise River. The Wise River flows through the Pioneer Mountains along the Pioneer Mountains Scenic Byway. During the river's 25.6 mile decent into the Big Hole, it drops 500 feet, creating long riffles dotted with pocketwater. The Wise River is a very dynamic river offering a wide range of fishing situations. Downstream of Grand Vista the river offers riffles, pools, and pocketwater. Upstream of Grand Vista the river opens up and flows through grassy meadows with undercut banks. Fortunately, there is plenty of access allowing the angler the opportunity to find a section that best fits his or her fishing abilities, be it pocketwater or slower, more meandering water.

The Wise River is not an easy river to wade. The rocks are extremely slippery. Cleats and a wading staff along with slow wading are advised. In May and June, the current is swift, sometimes flowing close to 800 cfs. However after mid June, the river starts to slow and continues to get easier as the season progresses, slowing to under 150 cfs by the end of July through October.

I was able to spend some time talking with a few local anglers regarding the Wise River, and I thank those of you who took the time to speak with me. These locals clearly had a warm spot in their heart for this river. Dave Decker, owner of the Complete Fly Fisher Lodge, was one of the locals I talked with. I asked Dave what it was he liked about the Wise River and he said, "I like the intimacy of the space, the smallness of it." Dave was excited when describing an evening on the Wise, "Evening dry fly fishing for six different kinds of trout is a throwback to a simple time when you can leap frog with a friend with five flies and a spool of 5X tippet." Dave also commented on the variety of angling techniques that can be used when fishing the Wise River. I too enjoy this aspect of the river. When searching for a fishing spot, do note that you

Upper Wise River. David Decker

A visit to the **Pioneer Mountains Crystal Park** would be a unique and enjoyable experience, especially for families. Crystal Park is located along Highway 73 midway between the town of Wise River and Browns Lake Trail. Crystal Park is open for day use and has a fee per car. Facilities include three picnic sites with tables and grills, information signs, toilets, and a paved trail with benches and an overlook. Quartz crystals are scattered liberally through the decomposed granite of the unique 220-acre site that's been reserved by the Forest Service for the popular hobby of rock hounding; your treasure quest, quartz crystals. The crystals found at Crystal Park can be clear, cloudy, white, gray, or purple (the highly sought after purple crystals are called amethyst crystals). Most of the crystals have little value other than as collector's items.

Another exploratory visit could include **Bannack State Park,** south on 278 to Bannack Road.

If returning to the town of Wise, you have two alternative routes. You can take 278 east of Bannack to I-15 and travel north through Dillon and Melrose. Turn west on 43 back to Wise. Or, you can take 278 west of Bannack and work your way north through Wisdom and continue on 43 to Wise.

Inset. Beautiful cutthroat. David Decker   *Above. Meadow area. David Decker*

can continue along the road and find another spot to fish that may be very different in its structure and type of fishing.

As you drive south or upriver from the town of Wise River, the first five or so miles are private. There are several campgrounds along the next 12 miles, however. Ten miles south of town is the Pettingill or Pattengail Recreation Site with a vault restroom, NO water, and three camp/RV sites. Fourth of July Campground is 12 miles south of town with drinking water, vault restrooms, and five camp/RV sites. 13 miles south is Lodgepole Campground with drinking water, vault restrooms and 10 camp/RV sites. Willow Campground is 14 miles south of town with drinking water, vault restrooms and 5 camp/RV sites. Near the headwaters is Mono Creek Campground, 22 miles south of town with drinking water, vault restrooms, and five camp/RV sites. Further south is the town of Elkhorn. For those that enjoy a hot soak, Elkhorn Hotsprings would be a nice way to spend the evening. Elkhorn has a restaurant with bar and cabins. Nearby camping is available at Grasshopper Campground at the headwaters to Grasshopper creek.

The western side of the Wise River has many small tributaries that flow from lakes. These tributaries and lakes could be fun to fish and discover. Many of these tributaries have dirt roads that follow them up to the lakes. An example would be Grouse Creek accessed from Pattengail Creek Road. Two other tributaries on the west side are Pattengail and Lacy creeks. Tributaries on the east side include Mono and Jacobson creeks. A good map to have on hand is the Southwest Montana, Interagency Visitor Map–Pioneer Mountains Scenic Byway. This map can be purchased through the Beaverhead-Deerlodge National Forest Service office in Dillon, Montana. Worthy lakes to explore on the west side include: Bobcat lakes, Schwinger Lake, Lake of the Woods and Odell Lake.

▶ **Fishing regulations:** Central District, Region 3.

Third Saturday in May through November 30. Combined trout, five daily and, in possession, only one over 18 inches. All grayling and cutthroat must be released. The best time to visit would be the end of June through October. Crowds of anglers will descend on the Big Hole River mid-May through June, fishing both the Salmonfly and caddis hatches. In October, large browns will move up into the Wise in preparation for spawning. Do change your rigging if targeting these 8–9 pound browns. A typical 5X dry fly rig will not be sufficient. Dropping down to 3X and using a 5-weight rod is advised.

➤ **What to catch:** Trout include brook, brown, rainbow, cutthroat and cutbow. Arctic grayling are a possibility and mountain whitefish are throughout. The average size is 10 inches. Brook trout are mostly located close to the headwaters, while the rainbow and browns are in the lower reaches.

➤ **Hatches:** Refer to the Montana Hatch Chart

The Wise is a wonderful dry fly fishery that receives little pressure. A small assortment of attractor patterns, with a few caddis and terrestrials is all that is needed. Attractors may include: Royal Wulffs, Renegades, PMXs, Humpies, and so on.

➤ **Tackle and strategy:** The Wise River is a small river. This would be a great opportunity for a 3- or 4-weight rod. The water is clean and clear a 9-foot 5X leader is recommended. When prospecting, look for depressions, boulders, undercut banks, foam lines, and woody structure along the banks. During the heat of the summer the trout do get spooky, a slow and careful approach is important.

Above right. Nice pocketwater. David Decker
Below right. Brown on a caddis. David Decker

CLOSEST FLY SHOP/ OUTFITTER
Troutfitters (guest accommodations) WiFi
62311 MT-43
Wise River, MT 59762
406-832-3212
www.bigholetroutfitters.com

CLOSEST LODGE
Big Hole Lodge (fly shop on premises)
36894 Pioneer Mountains Scenic Byway
Wise River, MT 59762
406-832-3252
www.flyfishinglodge.com

The Complete Fly Fisher Lodge
(fly shop on premises)
66771 Highway 43
Wise River, MT 59762
406-832-3175
www.completeflyfisher.com

CLOSEST CAMPGROUNDS
Visit: www.fs.usda.gov
State Montana, Beaverhead-Deerlodge National Forest and search under Wise River Ranger District.
Many campgrounds can be found along the Big Hole river as well.

BEST HOTEL
The Wise River Club
65013 Hwy. 43
Wise River, MT 59762
406-832-3258
www.wiseriverclub.com
Rooms, cabins, RV sites

CLOSEST RESTAURANT/BAR
The Wise River Club
First opened in 1896 and known for serving the Moscow Mule (vodka, ginger beer and lime) along with great steaks and hamburgers. An ice cream parlor is next door.

CLOSEST BEST GOOD DRINK
Mother Lode Casino and Crystal Room Restaurant

NEAREST HOSPITAL/URGENT TREATMENT CENTER
Saint James Healthcare
400 South Clark St.
Butte, MT 59701
406-723-2500
www.healthgrades.com

WIRELESS AND CELL PHONE SERVICE
It is important to note there is no cell service in Wise River. In nearby Wisdom it is spotty at best. In the town of Divide, at the time of this writing AT&T was the only cell provider with service. If you are arriving from the Bitterroot Valley, Sula is the last place for cell service before driving the Chief Joseph Pass. Butte has good cell service.

ACCESSIBILITY
2

WADING DIFFICULTY
4

WILDLIFE ALERT
General Montana wildlife safety precautions

Downtown Livingston at night. Peter Lami

References

Marcuson, P. (2008). *Fishing the Beartooths: An angler's guide to more than 400 prime fishing spots* (2nd ed.). Guilford, CT: Lyons Press.

Fothergill, C., & Sterling, B. (1988). *The Montana angling guide.* Battlement Mesa, CO: Stream Stalker.

Romans, B. (2010). *Montana's best fly fishing.* Mechanicsburg, PA: Stackpole Books.

Wilderness Adventures Press. (2011). *Montana's best fishing waters.* Belgrade, MT: Author.

Rosenbauer, T. (2011). *The Orvis guide to small stream fly fishing.* Guildford, CT: Lyons Press. www.bigskyfishing.com

www.glaciertoyellowstone.com

www.montanaflyfishingmagazine.com

www.montana.tu.org

Please protect our precious waters. Peter Lami

Philanthropy

We at Stonefly Press feel that it's important to view ourselves as a small part of a greater system of balance. We give back to that which nourishes us because it feels natural and right.

Stonefly Press will be donating a portion of our annual profits to conservation groups active in environmental stewardship. We encourage all our readers to learn more about them here, and encourage you to go a step further and get involved.

American Rivers
(americanrivers.org)

Bonefish & Tarpon Trust
(bonefishtarpontrust.org)

California Trout
(caltrout.org)

Coastal Conservation Association
(joincca.org)

Friends of the White River
(friendsofwhiteriver.org)

Riverkeeper
(riverkeeper.org)

Trout Unlimited
(tu.org)

Western Rivers Conservancy
(westernrivers.org)

Index

A
accessibility scale explanation, xxi
accommodations. *See* lodgings
across the stream fishing, xxx
Alvin, Dave, 29

B
Bannack State Park, 111
bars. *See* restaurants and bars
bears, safety tips, xviii
bed and breakfasts. *See* lodgings
beginners, good streams for
    Hyalite Creek, 37
    Swift Creek, 59
    Thompson River, 67
Bighorn Lake, xxxiv
Bighorn River, xxxiv
Billings, Montana, xxxiv
Billings region, xxxiv–25
Bitterroot River. *See* East Fork, West Fork of the Bitterroot River
Blackfoot River. *See* North Fork of the Blackfoot River
Blue Joint Creek, 103
Blue Ribbon river, 45
Bob Marshall Wilderness, 48
Boulder River
    access points, 73
    fishing regulations, 74
    hatches, 74. *See also* hatch chart, all regions
    map, 72
    tackle and strategy, 74
See also West Fork of the Boulder River
bow-and-arrow cast, xxx
Bozeman, Montana, 26
Bozeman region, 26–47
brook trout, streams containing
    Blue Joint Creek, 103
    Boulder River, 74
    East Rosebud Creek, 9
    Gallatin River, 30
    Hyalite Creek, 37
    Lake Creek, 64
    Little Blackfoot River, 90
    Little Prickly Pear Creek, 76
    Monture Creek, 85
    Rock Creek (southeast Montana), 5
    Seymour Creek, 107
    Stillwater River, 17
    Swift Creek, 59
    Thompson River, 68
    West Rosebud Creek, 9
    Wise River, 113
Brown, Dave, 52
brown trout, streams containing
    Boulder River, 74
    East Fork of the Bitterroot River, 100
    East Rosebud Creek, 9
    Gallatin River, 30
    Lake Creek, 64
    Little Blackfoot River, 90
    Little Prickly Pear Creek, 76
    Lower Madison—Beartrap Canyon, 45
    Monture Creek, 85
    North Fork of the Blackfoot River, 82
    Rock Creek (southeast Montana), 5
    Rock Creek (southwest Montana), 96
    Ruby River, 41
    Stillwater River, 17, 21
    Thompson River, 68
    West Fork of the Boulder River, 23
    West Rosebud Creek, 9
    Wise River, 113
Bull Trout Catch Card, xxiii
bull trout, streams containing
    Blue Joint Creek, 103
    East Fork of the Bitterroot River, 100
    Lake Creek, 64
    Middle Fork of the Flathead River, 56
    North Fork of the Blackfoot River, 82
    North Fork of the Flathead River, 51
    Rock Creek (southwest Montana), 96
    Swift Creek, 59
    Thompson River, 68

C
campgrounds, Billings region
    Custer National Forest campgrounds, 7
    East Rosebud Lake Campground, 15
    Emerald Lake Campground, 9, 11
    Greenough Lake Campground, 5
    Itch-Kep-Pe Park, 21
    Jimmy Joe Campground, 13
    Limber Pine Campground, 5
    Perry's RV Park and Campground, 7
    Pine Grove Campground, 9, 11
    Red Lodge KOA, 7
    Rosebud Isle fishing access site, 11
    West Boulder Road campground, 25
campgrounds, Bozeman region
    Alder KOA, 43
    Bozeman KOA, 31, 35
    Canyon Campground, 43
    Cottonwood Campground, 41
    Ennis RV Village, 47
    Hood Creek Campground, 39
    Langohr Campground, 39
    Red Mountain Campground BLM Public Land, 47
    Sunrise Campground, 35
campgrounds, Helena region
    Kading Campground, 91
    Monture fishing access site, 87
    Riverfront RV Park, 91
    Sleeping Giant Wilderness Area, 79
campgrounds, Missoula region
    Bitterroot Flat, 97
    Dalles Campground, 97
    Fourth of July Campground, 112
    Grasshopper Campground, 112
    Harry's Flat, 97
    Jellystone Park RV Resort, 93
    Jim and Mary's RV Park, 93
    Missoula KOA, 93
    Mono Creek Campground, 112
    Norton Campground, 97
    Pettengill Recreation Site, 112
    Rombo Campground, 103
    Seymour Creek Campground and Picnic Area, 109
    Siria Campground, 97
    Sula Country Store and Resort, 101
    Willow Campground, 112
campgrounds, Whitefish region
    Clark Memorial Camping, 69
    Cooper King Campground, 69
    Ford, Schnaus, and Ben Rover cabins, 53
    Glacier Campground, 49
    KOA Campgrounds of Whitefish, 49
    Montana State Parks, 49

Burnt Trees. Peter Lami

Mountain Meadow RV Park, 49
Thompson Falls State Park, 69
Whitefish Lake State Park, 57
Whitefish RV Park, 49
casting techniques, xxviii–xxxii
children, good streams for
    Hyalite Creek, 37
    Swift Creek, 59
color changes in water, xxvi
cutbow trout, streams containing
    Blue Joint Creek, 103
    Middle Fork of the Flathead River, 56
    North Fork of the Flathead River, 51
    Rock Creek (southwest Montana), 96
    Stillwater River, 17
    Wise River, 113
cutthroat trout, streams containing
    Middle Fork of the Flathead River, 56
    North Fork of the Flathead River, 51
    Rock Creek (southeast Montana), 5
    Rock Creek (southwest Montana), 96
    Stillwater River, 21
    Thompson River, 68
    Wise River, 113
cutthroat trout, rainbow, streams containing
    Ruby River, 41
cutthroat trout, westslope, streams containing
    East Fork of the Bitterroot River, 100
    Gallatin River, 30
    Lake Creek, 64
    Little Blackfoot River, 90
    Middle Fork of the Flathead River, 56
    Monture Creek, 85
    North Fork of the Blackfoot River, 82
    North Fork of the Flathead River, 51
    Ruby River, 41
    South Fork of the Flathead River, 48
    Swift Creek, 59
cutthroat trout, Yellowstone, streams containing
    East Rosebud Creek, 9
    Gallatin River, 30
    Hyalite Creek, 37
    Stillwater River, 17, 21
    West Fork of the Boulder River, 23
    West Rosebud Creek, 9

D
dapping and jigging, xxx
Decker, Dave, 111
downstream fishing, xxxi
drop-offs, xxvi
dry flies, xxxi

E
East Fork of the Bitterroot River
    access points, 99
    fishing regulations, 99–100
    hatches, 100. *See also* hatch chart, all regions
    map, 98
    tackle and strategy, 100
East Gallatin River
    access points, 33
    fishing regulations, 33
    hatches, 33. *See also* hatch chart, all regions
    map, 32
    tackle and strategy, 34
East Rosebud Creek
    access points, 13
    fishing regulations. *See also under* West Rosebud Creek
    hatches. *See also under* West Rosebud Creek. *See also* hatch chart, all regions
    map, 12
    tackle and strategy. *See also under* West Rosebud Creek

F
fishing licenses, xxiii
fishing regulations, xxiii. *See also* specific streams
Flathead River. *See* Middle Fork, North Fork of the Flathead River
floating, as fishing strategy, 55
fly lines, xxv
fly rods, xxv
fly selection, xiii
fly shops and outfitters, Billings region
    Bighorn Fly and Tackle Shop, 1
    Brant Oswald Fly Fishing Services, 25
    Dan Bailey's Fly Shop, 25
    East Rosebud Fly and Tackle, 1
    Fly Fishing Only Adventures, 3, 7
    George Anderson's Yellowstone Angler, 25
    Hatch Finders Fly Shop, 25
    Kinsey Outfitting, 25
    Long Outfitting, 25
    Montana Trout Scout, 7
    Stillwater Anglers Fly Shop and Outfitters, 11, 17
    Sweet Cast Angler, 25
    Sweetwater Fly Shop, 25
    Sylvan Peak Mountain Shop, 3
fly shops and outfitters, Bozeman region
    Bozeman Angler, 35
    East Slope Outdoors, 31
    Fins and Feathers of Bozeman, 31, 47
    Flatline Outfitters Fly Shop, 43
    Four Rivers Fishing Company, 43
    Gallatin River Guides, 31
    Greater Yellowstone Flyfishers, 31, 47
    Grizzly Outfitters, 31
    Madison River Fishing Company, 47
    Montana Troutfitters, 35
    River's Edge, The, 35
    River's Edge West Fly Shop, The, 31, 47
    Stonefly Inn and Fly Shop, 43
    Tackle Shop, The, 47
    Thompson's Angling Adventures, 47
    Wild Trout Outfitters and Guide Service, 31
fly shops and outfitters, Helena region
    Blackfoot Angler and Supplies, 83, 87
    Cross Currents Orvis Fly Shop, 71
    Montana Fishing Outfitter, 71
    Montana Fly Goods Company, 71
    Montana River Outfitters, 79
    Osprey Expeditions, 71
    PRO Outfitters, 71
    Stonefly Fly Shop, The, 91
fly shops and outfitters, Missoula region
    Angler's Roost, 101
    Bitterroot Fly Company, 101
    Blackfoot River Outfitter, 93
    Chuck Stranahan's Flies and Guides, 101
    Fishaus Fly Fishing, 101
    Fisherman's Mercantile and Motel, 96, 97
    Flint Creek Outdoors, 97
    Freestone Fly Shop, 101
    Grizzly Hackle, 93
    Kingfisher Fly Shop, The, 93
    Missoulian Angler, 93
    Montana Hunting and Fishing Adventures, 101
    Osprey Outfitters Guide Service, 101
    Trout Bums Fly Shop, 97
    Troutfitters, 113
fly shops and outfitters, Whitefish region
    Glacier Outdoor Center, 57
    KRO (Kootenai River Outfitters), 65
    Lakestream Outfitters and Fly Shop, 49, 55
    River Otter, The, 53
    S & S Sports, 69
    Stumptown Anglers, 49
foam lines, xxvi
food. *See* restaurants and bars

G
Gallatin River
    access points, 29
    fishing regulations, 30
    hatches, 30. *See also* hatch chart, all regions
    map, 28
    tackle and strategy, 30
    See also East Gallatin River
Glacier National Park, 48
golden trout, streams containing
    East Rosebud Creek, 9
    West Rosebud Creek, 9

grayling, streams containing
    Hyalite Creek, 37
grayling, Arctic, streams containing
    Hyalite Creek, 37
    North Fork of the Flathead River, 51
    Ruby River, 41
    Wise River, 113
guides
    Bighorn River, Bighorn Lake, xxxiv
    Gallatin River, 30
    Middle Fork of the Flathead River, 55
    Rock Creek (southeast Montana), 3
    Stillwater River, 17
    West Fork of the Bitterroot River, 105
    See also fly shops and outfitters

H
hatch chart, all regions, xiv–xv. See also specific streams
hatches, matching, xxxi
Helena, Montana, 70
Helena region, 70–91
hotels. See lodgings
Hyalite Creek
    access points, 37
    fishing regulations, 38
    hatches, 38. See also hatch chart, all regions
    map, 36
    tackle and strategy, 39

I
invasive species, avoiding transportation, xxiii

L
Lake Creek
    access points, 63
    fishing regulations, 64
    hatches, 64. See also hatch chart, all regions
    map, 62
    private access, 63
    tackle and strategy, 65
leaders, xxvi
Leisenring Lift, xxxiii
Little Blackfoot River
    access points, 89
    fishing regulations, 90
    hatches, 90. See also hatch chart, all regions
    map, 88
    tackle and strategy, 90–91
Little Prickly Pear Creek
    access points, 77
    fishing regulations, 78
    hatches (see hatch chart, all regions)
    map, 76
    tackle and strategy, 79

Livingston, Montana, 24
locating fish, xxvi–xxvii
lodgings, Billings region
    Beartooth Hideaway Inn, 7
    Comfort Inn, 7
    Grand Hotel Bed and Breakfast, The, 25
    Lupine Inn, 7
    Magpie Nest, 17
    Murray Hotel, The, 25
    Pollard Hotel, 7
    River Haven Bed and Breakfast, 17
    Stillwater Lodge, 11
    Super 8, 21, 25
    Yellowstone River Lodge, Cabins and B&B, 21
    Yodeler Motel, 7
lodgings, Bozeman region
    320 Ranch, 31
    Best Western Plus GranTree Inn, 35
    Big Hole C4 Lodge, 43
    Cinnamon Lodge, 31
    Covered Wagon Ranch, The, 31
    Gallatin River Lodge, 31, 35
    Healing Waters Lodge, 43
    Lone Mountain Ranch, 31
    Rainbow Ranch Lodge, 31
    Ruby Valley Lodge, 43
lodgings, Helena region
    Jorgenson's Inn and Suites, 71
    PRO Outfitters' North Fork Crossing Lodge, 83
    Rocking Z Guest Ranch, 77
    Sportsman Motel, 83
    Three Bears Motel, 83
lodgings, Missoula region
    Angler's Lodge, 101
    Big Hole Lodge, 113
    Big Horn Bed and Breakfast, 97
    Blue Damsel Lodge, 97
    Boulder Creek Lodge, 97
    Broadway Hotel, 97
    Complete Fly Fisher Lodge, The, 113
    Ekstrom's, 97
    Holiday Inn Missoula Downtown, 93
    Inn at Philipsburg RV Park, The, 97
    Townhouse Inn Hamilton, 101
    Triple Creek Ranch, 101
    Wise River Club, The, 113
lodgings, Whitefish region
    Belton Chalet / Grill and Tap Room, 57
    Downtowner Inn, 49
    Falls Motel, 69
    Gentry River Ranch, 53
    Glacier Guides Lodge, 57
    Good Medicine Lodge, 49
    Grouse Mountain Lodge, 49
    KRO (Kootenai River Outfitters) Ranch, 63–64
    Lodge at Whitefish Lake, The, 61

    Pine Lodge, 49
    River Front, 69
    Spotted Bear Ranch, 48
Lower Madison—Beartrap Canyon
    access points, 45
    fishing regulations, 45
    hatches, 46. See also hatch chart, all regions
    map, 44
    tackle and strategy, 46

M
maps. See specific streams
mending, xxx
Middle Fork of the Flathead River
    access points, 55
    fishing regulations, 55–56
    hatches, 56. See also hatch chart, all regions
    map, 54
    tackle and strategy, 56–57
Missoula, Montana, 92
Missoula region, 92–114
Mitchell, Jim, 105
Montana Stream Access Law, xxiv
Monture Creek
    access points, 85
    fishing regulations, 85
    hatches, 85. See also hatch chart, all regions
    map, 84
    tackle and strategy, 85–86
moose, safety tips, xviii–xix
mountain lions, safety tips, xix
Mystic Lake, 9

N
North Fork of the Blackfoot River, viii
    access points, 81
    fishing regulations, 81
    hatches, 82. See also hatch chart, all regions
    map, 80
    tackle and strategy, 82
North Fork of the Flathead River, x
    access points, 51
    fishing regulations, 51
    hatches, 51–52. See also hatch chart, all regions
    map, 50
    tackle and strategy, 52
nymphing, xxxi

O
outfitters. See fly shops and outfitters
overhead cast, xxviii
over-lining for small streams, xxv

P
photographing fish, xxxii
pile cast, xxxi
Pioneer Mountains Crystal Park, 111
pools, xxvi
possession limit, xxiii
practice cast, xxviii

R
rainbow trout, streams containing
    Boulder River, 74
    East Fork of the Bitterroot River, 100
    East Rosebud Creek, 9
    Gallatin River, 30
    Hyalite Creek, 37
    Lake Creek, 64
    Little Prickly Pear Creek, 76
    Lower Madison—Beartrap Canyon, 45
    Middle Fork of the Flathead River, 56
    Monture Creek, 85
    North Fork of the Blackfoot River, 82
    North Fork of the Flathead River, 51
    Rock Creek (southeast Montana), 5
    Rock Creek (southwest Montana), 96
    Ruby River, 41
    Seymour Creek, 107
    Stillwater River, 17, 21
    Thompson River, 68
    West Rosebud Creek, 9
    Wise River, 113
reach cast, xxx–xxxi
redband trout, streams containing
    Lake Creek, 64
Red Lodge, 3
reels, xxv
releasing fish, xxxii
restaurants and bars, Billings region
    2nd Street Bistro, 25
    307 Bar and Grill, 21
    Apple Village Restaurant, 21
    Bear Creek Saloon and Steakhouse, 7
    Bogart's, 7
    Bridge Creek Backcountry Kitchen and Wine Bar, 7
    Cafe Regis, 3, 7
    Carbon County Steakhouse, 7
    Coffee Factory Roasters, 7
    Cowboy Bar and Supper Club, 11
    Fishtail General Store, 9
    Foster and Logan's Pub and Grill, 7
    Gil's Goods, 25
    Grand Hotel, The, 25
    Grizzly Bar and Grill, 11
    Holly's Road Kill Saloon, 25
    Itti Bitti Bistro, 11
    Katabatic Brewery, 25
    Mas Taco, 7
    Mint Bar and Grill, The, 25
    Montana Jack's, 11
    Montana's Rib and Chop House, 25
    Murray Bar, The, 25
    Neptune's Brewery, 25
    New Atlas Bar, 17, 21
    Owl Lounge, The, 25
    Prindy's, 7
    Pub at the Pollard, The, 7
    Red Lodge Ales Brewing Company, 7
    Rosebud Cafe, 11
    Sport Bar and Grill, The, 25
    Uncle Sam's Eatery, 21
    Vintage One Bistro, 7
restaurants and bars, Bozeman region
    Bacchus Pub, 35
    Blue Anchor Bar, 43
    Corral Bar, Steakhouse and Motel, 31
    Dave's Sushi, 35
    Garage Soup Shack and Mesquite Grill, The, 35
    Lone Peak Brewery, 31
    MacKenzie River Pizza, 35
    Main Street Overeasy, 35
    Mama Mac Bakery and Sandwich Shop, 31
    Montana Ale Works, 35
    Nova Café, The, 35
    Old Hotel, 43
    Plonk, 35
    Wagon Wheel, 43
restaurants and bars, Helena region
    Avon Family Café, 91
    Benny's Bistro, 71
    Brewhouse Pub and Grill, 71
    Frenchman and Me, The, 79
    Lambkins of Lincoln, 83
    MacKenzie River Pizza Company, 71
    Maryville House Bar and Restaurant, 77
    Mediterranean Grill, 71
    New Steve's Café, The, 71
    Park Avenue Bakery, 71
    Steve's Café "Original," 71
    Stray Bullet Café, 83
    Trixi's Antler Saloon and Family Diner, 83
    York Bar, 71
restaurants and bars, Missoula region
    Big Dipper Ice Cream, 93
    Bitter Root Brewing, 101
    Bob Marshall's Biga Pizza, 93
    Bradley O's Steakhouse and Saloon, 101
    Caffe Dolce, 93
    Coffee Cup Café, 101
    Depot Restaurant and Bar, 93
    Edge Restaurant and Sports Bar, The, 101
    Ekstrom's, 97
    Hob Nob, 93
    Iron Horse Brew, 93
    Loft Café, The, 101
    Mother Lode Casino and Crystal Room Restaurant, 113
    Pearl Café, 93
    Philipsburg Brewing Company, 97
    Plonk, 93
    Silver Mill Restaurant, 97
    Sleeping Child Farms and Farm Table Restaurant, 101
    Spice of Life Café and Catering, 101
    Sula Country Store, 101
    Sunshine Station, 97
    Wise River Club, The, 113
restaurants and bars, Whitefish region
    Amazing Crepes and Catering, 49
    Buffalo Café, 49
    Great Northern Bar and Grill, 49
    Great Northern Brewing, 49
    Jersey Boys Pizza, 49
    Minnie's Montana Café, 69
    Mother Lode Casino and Crystal Room Restaurant, 69
    Palace Bar, The, 49
    Subway, 69
    Thompson Grill, 69
riffles, xxvi
rising trout, xxxi
Rock Creek (southeast Montana)
    access points, 3, 4
    fishing regulations, 5
    hatches, 5. See also hatch chart, all regions
    map, 2
    tackle and strategy, 5
Rock Creek (southwest Montana)
    access points, 95
    fishing regulations, 96
    hatches (see hatch chart, all regions)
    map, 94
    tackle and strategy, 97
rocks as habitat, xxvii
roll cast, xxix
Rosebud Creek. See East Rosebud Creek, West Rosebud Creek
Ruby River
    access points, 41
    fishing regulations, 41–42
    hatches, 41. See also hatch chart, all regions
    map, 40
    tackle and strategy, 42
runs, xxvi

S
safety tips
    weather, xxii
    wildlife, xviii–xx
seams, xxvi
Seymour Creek
    access points, 107
    fishing regulations, 107
    hatches (see hatch chart, all regions)
    map, 106
    tackle and strategy, 107–108

slow water, xxxi
snakes, safety tips, xix
spring runoff, xi
Stillwater River
    access points, 17
    fishing regulations, 18
    hatches, 18, 19. *See also* hatch chart, all regions
    map, 16
    tackle and strategy, 18
    See also West Fork of the Stillwater River
strategies for fishing small streams, xxv. *See also* specific streams
streamers, xxxii
Swift Creek
    access points, 59
    fishing regulations, 59
    hatches, 59. *See also* hatch chart, all regions
    map, 58
    tackle and strategy, 60
Szofram, Andy, 3

T
tackle, xxv
    and strategy (*see* specific streams)
    shops (*see* fly shops)
Tenkara fly rod fishing, 105
Thompson River
    access points, 67
    fishing regulations, 68
    hatches, 68. *See also* hatch chart, all regions
    map, 66
    tackle and strategy, 68
ticks, safety tips, xx
Trayser, Austin, 30

U
undercut banks as habitat, xxvii
upstream fishing, xxx

W
wading challenge explanation, xxi
walk-and-wade creeks, 63
water conditions, observation of, xxvi–xxviii
water features, xxvi–xxvii
weather, safety tips, xxii
Weiker, Rob, 55
West Fork of the Bitterroot River
    access points, 103
    fishing regulations, 99–100
    hatches, 103–104. *See also* hatch chart, all regions
    map, 102
    tackle and strategy, 104–105
West Fork of the Boulder River
    access points, 23
    fishing regulations, 23
    hatches, 23. *See also* hatch chart, all regions
    map, 22
    tackle and strategy, 23–24
West Fork of the Stillwater River, 21
West Rosebud Creek
    access points, 9
    fishing regulations, 9
    hatches, 9, 11. *See also* hatch chart, all regions
    map, 8
    tackle and strategy, 11
Whitefish, Montana, 48
whitefish, streams containing
    Boulder River, 74
    East Fork of the Bitterroot River, 100
    Little Blackfoot River, 90
    Lower Madison—Beartrap Canyon, 45
    Ruby River, 41
    Stillwater River, 17
    Thompson River, 68
whitefish, mountain, streams containing
    East Rosebud Creek, 9
    Gallatin River, 30
    Little Prickly Pear Creek, 76
    Middle Fork of the Flathead River, 56
    North Fork of the Blackfoot River, 82
    Ruby River, 41
    West Fork of the Boulder River, 23
    West Rosebud Creek, 9
    Wise River, 113
Whitefish region, 48–69
Wild and Scenic rivers
    Middle Fork of the Flathead River, 55
    North Fork of the Flathead River, 51
Winstrom, Robert, 63
Wirth, Zack, 77
Wise River
    access points, 111
    fishing regulations, 112
    hatches, 113. *See also* hatch chart, all regions
    map, 110
    tackle and strategy, 113
woody structure as habitat, xxvii

Y
Yellowstone National Park, 29

Driving the Beartooth Pass. Peter Lami

www.ingramcontent.com/pod-product-compliance
Lightning Source LLC
Chambersburg PA
CBHW041521220426
43669CB00002B/18